Webs of Power

Webs of Power

Women, Kin, and Community
in a Sumatran Village

Evelyn Blackwood

ROWMAN & LITTLEFIELD PUBLISHERS, INC.
Lanham • Boulder • New York • Oxford

ROWMAN & LITTLEFIELD PUBLISHERS, INC.

Published in the United States of America
by Rowman & Littlefield Publishers, Inc.
4720 Boston Way, Lanham, Maryland 20706
http://www.rowmanlittlefield.com

12 Hid's Copse Road
Cumnor Hill, Oxford OX2 9JJ, England

British Cataloguing in Publication Information Available

Library of Congress Cataloging-in-Publication Data

Blackwood, Evelyn.
  Webs of power : women, kin, and community in a Sumatran village / Evelyn Blackwood.
    p. cm.
  Includes bibliographical references.
  ISBN: 978-0-8476-9911-7
    1. Women, Minangkabau—Social conditions. 2. Minangkabau (Indonesian
  people)—Social conditions. 3. Sex role—Indonesia—Sumatera Barat. 4. Matrilineal
  kinship—Indonesia—Sumatera Barat. I. Title.

DS632.M4 B53 2000
305.3'09598'1—dc21   99-045666

Printed in the United States of America

♾™ The paper used in this publication meets the minimum requirements of American
National Standard for Information Sciences—Permanence of Paper for Printed Library
Materials, ANSI/NISO Z.39.48–1992.

Contents

Figures

MAPS

Preface

This monograph is based on one-and-a-half years of fieldwork in the village of Taram, West Sumatra, during 1989 and 1990 and a return trip in the summer of 1996. During my first stay I made arrangements to stay in the house of one of the wealthier women in Tanjung Batang. The first time I was introduced to my host, she served me tea in her formal living room with its beautiful set of upholstered chairs with carved wood backs. That occasion was one of the few times she used her formal living room while I was there. I rented a room in her house, which I used as my bedroom and study.

Being a permanent feature in the house, I was accepted as part of the family and called my host Ibu (mother). We quickly fell into a routine. Most evenings we ate dinner in her informal living room, sitting on the floor on mats, despite the fact that she had a couch, chairs, and a dining table in this room as well. There we stayed after dinner to watch TV until Ibu fell asleep or the electricity went out (which it did many nights around seven or eight o'clock in the evening). On many evenings we were joined by Ibu's daughter, plus friends or neighbors. When Ibu retired for the night, I withdrew to the privacy of my room to read.

The times during the day when I stayed home to work on my notes, the village seemed blissfully quiet to my urban American senses. Because Ibu's house was away from the main road, there was little traffic noise, except for infrequent motorcycles rushing down the village paths, or tractors trundling by heading for the rice fields. The quiet was punctuated only by the shouts of children, conversations of adults walking by, the bleating of goats tethered nearby, and the ever-present clucking and crowing of chickens.

Over time I recognized the village as a vibrant, thriving locale, whose everyday moments were replete with the daily concerns of living, the machinations of kin affairs, and the continual negotiation of Minangkabau and Indonesian identities.

As I observed the control that women have as elders in their kin groups, I came to question much of the "official" discourse about gender and men's authority. Therefore I sometimes went to great effort to have people spell out exactly what they meant by things like "household head," or "head of the lineage." I questioned what was meant when people said their *penghulu* "made" the decision or "owned" the land. I found that always behind such simple statements were much more complicated processes involving both men and women. These complex processes are the subject of this book.

My style in writing this monograph has been to present the Minangkabau in their everyday lives and to avoid terms or usages that tend to exoticize or make their lives seem unfamiliar. To aid in this effort, I translate the statements that people made to me somewhat loosely to conform to familiar English idioms. Throughout the text I generally use English translations for specific Indonesian and Minangkabau words but I include the original words in parentheses for the area specialists. The Minangkabau language is distinct from Indonesian, although there is quite a degree of overlap. I note some Minangkabau terms with the notation (M.) in parentheses.

In the text I refer to the people whom I interviewed and with whom I worked as consultants, not informants. This reference is my way of acknowledging their knowledge and insight into Minangkabau history and culture. I have chosen to use the actual name of the village where I worked since it is already known to the state officials from whom I received permission to do this study. The same village was also studied by Harsja Bachtiar in the mid-1960s and was identified by name in his subsequent publication, to which I refer at times in the text for comparative purposes. The names of the hamlets within Taram and of people in the village have been changed to maintain their privacy. To convey a sense of people's lives, I developed five composite families for this text, which, although based on actual families, are a blend of a number of individuals in the village. My purpose in using a few individuals to convey the stories of the people of Taram is both to bring their lives into greater focus and to further disguise the identities of the actual people whose stories I relate. I indent text that describes family histories and local events.

I am indebted to a number of people who helped me through fieldwork and ongoing writing projects. I am extremely grateful to Jane Collier and Sylvia Yanagisako, whose comments and suggestions have been invaluable and whose intellectual influences are apparent throughout this work. I would also like to thank Renato Rosaldo for his assistance during the writing of my dissertation. Other people who have been kind enough to read assorted drafts of chapters and give me very helpful comments include Carolyn Martin Shaw, Maila Stivens, Rita Kipp, Peggy Sanday, Don Kulick, Gracia Clark, and Alice Dewey. For her tremendous moral support during the last couple years of completing this book, I am particularly indebted to Diana Hardy.

Some of my research appeared in much earlier form in: "Big houses and small houses: Doing matriliny in West Sumatra," *Ethnos* 64, no. 1 (1999): 32–56; "Women, land and labor: Negotiating clientage and kinship in a Minangkabau peasant community," *Ethnology* 36, no. 4 (1997): 277–93; and "Senior women, model mothers and dutiful wives: Managing gender contradictions in a Minangkabau village," in *Bewitching Women, Pious Men: Gender and Body Politics in Southeast Asia*, ed. A. Ong and M. Peletz (Berkeley: University of California Press, 1995), 124–58.

Several foundations and organizations have provided invaluable support along the way. These include the Department of Anthropology and the International Studies Program at Stanford University, the East-West Center (Joint Doctoral Research Award), the Woodrow Wilson National Fellowship Foundation (Women's Studies Grant), the Purdue Research Foundation, Purdue University School of Liberal Arts (Faculty Development Grant), and the Association for Asian Studies/Southeast Asia Council (Small Grant). The original fieldwork was carried out under the sponsorship of the Indonesian Institute of Sciences (LIPI) and Dr. Sayogyo at the Agricultural Institute of Bogor (IPB). I am grateful to a number of people in Indonesia who generously gave of their time and assistance: Harsja Bachtiar, who took the time to discuss his work with me; Joke van Reenen, Abdul Aziz Saleh, Imran Manan, Flud Van Giffen, and Haidir at Andalas University; and Ellysa Noerham (Bu Elly) at the Department of Education and Culture in Payakumbuh, who took me under her wing to talk to me about Minangkabau women as well as give me instruction in Bahasa Minangkabau. I am also grateful for the assistance I received from several government officials at both the province and kabupaten level: Edwar Pamunchuk, Achmad Noor and M. Gaus, Baharuddin, Rinaldy, Tamzil, Rusydi Alwie, and particularly Syahyu Dasril, the PPL extension officer in Taram, with whom I had several discussions concerning state agricultural policies and programs.

I never would have arrived in West Sumatra without the kind assistance of Faisal at the Indonesian Consulate in San Francisco, and his family in Jakarta, Yasni and Rahimi Sutan, and his sister and her family in Payakumbuh, Fauziah Bakar. I am deeply grateful for their hospitality. Sinardi and Ing Susilo provided good food and good company in Taram. Sjamsir Sjarif gave me some initial helpful suggestions concerning fieldwork with the Minangkabau and translated some difficult tapes for me. I am very thankful to Dt. Karut for his patient exposition of *adat*. While I was in the field, I was fortunate to have my colleague, Jennifer Krier, doing fieldwork nearby. She was a great morale booster and provided some crucial relief from the isolation of fieldwork. Finally, I want to thank Nelfita for giving me a different perspective on life in West Sumatra.

Because I use fictitious names for the individuals in Taram with whom I worked, I cannot thank them by name. My great thanks go to my wonderful host and adopted mother in Taram, who was immeasurably kind and generous to me, for putting up with me all those months. I can never repay the debt I owe her. I apologize many times over for not always representing relations in the village as she preferred to portray it. I can only hope that my version conveys a sense of the depth, struggle, and meaning of her life and of others in the village, as well as my great respect and love for her.

I am also deeply indebted to the many wonderful people in Taram, who allowed me to take part in their lives, attend their ceremonies, and ask questions about everything. They were not just my consultants but my support and my friends. Thanks are not enough for the way they so willingly shared their struggles with me.

Lah sampai.

Families in the Village

Family 1: Santi's family

Santi: the senior woman, widowed   **Dt. Mangkuto**: titled man, her nephew
Irwati: daughter, university-educated, married, lives in Padang

Servant kin:
>   Rahmah: *haji* and grandmother
>   Mariam: Rahmah's sister, also *haji*
>>   Aziana: Mariam's daughter, married Dt. Kuning
>   Jasir: wage laborer
>   Tisra: Jasir's wife, runs a food stall, comes from another village

Family 2: Yenita's family

Yenita: the senior woman   **Dt. Bandaro**: titled man, her son
Nurani: eldest daughter, rice merchant, lives in her own house, moving into
  senior woman role
>   Reni: granddaughter, works in the civil service
>   Ahmad: Reni's husband, comes from another village
Dela: second daughter, lives with her mother
>   Dt. Sati: Dela's husband, owns rice mill with his sister
>   Fina: Dt. Sati's sister

Client kin:
>   Sahril: sharecropper
>   Intan: his wife, sharecropper with her husband

Family 3: Fitriani's family

Fitriani: the senior woman, owns very little land
Wira: eldest daughter, widowed, lives at home
Lina: second daughter, farmer, lives with her husband next door
Efran: son, married, lives in village

Dt. Sango: titled man, her nephew

Client kin:
> Anna: the rice miller
> Esi: her daughter, getting married
> Henita: poor, retired farm worker

Family 4: Hartati's family

Hartati: the senior woman, widowed, her husband was Yonalis's son
Yetri: eldest daughter, lives at home
Siti: Hartati's sister, lives with her

Dt. Rajo: titled man, her brother

Client kin:
> Leli: farm worker, partially retired
> Yeni: eldest daughter, farm worker

Family 5: Yonalis's family

Yonalis: the senior woman
Ema: eldest daughter, returned from *rantau*, lives at home
Nurma: second daughter, lives next door, moving into senior woman role

Dt. Kuning: titled man, her nephew, newly titled, married Aziana

Client kin:
> Noni: separated from her husband

Note on Orthography

The plural form is not distinguished from singular in Indonesian. In some cases I add an English *s* to the Indonesian term for easier reading but with terms such as Minangkabau, I use the same word for singular and plural.

Abbreviations

Dt.	*Datuk*, term of address for a titled man
Ind.	Indonesian
LKAAM	*Lembaga Kerapatan Adat Alam Minangkabau*, Association of Adat Councils of the Minangkabau World
LKMD	*Lembaga Ketahanan Masyarakat Desa*, village security council
LMD	*Lembaga Musyawarah Desa*, village council
M.	*Bahasa Minangkabau*, the Minangkabau language
PKI	*Partai Komunis Indonesia*, Indonesian Communist Party
PKK	*Pembinaan Kesejahteraan Keluarga*, Family Welfare Organization
PUSKESMAS	*Pusat Kesehatan Masyarakat*, community health center
REPELITA	*Rencana Pembangunan Lima Tahun*, five-year development plan
SD	*Sekolah Dasar,* elementary school
SMA	*Sekolah Menengah Atas*, high school
SMP	*Sekolah Menengah Pertama*, middle or junior high school

1

✛

Introduction:
Matriliny, Gender, and Power

This study analyzes the cultural and political construction of gender, kinship, and power in a Minangkabau village in West Sumatra, Indonesia. This village is known for its production of quality rice and its adherence to *adat* (local customs, beliefs, and laws). Yet it is neither isolated nor central, nor is it simply exploited by the state or at the mercy of the world economy. It is, however, located firmly in the midst of a number of social processes. Earlier peasant studies of Southeast Asia used terms such as proletarianization, domination, or modernization to describe these processes, but these terms no longer capture the complexity of changes going on.

Rural Minangkabau villages participate in and are shaped by discourses of nationalism, Islamic reformism, agricultural development, and globalization. As such, they typify many rural communities in Indonesia and Southeast Asia, yet at the same time they contain intriguing contrasts. Where kinship in Southeast Asia tends to be predominately bilateral (cognatic) or patrilineal, the Minangkabau are one of the few strongly matrilineal and Islamic groups in the region.[1] In rural Minangkabau villages matrilineal kinship forms the basis of local social relations. Families and lineages are oriented around the mother and her daughters and sons; rice farming and life-cycle ceremonies are organized by and through women and their brothers. This form of matriliny empowers women as controllers of land and houses, creating an obvious dissonance with the masculinist discourses of the state, Islam, and capitalism.

Although this study focuses on one village, it provides vital insights into the gendered processes of postcoloniality. A focus on one village brings to light the specific contestations, accommodations, and reconstitutions being made in rural

1

villages by both men and women. By focusing on personal, family, and community responses, this book explores the microprocesses at the heart of globalization.

HEGEMONY AND VILLAGE LIFE

Positioning the "local," in this case a village, in relation to national and global processes has become a central tenet of anthropology. Although distinct categories of "local" and "global" are increasingly problematic as useful identifiers in what many see as a globalized world, the analysis of the relation of communities to larger social, economic, and political formations remains an important task in anthropology. One aim of this book is to explore the discourses that flow through the village to show how rural Minangkabau are constrained by such discourses, yet at the same time how they manipulate these discourses to their own advantage.

I situate the "local" at one point in time in the late twentieth century, a time in which the Minangkabau of West Sumatra are partners in the New Order state of Indonesia.[2] But what appears as "local" and fixed is always part of and interacting with a number of other historical and economic processes. For Indonesia this history starts with the end of World War II, the overthrow of Dutch colonial rule, and the beginnings of an independent nation. As the nation began to create itself, it set in motion a number of economic and social transformations that would have serious ramifications for village life. Minangkabau history, however, does not begin with the state. A population identified as Minangkabau and living in the highlands of West Sumatra precedes both the Indonesian state and the Dutch who controlled the East Indies for over two hundred years. The earliest colonial records of the Minangkabau show them to be avid farmers, traders, and merchants in the process of becoming devout Muslims.

The Minangkabau people are one of the many ethnic groups that have been incorporated into the state of Indonesia. The Indonesian state was formed in 1945 from a Dutch-created territory that contains hundreds of ethnic groups on some 13,000 islands (see map 1.1). For over two hundred years the Dutch controlled large parts of these islands through the Dutch East Indies Company. Following formation of the Indonesian State and the nationalization of Dutch plantations in 1957, the Dutch presence in Indonesia was dramatically reduced. Their legacy of political and legal institutions, however, continues to be formative. During the early years of the new state, which was located physically and ideologically on the island of Java, there was considerable unrest and rebellion in islands other than Java and Bali, reflecting the difficulties of creating a postcolonial nation out of disparate entities. The designation "Outer Islands" for the vast majority of the islands of the Indonesian archipelago was a clear reflection of the political divisions and tension within the early state.

With Suharto's rise to power and the establishment of the New Order government in 1965–66, the Indonesian state cut off all grass-roots political movements

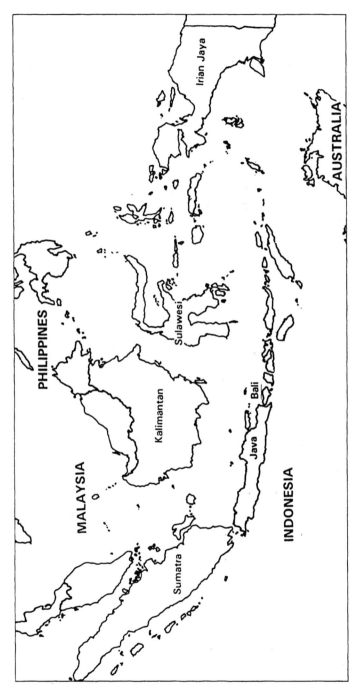

Map 1.1 The Indonesian Archipelago

and effectively monopolized all political power within the state bureaucracy. In moving away from Sukarno's accommodation of differing political views, including those of the PKI (Indonesian Communist Party), the state began consistently to emphasize development based upon integration into the world capitalist economy. Since that period the state has predominated in the exercise of social control, in the management of production, in the distribution of resources, and in cultural production (Langenberg 1986). Further, the rulers of the new state have built a substantial ideological structure to legitimate their considerable power and authority.

The Indonesian Constitution established in 1945 declared the equality of all Indonesian citizens. In articulating democratic goals, the state set the terms for a modern citizenry without distinctions of rank (see Dick 1985). The actual effect of this ideology of equality was to undermine the political power of local ethnic groups. By claiming that all its citizens were equal, the state undercut local claims to political power based on principles of kinship and bolstered the power of state officials who served under the authority of the state only. Although many state officials have risen to positions of power because of elite kin ties, the importance of wealth, education, and class have equal or greater currency in the contemporary discourse of power.

The state uses many means to bring its citizens into conformity with its ideology. The primary means of indoctrination is the *Pancasila*, the five guiding principles of the Indonesian state, which were developed under Sukarno's leadership (Morfit 1986).[3] All state organizations must acknowledge these principles as their sole foundation, a requirement that was expanded in the 1980s to include all social and political organizations (Hefner 1997). Civil servants are required to take an annual refresher course on these principles and are encouraged to work them into all aspects of their life. Schoolchildren learn the *Pancasila* by heart, ensuring that future generations will uphold these principles.

Beginning in 1968, the New Order government established five-year development plans (REPELITA, *Rencana Pembangunan Lima Tahun*) to guide the state's development efforts. To hasten Indonesia's progress as a "developing nation," the state formulated an ideology aimed at creating an Indonesian citizenry in step with the "modern" world. The ideology of modernization asserted that Indonesians should strive to be well-educated and forward-looking. Typical of many other developing countries, Indonesia viewed its rural population as outdated and backward farmers uninterested in joining the modern world (Dove 1988). By creating a dichotomy between rural ethnic groups and the "modern" state, the state established itself as the sole authority on progress while at the same time invalidating local practices and beliefs.

State agricultural policies furthered this process. The Indonesian state began a concerted drive for agricultural development in the late 1960s. They instituted massive programs to encourage the use of new varieties of high-yielding rice, new equipment, fertilizers, and pesticides, in the hopes of increasing rice production (Mears 1981, Rieffel 1969, Tinker and Walker 1973). Though the programs were not always successful at first, intensive government efforts and farm subsidies slowly led to the adoption of these new practices. These programs were put in place through a continuously expanding network of farm programs and extension officers whose top-down approach ignored any benefits of local production practices and stressed reeducation of farmers to "modern" techniques.

A number of other changes have been instituted since Indonesian independence. The state has sought to improve education by building elementary and junior high schools throughout the nation in local villages. With the greater accessibility of schools many more Indonesian families are able to provide an education for their children, at least through elementary school. The state has also made concerted efforts to expand the nonfarm sector of the economy, in part by allowing multinational corporations to set up factories for export production within the borders of the state. Since the mid-1960s, the expansion of education and nonfarm wage labor in Indonesia and the increasing availability of consumer goods through the market have contributed to an increased commodification of daily life.

Although the Indonesian state is not a monolithic entity, Minangkabau identity since 1945 has developed to a certain extent in response to the state's own strategies of unification and development. Yet despite the state's power to create and instill new definitions and identities for its citizens, its dominance is not total or exclusive (see Williams 1977). The concept of hegemony is useful here to understand the relation of the local to the state (see Gramsci 1971, Ortner 1990, and Williams 1977). Hegemonic or dominant ideologies define what is permissible, even thinkable; they serve as the standard against which actions are measured, producing codes, regulations, and laws that perpetuate a particular ideology. A dynamic concept of hegemony recognizes that any one relation or subjective identity is multiply constructed and constantly shifting (Hall 1988, Grewal and Kaplan 1994). Dominant ideologies generate discourses that stabilize, normalize, and naturalize behavior (Yanagisako and Delaney 1995), yet within any dominant ideology there are emergent meanings, processes, and identities vying for legitimacy, authority, and recognition (Williams 1977).

Even as postcolonial states in Southeast Asia try to ensure control over their borders, the many ethnic groups within their boundaries provide alternative hegemonies through which people continue to frame their lives. I call these ethnic groups "alternative" hegemonies, rather than counter-hegemonies, because they did not arise in opposition to the state, in the way Gramsci (1971, see also Hall 1988) first described hegemonic processes in the advanced capitalist nations of Europe. Williams (1977) was not particularly concerned with the place of ethnic minorities in a larger state, but his warning about overvaluing the totality of the hegemonic state is equally applicable to my analysis here. As Williams notes, "it is misleading ... to reduce all political and cultural initiatives and contributions to the terms of the hegemony" (1977:113). Not all social processes within the state are a product of its conditions.

Many of the current transformations in Southeast Asia are responses to the dictates of the state, as a number of excellent studies have shown. Kahn (1976, 1993) for instance argues that state administration, markets, wage labor, and new tenancy practices dominate Minangkabau village life.[4] Stivens (1996) asserts that Negeri Sembilan women recreate matrilineal discourses and practices in resistance to larger state and global efforts to delegitimate matriliny. The model of resistance provides a powerful tool to understand relations between local and global forces. Focus on the "everyday" quality of these resistances, a perspective that has become popular in studies of the micro-politics of peasant and village life, redirects attention to the multitude of ordinary, daily practices through which individuals contest and negotiate power. Yet one of the problems with this model lies in its failure to recognize the continuing importance of key elements of social life, such as "reciprocity, altruism, and the creative power of the imagination" (Brown 1996:734, see also Gutmann 1993, Ortner 1984, 1995). In the extreme it turns every action into a reaction (Ortner 1995).

Although I do not discount the power of the state to impose its will, I argue that hegemonies are not necessarily the dominant discourse against which all other discourses and actions must be measured (see also Hall 1988). I foreground the ability of local communities to reconstitute and recreate themselves even in the context of more powerful social processes. Instead of looking to the state and its policies to understand the lives of its citizens, I look at the local level where state ideologies take root. State principles of equality and modernization, expressed through the media, in political speeches, and in the schools, are certainly part of Minangkabau consciousness. My aim in this book, however, is to show how the Minangkabau interweave state and other hegemonic discourses with their own understandings of rank and gender, kinship and matriliny.

GENDER AND NARRATIVES OF POWER

Another important focus of the book is the question of gender and power. Part of my effort in exploring the interplay of national, global, and local discourses is to see how it plays out in the lives of rural Minangkabau women. Throughout this book I examine how Minangkabau women negotiate their identities in the face of a rapid and ongoing agricultural revolution and in light of ideologies of Islamic reformism and the Indonesian state that portray women as models of domesticity. In chapter 4, for instance, I explore the state representations of households as domestic spheres and men as household heads and the way daughters incorporate these representations as they establish their own houses. These ideologies stand in sharp contrast to gender practices in a village where women with their kinsmen create and maintain powerful social networks. Although I do not dispute the significance of hegemonic state discourses on women's lives, what I bring to the fore in this book is the way Minangkabau women constitute and reconstitute themselves as heirs and heads of households despite the circula-tion of alternative discourses of masculine hegemony.

Before I can do that I need to address some of the contradictions about gen-der and power that have been central to studies of the Minangkabau. The Minangkabau have long held a place of prominence in anthropological stud-ies due in part to the question of matriarchy.[5] The possibility of a Minang-kabau matriarchy was firmly rejected by anthropologists, who claimed that authority resides with the mother's brother, not the mother.[6] That authority was typically defined as follows: "The *mamak* [mother's brother] is the guardian of the *kemanakan* [sister's children, variant spelling] and is respon-sible for [their] well-being.... For this, the *mamak* is endowed with authority as *tungannai* [house elder] or *penghulu* [titled man]" (Kato 1982:60). Set in place in the first half of the 1900s, this hegemonic view remained firmly entrenched despite questioning by several feminist anthropologists. To make matters more complicated, Minangkabau villagers themselves are quick to assert the hegemonic view of men's formal authority over their kin. In tack-ling this dilemma, I revisit some of the basic assumptions about the relations between gender and power.

Some early feminist anthropologists constructed a universalist theory of women's subordination to men based on a structural opposition between domes-tic/public and nature/culture (see Rosaldo 1974, Ortner 1974). Ortner (1974), for instance, argued that women have less access to prestigious (public) roles and thus are subordinate to men. Feminist anthropology quickly moved beyond this early view of women as a homogeneous group characterized by a shared oppres-sion. Ortner herself later rejected this unidimensional analysis in favor of a view of culture multiply constituted through hegemonic practices in which women and men are differentially placed, not always to the disadvantage of women (Ortner 1990, see also Rosaldo 1980). The dissatisfaction with singular narratives of subordination led to work that firmly positioned women as actors in the negoti-ation of social meaning (see, for example, Atkinson and Errington 1990, Gins-burg and Tsing 1990, Sanday and Goodenough 1990, Stivens 1994). Noting that there is no single gender model or ideology within a culture, anthropologists argued that any discussion of gender relations must be framed in culturally spe-cific terms and meanings reflecting local contexts (Yanagisako and Collier 1987, di Leonardo 1991, Strathern 1987, Valle 1993). This view was echoed by transnational feminists who argued that feminist practice needs "to address the concerns of women around the world in the historicized particularity of their relationship" to scattered hegemonies (Grewal and Kaplan 1994:17; see also Mohanty 1988, Parpart 1993). Feminist anthropologists in the 1990s have devel-oped more nuanced and complex theories of gender and social relations. Under the influence of post-modern thinkers such as Foucault, analyses of power, resist-ance, multiplicity, and fractured identities have come to the fore in a number of studies.

Gender in Southeast Asia

Feminist anthropologists have long argued that women have control and power within particular social relations, and are therefore not powerless.[7] Only recently has attention been directed at the gendering of the concept of power and the way Western narratives of power and control privilege men. Rural Southeast Asia provides an important forum for rethinking gender and power because of the prevalence of women's landholding, control of finances, and control of agricultural resources. Scholars have long suggested that gender relations are relatively egalitarian in certain domains of Southeast Asian cultures (Papanek and Schwede 1988, Stivens 1994, Van Esterik 1982). These scholars point to the many rural areas in Southeast Asia where peasant women own and work their own land or land they control jointly with their husbands.[8] Work on peasant communities in Negeri Sembilan, Malaysia, has shown that women were powerfully situated as controllers of matrilineal land (Stivens 1985, 1996, Peletz 1988, 1996).[9]

Works on gender in Southeast Asia provide rich yet contradictory views of women, attesting to the futility of any singular rendering of Southeast Asian "women." The multiplicity of women's subject positions is consistent with the insights of feminist theory that gender is a process generated in discrete locales and through particular histories. Women do not constitute an undifferentiated category.[10] With its emphasis on gender in the context of "Southeast Asian modernities," Ong and Peletz's anthology (1995) highlights the hybridity and fluidity of gender forms "negotiated, transmitted or disrupted in the margins of cultural hegemonies and national narratives" (1995:9). The weight of dominant and competing discourses (whether Javanese patriarchy, Islamic fundamentalism, or male-dominated politics, among others) suggests to them the "indeterminacy and ambivalent nature of gender processing" (1995:10). In Sears' (1996) rich anthology exploring the representations of "the feminine" in Indonesia, Sears argues against essentializing or artificial notions of Indonesian women. Her aim is "to understand what has circumscribed feminine behavior in nineteenth and twentieth century Indonesia by revealing the shifting and illusive margins of feminine identities" in Indonesia (1996:4).

While these anthologies use tropes of marginality and circumscription to represent women, Karim's (1992, 1995) work on Malaysian women argues for an analysis of gender based on Southeast Asian frames of references. Asserting that belief in the prevalence of social inequality is a western feminist assumption, she presents the concept of bilateralism as a more powerful way to understand social relations. She defines bilateralism as "the need to maintain social relationships through rules of complementarity and similarity rather than hierarchy and opposition, and the need to reduce imbalances in power through mutual responsibility and cooperation rather than oppression and force" (1995:16). She suggests that in Southeast Asia the flexibility of gender provides an important source of women's power that is often overlooked because it falls outside the frame of Western ideals and values. Does the operation of power through "informal" means consign it to the periphery,

Karim asks, or is the concept of periphery and centrality "merely discourses of feminist anthropologists based on Western values of work" (1995:19).

These multiple views of gender in Southeast Asia raise persistent questions about Western narratives of gender. Does Western scholarship privilege certain domains and discourses that are then imposed in analyses of other cultures? This is precisely the argument feminist anthropologists have made in their efforts to deconstruct Western dichotomies such as domestic/public or nature/culture (see Yanagisako and Collier 1987). Karim in turn critiques both feminists and other Western scholars who have privileged social relations of inequality and formal power over other possible interpretations.

WESTERN NARRATIVES OF KINSHIP AND AUTHORITY

In the Western binary model of domestic and public, women were reproducers and "natural" members of the mother-child dyad in the "domestic" sphere, while men were associated primarily with the public domain of power and politics (Yanagisako 1979, Collier and Yanagisako 1987). The domestic domain was the sphere of child-rearing and affective ties, while the politico-jural domain constituted the realm of rules and legitimate authority. In arguing against this dichotomy Yanagisako (1979) pointed out that anthropologists have mistakenly limited family relations to the basic activities of day-to-day life, despite the fact that families and domestic groups cross-culturally do not all carry out the same activities nor attach the same meanings to these activities. The concept of the "domestic sphere" created boundaries in many cases where none existed.

This dichotomy meant that in studies of unilineal systems of descent, men were assumed to be the authority figures, a dictum that was maintained in matrilineal theory, where the mother's brother was found to be the locus of authority within the lineage. Schneider's (1961a) definition of matriliny rests on the assumption that power was vested in men. Since men were thought to be the actors and agents of corporate affairs, corporate descent groups were literally groups of kinsmen. For those theorists who identified corporate kin groups with social structure, political authority became synonymous with the (male) heads of kin groups. Following this reasoning, most scholars took for granted that authority in kin-based societies was found in the "formal" lineage structure with its men functionaries, elders, and chiefs responsible for adjudicating inter-lineage disputes (see Schneider and Gough 1961, Kahn 1980, Watson 1991).

The extent of men's authority in Minangkabau society has remained in dispute as anthropologists try to unravel the knotty problems of domestic vs. public and formal vs. informal in Minangkabau kinship. The Minangkabau case has always disturbed universalistic assumptions about women's place in the world. Even those who wrote complacently about Minangkabau men's authority were forced to note some disturbing peculiarities. There were occasional odd notes that, for

instance, "the oldest common ancestress ... actually stood above the *mamak*
[mother's brother]" (Willinck 1909, quoted in F. Benda-Beckmann 1979:84).
Maretin noted that within the family council "the women played a very active
role, especially the oldest woman of the family" (1961:175). In a slightly different version, Bachtiar stated that "the elder woman may have the most to say in a
family discussion when the *kaum* [matrilocal extended family group] decides on
any action to be taken in its behalf" (1967:368).

Seizing on this evidence, some scholars sought to dislodge the narrative of men's
authority by exploring the power Minangkabau women have within the household.
One line of argument taken by some feminist scholars was to show that Minangkabau women also participate in "formal" spheres of power, such as ceremonial
affairs and dispute settlement (see Prindiville 1985, Tanner and Thomas 1985).
Another line of argument supported the view that Minangkabau women have
power within the household while men have power in the public domain (see Kahn
1976, Ng 1987, Schwede 1991, Tanner 1971, 1974, Reenen 1996). Tanner (1971,
1974), for instance, emphasized that women hold power informally, drawing a distinction between household affairs where women predominate and the "public"
arena of politically active men. In a slightly different version of the domestic motif,
Franz von Benda-Beckmann noted in his analysis of property relations that,

> in matters internal to the group[,] authority is also vested in the position of the eld-
> est woman of the group.... She wields the highest authority within the house. But her
> authority is not restricted to purely domestic matters. For the oldest woman is the
> one ... who controls and keeps the property, who has the dominant voice in the dis-
> tribution of the group's property and any surplus the group's property may have
> yielded. (1979:83–84)

Benda-Beckmann found that women's authority within the house actually
reached beyond the house to include control over the use and distribution of lineage property. In all these cases there was clear evidence that women were dominant in household affairs.

Both of these lines of argument, however, left intact dichotomous models of
power. Those who located Minangkabau women's authority in the domestic
sphere reinforced a dichotomy between men's and women's authority, confirming the traditional view that men held overarching authority. Women's authority
included domestic and even "economic" matters but men's authority resided
above everything else. Further, by including subsistence production within the
realm of "household" affairs, women's control of economic matters was rein-
scribed within the "domestic" domain.

In these scholarly accounts, narratives of Minangkabau gender and power fall
prey to Western binary terms of the domestic/public and official/practical, leaving the definition of power uncontested. One way past these dichotomies is to
reveal the assumptions behind narratives of authority and power. Power in the

Western sense is identified with "activity, forcefulness, getting things done, instrumentality, and effectiveness brought about through calculation of means to achieve goals" (Errington 1990:5). In a now classic piece, Anderson (1981) argues convincingly that Southeast Asians hold a distinctly different notion of power than Westerners. In taking up his argument Errington noted that "the prevalent view in many parts of island Southeast Asia ... is that to exert force, to make explicit commands, or to engage in direct activity—in other words, to exert 'power' in a Western sense—reveals a lack of spiritual power and effective potency" (Errington 1990:5). Applying Eurocentric ideas of power to Southeast Asia results in skewed interpretations of hierarchy and gender; it is the immobile center who holds the most power.

Ironically, this model of Southeast Asian "power" overlapped suspiciously with notions about men and women. The immobile centers, the kings and sultans, were invariably men, while women, as the aggressive outspoken managers of households, lacked real power (particularly in the cases of Java, the Philippines, and Malaysia). Southeast Asian women thus appear to be conniving and calculating in their efforts to manipulate men to get their wishes. Recent work on Javanese culture has prompted a rethinking of Southeast Asia "power." Brenner (1995) points out that rather than being neutral about gender, the dominant Javanese ideology of power is male-biased. What was taken as an objective discourse on power in other studies was actually an account that substantiated men's claims to power.

Karim provides another interesting twist on the question of power in Southeast Asia. She argues that the emphasis on public power, or power vested in "official" titles and those who speak publicly at "official" gatherings, accords with Western narratives of power. In Southeast Asia power may be manifest in the formal spheres of politics and religion dominated by men, but women's activities within the informal spheres are equally as significant in terms of prestige and power. "From my observation, in reality, to do things through informal structures *is* the proper way, and one which is fully acceptable within the confines of custom (*adat*)" (Karim 1995:18). For Karim, power actually operates within the informal sphere in Southeast Asia. Her analysis suggests that identifying power with men comes from reifying "public" aspects of power as "real" power rather than understanding how power actually works in social relations.

Two recent ethnographies on Southeast Asia provide another angle for understanding power. Both center on the "domestic" domain in an effort to rethink the political significance of women's actions in an area traditionally considered "female." In a study of the Langkawi fishing community in Malaysia, Carsten (1997) found that Langkawi women and men seem conveniently divided in their tasks, with women involved in domestic reproduction and men in the fishing economy and in political and religious activities. While it is true that women are associated with domestic reproduction and the house, she argues, the house itself is not simply a domestic unit. The everyday tasks in which women engage are more than domestic activities. Langkawi households are not domestic units but sites of "feeding, fostering, marriage, and having children" that are central to the symbolic reproduction of the larger community (Carsten 1997:18). In carrying out what appear to be domestic activities, women reproduce the wider community. In Carsten's interpretation mundane household practices produce village identity (see also Karim 1992, 1995, Rudie 1994).

Brenner's (1998) work on a Javanese community in Solo is equally insistent on claiming the "domestic domain" as a key site in cultural production. Arguing for a new and culturally specific understanding of the "domestic," Brenner explores the significance of women's centrality in the family and household, showing that "as the primary agents of domestication in the household, [women], often to a greater extent than their husbands, took on the responsibility for generating material, cultural, and social value for their families" (1998:17). Brenner's focus on the domestic sphere reveals it as "the locus of [the family's] power in the community and wider society" (1998:17).

These works highlight the significance of women's "domestic" or "informal" actions in the production of meaning. In creating shared identities or generating material, cultural, and social value, women control social relations and their meanings. Sanday's rethinking of the term "matriarchy" also invokes this broader definition of power. She envisions matriarchal power to be women's ability to "authenticate and regenerate or ... nurture the social order." This is not power *over* subjects but "female power (in their roles as mothers and senior women) to conjugate—to knit and regenerate social ties..." (1998:2). These critiques point to the many ways in which Western narratives of power are based on and limited by assumptions about gender.

RESISTING AUTONOMY

If Western narratives of power have limited anthropology's ability to analyze gender relations, they have also limited the ability to conceptualize women's actions. The concept of autonomy is frequently used to describe situations in which women have economic and social power, but as I shall argue, this concept obscures more than it reveals. For instance, in studies of rural women in Negeri Sembilan, Malaysia, where women retain many prerogatives and social advantages due to their right to inherit agricultural land, women are said to have economic "independence" from their husbands (Stivens 1992, 1996). Ong (1987, 1990) points out that Malay women in general have considerable autonomy and control in everyday life due to a combination of factors such as *adat* practices, kindred relations, cash-crop gardens, and petty trade. Similarly, for the Mendi of the southern New Guinea highlands, Lederman (1990) characterizes Mendi women's ability to maintain their own exchange relations independently of their husbands' exchange or clan interests by the term "autonomy." These studies make important contributions to the analysis of gender relations. I mention them here only because they are indicative of an ethnographic commonplace to sum up women's economic control with the term "autonomy."

The term, which made its appearance in nineteenth century philosophical debates about the individual versus society (see Sharma 1990, Stivens 1994), invokes notions of precultural human beings whom society must force to its conventions. "Autonomy" signifies independence, ability to act alone, and freedom from outside constraint. Stivens notes that the construction of women as "relatively autonomous" reflects "modernist ideas about the possibility of attaining a free and autonomous self" (1994:36). It is used by Western feminists to signify women's separation or freedom from men's control, or as Stivens (1994) suggests, to judge how close their state comes to the "allegedly free and autonomous" male self. Consequently, when the term "autonomy" is invoked it signifies women's freedom from marital constraints and their ability to act as their own agents apart from their husbands.[11]

Use of the concept of autonomy is problematic, however, because it tends to obscure other social relationships and other ways of being.[12] Its signification of a "free-floating, culturally complete" individual (Rudie 1993:103) is at odds with notions of self in other cultures. Women may be autonomous in relation to their husbands but that is not the only way to represent women. In her discussion of Malay women, Rudie states that their sense of self derives from being a complementary family person. Women operate within a nexus of relations that surpass the husband/wife relationship. Carsten's (1997) discussion of Malay women's impact on the wider community also extends the analysis beyond the marital relationship.

Analysis of women's autonomy in relation to their husbands or other men is an important part of gender studies but it only provides a partial perspective. "Autonomy" as a concept misses the complex and dynamic ways that women wield power over those under their control or influence. What other relations are women involved in? How do women work to create relations with others? What tactics do they use to maintain these relations? What categories of people typically come under their influence? With whom do they align themselves to build these relations? Feminist anthropology has shown that women have decision-making power, control land, have rights in its produce, and even maintain trade and exchange relations, but the ramifications of that power need to be drawn out further.

RETHINKING POWER: A FEMINIST REVISION

Feminist revision is always about a new way of looking at all categories (Behar 1995:6).

There are many definitions of and perspectives on power. As Margolis (1989) notes in her discussion of power theory, traditional definitions focus on the ability of one or more actors to produce intended effects on other actors. This definition has been well critiqued for its failure to take into account structural inequalities that privilege one or the other actors. Marxist theorists define power as the ability to control resources and the relations embodied in those resources. In Marxist-informed analyses of gender relations, much attention has been given to women's control over or access to (material) resources, but less to the social relations that are necessarily part of productive activities.

Another way to understand power that I find useful in this book is to look at its expression in the creation and negotiation of social identities.[13] The negotiation of social identities such as class, rank, or ethnic identity is one of the basic processes through which the social order is legitimated and explained. As Margolis states, "the creation of an identity is itself one of the strongest expressions of power" (1989:399). Individuals are situated within webs of socially produced identities that empower or disable them in any given context. Social identities bestow certain claims, entitlements, and rights to individuals and groups, which in turn privilege or disadvantage them in everyday practice (Moore 1992). Thus, the control over social identities, which are based on socially constructed differences, form the nexus of power in rural communities. From the angle of social identities, power operates in a number of ways: in the ability (1) to name someone or the services they may or must provide, or the material resources they can or cannot claim; (2) to determine how human energy will be spent, for whose benefit and return; (3) to make decisions on behalf of a group; (4) to define a need and what would satisfy it; (5) to define issues as nonissues; (6) or to define one's right (or the rights of all others in the same category) as fore-ordained or normative (see Fraser 1989, Margolis 1989).

I also want to draw on Foucault's (1980) insights into power/knowledge relations here to provide a sharper edge to this perspective. Power in Foucault's sense of the word works in many contexts and at multiple levels. His analysis of power redirects attention to the multiplicity of ordinary, daily practices through which individuals contest and negotiate power. Drawing on these various perspectives on power, I see power expressed in the construction and reconstitution of social relations and in the ability to construct and maintain social identities. Rather than imagining single nodes of power, such as those vested, for instance, in positions of authority (titled men, chiefs, or elders), I envision power residing in a multiplicity of nodes and interlinkages that together constitute the processes and practices of social life.

I use this perspective on power throughout the book to elucidate the complexities of women's power in a rural Minangkabau village.[14] In this book I devote my attention to the way women shape and control social relations and cultural processes. Where others focus on the ordinary and daily aspects of women's power in domestic and market relations or in informal practices (see, for example, Brenner 1998, Carsten 1997, and Karim 1995), the Minangkabau case provides an opportunity to expand the view of rural women beyond that of wife and mother. In rural Minangkabau villages women's kinship and production relations extend throughout the community. I explore various arenas in turn—household practices, lineage relations, ceremonial practices, and agricultural production—to show the webs of power through which women (and men) constitute and reconstitute social life.

In the following chapters I carry out my revisioning of Minangkabau women's lives—filling in the gaps and silences about Minangkabau women within the household, within the lineage, and within agricultural production—to develop a more complex rendering of the processes of power in a Minangkabau village. In chapter 2, I revisit the question of Minangkabau men's "formal" authority through an analysis of a clan deliberation. In chapters 3 and 4, I discuss the way Minangkabau mothers and daughters invoke matrilineal *adat* to constitute and reconstitute themselves as heirs, heads of households, and controllers of land and kin. In chapter 5, I explore the meaning of ceremonial practices and the way elite women control those meanings to preserve their dominance in the village. Here and in each chapter I attend to the differences among women in terms of economic status, kinship rank, and education to reflect the multiplicity of women's subject positions. Chapter 6 analyzes the way status is contested and negotiated among women and families of different kinship ranks. Chapter 7 explores the extent of elite women's control of agricultural production and labor in the village and how changing production relations threaten to dislodge long-standing relations between elite women and their subordinate kin.

RETHINKING KINSHIP IN MATRILINEAL SOCIETIES

One final theme that has bearing on a book on matriliny is the study of kinship itself. In this final section I critique and reconceptualize the categories of kinship and matriliny. Those who study kinship no longer claim that it is a universal or primordial subject. Earlier studies of kinship assumed that biology was the obvious and determining factor and motive of kin ties. Folk views concerning the naturalness of kinship as a relationship based on physical ties only served to confirm this assumption. Following Schneider's (1968, 1984) critique of kinship theory, it became clear that kinship was more than anything "a category of Western culture; its anthropological stature was due far less to what the ethnographic facts might warrant than to the persistence of a deep-seated ... Western presumption laconically expressed in the maxim that 'blood is thicker than water'" (Faubion 1996:68–69). With kinship bereft of its moorings in biology and lacking its dominance as a distinct sphere of culture, many anthropologists became skeptical of its ability to say anything meaningful about the groups they study.

A new generation of anthropologists revitalized kinship studies by generating new puzzles and new answers within the fields of gender and kinship (see, for example, Yanagisako and Collier 1987). New studies in kinship avoid assumptions about its naturalness or its importance as a major structuring principle. Kinship appears as one form of social relatedness rather than the basic structure of society. In a move away from discussions of abstract principles, Carsten, for instance, argues that "[k]inship is not a lifeless and pre-given force which in some mysterious way determines the form of people's relations with each other. On the contrary, it consists of the many small actions, exchanges, friendships and enmities that people themselves create in their everyday lives" (1997:23). Kinship in this view is not a taxonomic principle but a proposition, an assertion about a particular relationship by people embedded in particular situations (see Bourdieu 1977, Faubion 1996, Hobart 1991). The new kinship returns as an idiom of social practice, a set of ideas—about relatedness, "blood," sociality, friendship, obligation, and origin—that give meaning to social relations.

In like manner I view kinship as a flexible idiom for social relations rather than a stable social structure providing rules that are enacted from generation to generation. In taking this view to the analysis of matriliny, I am not concerned with how kinship governs or structures behavior, but how the practice of kinship provides the orientation for and idiom of village life. The Minangkabau use kinship to define closeness of relationship among village inhabitants. It can refer to those said to be related by genealogical tie (with varying degrees of certainty) as well as those adopted in (newcomers to the village or descendants of slaves). It is used to pass on property, define rank, and allocate and justify authority. It is not, however, a stable and unchanging structure. Like other cultural processes Minangkabau kinship is continually enacted, constituted, and recreated in everyday social practices. Thus I look to people's everyday lives to understand kinship. It is their social practices that constitute kinship, not the other way around.

Throughout this book I use the term "practices" in reference to kinship as a way to signify a less structured and more historically contingent meaning to processes usually glossed as rules and norms. I view kinship practices as the current reworking, negotiation, and articulation of both material and ideological processes of local, state, global, and historical significance. My usage of the term draws on Bourdieu's (1977) concept of *habitus*, which he defines as the principles for the generation of structures that are themselves the product of past practices. In arguing against the structuralist practice of creating "a closed, coherent system of purely logical relationships" (1977:37), Bourdieu claims that kinship structures "are the product of strategies (conscious and unconscious) oriented towards the satisfaction of material and symbolic interests" (1977:36), thus articulating the importance of economic and social conditions to the practice of kinship. In Bourdieu's terms, "practice" is action (everyday events) shaped by pre-existing structures (official kinship) as well as the contingencies of economic life. This view of kinship sees each event as a reconstitution of local practices (*habitus*) that may both reinforce and alter these practices. The term "practice" in this sense incorporates both structure and agency in its meaning (see Ortner 1984, see also Collier and Yanagisako 1990); it sees structure as constitutive but not determinant of people's actions or ability to shape their lives and communities.

Although I agree with Bourdieu that *habitus* excludes some conditions from thought (the doxa, taken-for-granted, unconscious part of ourselves, as well as the unthinkable; see also Durkheim 1938), I see agents as aware both of the pressures and the inequalities in the system. People may obey the norms of practice because they have more to gain from it than not, as Bourdieu suggests (1977:22), but their experiences and contradictory identities give rise to divergent practices that lead to minor shifts and reworkings of kinship relations.

To return to Minangkabau society, Minangkabau villagers operate within what I call a matrix of matrilineal practices that inform women's and men's actions and behaviors not only in lineage affairs, but within households, nuclear families, and production processes. The term "matrilineal practices" is used here to identify the core set of beliefs, values, and ways of being that provide the basic framework for acting in the world. I identify these practices as matrilineal, rather than matrifocal or matricentric or merely kin practices, to name a few possibilities, for several reasons. First, because I see kinship as a flexible idiom for social relations, I use the term "(matri)lineal" in a general rather than a definitive way to stand in for the range of kinship practices in the village. Second, I use the term because I believe that the kinship practices of (matri)lineal inheritance, control of ancestral property, and ranking lie at the heart of rural Minangkabau village life. And finally, I use the term "matri(lineal)" because these kinship practices are oriented around women and empower them as lineal heirs, heads of households, and controllers of land and kin.

"Tradition" and Matriliny

The discussion of matrilineal practices brings me to two final points concerning the concept of matriliny: the debates about its "classic" form and its "fate." The structuralist approach of earlier Dutch scholars was responsible for a highly formalized view of Minangkabau matriliny that became enshrined in standard anthropology texts (see, for example, Josselin de Jong 1952, Maretin 1961, and Schrieke 1955). The principles of "traditional" matrilineal organization were said to include transmission of land through the female line, lineage exogamy, uxorilocal postmarital residence, authority of the mother's brother, matrilateral cross-cousin marriage, and corporate ownership of land.

In the classic work on matriliny entitled succinctly *Matrilineal Kinship* and edited by Schneider and Gough, Schneider set out "the constant features of the structure of matrilineal descent groups" (1961b:xiii), which were said to exert "certain limiting conditions" on societies with matrilineal descent groups. Schneider noted that the actual system of any particular group would be "a product of those features in interactions with cultural and ecological conditions peculiar to the group" (1961b:xiv), thus distinguishing between the theoretical model and the actual system (of rules) in any particular society. Nevertheless, the key features of matrilineal descent groups were seen as necessary aspects of any working matrilineal system, giving them "their distinctive characteristics" (1961a:5). Schneider and Gough's massive comparative work enshrined the theoretical model as the ideal against which matrilineal systems were measured. It also oriented the research questions of subsequent generations of anthropologists, including those studying the Minangkabau, to questions concerning the maintenance and deterioration of matriliny (Watson 1991).

The Minangkabau present a curious paradox to scholars. Though the demise of Minangkabau matriliny has long been predicted (see, for example, Maretin 1961, and Schrieke 1955), "matrilineal organisation seems to retain an important place in modern Minangkabau" (Kahn 1976:64). The failure of the prediction, according to Kahn, was due to "a false conception of Minangkabau society both before and during the period of colonial rule" (1976:65). In an excellent historical study of the way the Minangkabau were constituted, Kahn (1993) suggests that Minangkabau intellectuals, Dutch orientalists, and colonial officials built images of Minangkabau in the "time of adat" that came to represent Minangkabau society. Stivens, like Kahn, provides strong evidence that the matriliny of Negeri Sembilan, a group whose ancestors originated from Minangkabau land, was and is constituted by "officials, the local 'middle class' and anthropologists" (1996:243). Scholars accentuated particular features and downplayed or ignored others at the same time that colonial officials instituted certain laws aimed at preserving what they assumed were traditional village lifeways. Thus, as Kahn argues, they created an image that was "not so much inaccurate as selective," an image that came to represent "traditional" Minangkabau society (1993:186).

Like Kahn and Stivens, I agree that the notion of "tradition" has held too much weight in studies of matriliny.[15] Having erected an edifice of matrilineal structures, scholars were forced to argue whether or not these structures were being maintained in "traditional" or ideal form. The arguments made by Kahn, Stivens, and others, insist to the contrary that kinship systems are always in process, never permanent edifices. Thomas and Benda-Beckmann's (1985) anthology on the Minangkabau, a compilation of important new work from the 1970s and 1980s, reflected the move to larger questions of change and continuity, rather than the survival of matriliny, arguing for the high negotiability of *adat* in social interaction. In works such as these the question was no longer how matriliny was "eroding," but how it was being reshaped.

Another problem with earlier structural accounts of matriliny was the presumed connection between social change and the "breakdown" or "survival" of matriliny. For many Minangkabau scholars any social change was equivalent to a breakdown, whether it was increased migration, loss of authority of the mother's brother, sale of matrilineal land, privately owned land, or increased nuclear families. The debate about the breakdown of matriliny is no longer a fruitful argument. It comes out of a structuralist framework that assumes the necessity of a coherent and autonomous system. Kinship is a much more complicated process than any simple rendering of it as a unilineal descent system (as intricate as that may get). Kinship is always in process, always negotiated, always producing contradictory practices. Yet I would not go so far as to suggest that matriliny (or patriliny) does not exist. Bolyanatz (1996) argues that matrilineal social relations may exist even though certain practices such as land inheritance do not fit the classic form of matriliny. In West Sumatra the movement of the husband into his wife's house as a permanent member and the more distant relation of the mother's brother to his kin represent changes from the "classic" pattern. Yet even though certain "principles" of matriliny have changed, or been reoriented, the core understanding animating village life revolves around the matrilineage, a group of kin constituted through women.

Because I aim to provide an in-depth understanding of women's power, I highlight the activities and perceptions of individual women and their families throughout the book. In order to make their lives more memorable and thus bring the issues to life more sharply, as well as to disguise the identities of the people being discussed, I have developed five composite families to stand in for the inhabitants of the village. Each family is identified by its senior woman and all its members are given fictitious names. These families are based on and closely resemble actual families in the village but the individuals within them are not in all cases the actual members of those families. In some cases several individuals are blended into one whose rank, age, and economic status is consistent with all the others. All the events described are actual events as well but in some cases they are attributed to people other than the original actors. As an aid to remembering these families, a list of the families and a short description of each person appears at the beginning of this book (see page xiii).

By presenting five families in this book, my aim is to give voice and recognition to individual women and men. But as a feminist anthropologist, I am aware that this effort is always duplicitous; even as it strives for cultural authenticity, it reveals the fiction of the anthropological endeavor (see Abu-Lughod 1990, Visweswaran 1994). Although the people in this book speak for themselves, their words are used to address my theoretical concerns. Yet even if their stories provide evidence for the questions I ask, I hope that they also open a window into the deeper meanings of people's lives.

In this book I aim for coherence and structure at the same time that I assert the negotiated, fluid, and contradictory qualities of social processes. By highlighting women's lives, I wish to convey not simply the centrality of women to all aspects of village life, but the power of women to construct social practice in the village. Despite the monumental strides of feminist anthropology within the discipline as a whole, persistent blind spots in relation to gender make this task essential.

My presentation in this book is only a partial vision of a rural Minangkabau village (see Haraway 1988), one that sees daily interactions as negotiations over identity, power, and meaning, while ignoring other possible interpretations. Although these daily interactions are in one sense the efforts of a dominant group to maintain control over subordinate groups (the view usually taken of peasant life), in another sense they reflect the efforts of families to create and maintain close social bonds through kinship. I view these interactions as a testament to both the viability and the complexity of the community. Although mine is a partial perspective, it underlines the creative ways in which negotiations of identity and power open new paths of meaning and integration within a richly cultured community.

NOTES

1. Although identifying any one group by a particular kinship "system" is problematic, groups in Kalimantan and Java are generally considered bilateral or cognatic, while groups in eastern and western Indonesia are considered (patri)lineal (see Errington 1990, Hüsken and Kemp 1991).

2. The New Order refers to the period of Suharto's presidency in Indonesia, which started in the late 1960s and ended tumultuously in the late 1990s.

3. The five principles of the *Pancasila* are: (1) belief in one God, (2) just and civilized humanitarianism, (3) Indonesian unity/nationalism, (4) democracy led by wisdom born of consultation, and (5) social justice for the Indonesian people (Morfit 1986).

4. Kahn's village site, Sungai Puar, depends heavily on petty commodity production rather than rice land. In contrast, village relations in my village site are oriented around land and lineage-based practices that rely heavily on possession of land.

5. For an intriguing rethinking of the "matriarchy" question, see Sanday 1998.

6. This interpretation was made in works such as Cole 1936, Josselin de Jong 1952, Loeb 1972, and Schrieke 1955, and was upheld by Schneider and Gough 1961.

7. See, for example, Weiner's (1976) analysis of Trobriander women's control of exchange relations, the power of women as sisters (Gailey 1987, Ortner 1981, Sacks 1982), and numerous works on women's control of the household/domestic sphere (for example, Lamphere 1974, Reiter 1975).

8. Other studies attesting to the prevalence of women's landownership in Southeast Asia include Fett 1983, Kassim 1988, Stoler 1977, and Wong 1987.

9. Unfortunately, mainstream peasant studies on Malaysia have given little attention to women's ownership and control of land. In Stivens' telling article on the topic of gender in Malaysian studies, she states that "until recently hardly any published accounts of Malaysian rural society ... actually counted the number of male and female owners of land" (1992:208).

10. Feminist work deconstructing the category "woman" includes, among many others, Butler 1990, Flax 1990, and Kondo 1990.

11. Important feminist studies that pushed the analysis of gender beyond that of husband and wife to women as mothers, sisters, and daughters include Gailey 1987, Ortner 1981, and Sacks 1982.

12. Yanagisako and Collier take a slightly different approach, arguing that equating women's decision-making power with autonomy "fails to investigate the social and cultural factors shaping women's decisions" (1987:38).

13. This interpretation of power draws on the works of Fraser 1989, Margolis 1989, and Moore 1992, among others.

14. This perspective is important not just for understanding women's power but for deconstructing some of the assumptions about men's power. Another ethnographic commonplace is the assumption that men in small-scale communities have power, particularly elders or chiefs, but what that power is, what it is based on, and how it works, is less well examined.

15. But unlike Kahn and Stivens, I give less weight to the determining effects of experts and officials on village practice.

2

Village Currents in West Sumatra

This chapter introduces the village of Taram and sets it within the broader historical context of West Sumatra (see Map 2.1). The village of Taram is located in the regency (*kabupaten*) of Lima Puluh Kota (literally, Fifty Cities), one of the original three provinces that form the core of the Minangkabau world. To the east lies the Bukit Barisan, the mountain range that separates West from East Sumatra and serves as the border of the Minangkabau world.

The village itself is an interesting mixture of old and new. Along some of the irrigation canals, wooden waterwheels are still in use to bring water from the canal to the level of the rice fields. The nearly 3,400 tons of rice produced annually are processed in rice mills operating powerful and noisy gas-driven rice hullers. The main road through the village is paved, but many smaller dirt roads branch off this main road. The brown Sinamar River runs through Taram so that most traffic into the village crosses the old steel bridge over the river.

Across the bridge in the center of town is the market. On non-market days the market is a jumble of empty wood and concrete structures. The jitneys, little minivans with two benches in the back for passengers, sit idling out front waiting for passengers to take to the nearby town of Payakumbuh. On market days the stalls are full of goods and produce: dried fish and eel, all kinds of vegetables, bolts of cloth, plastic buckets and dippers, tin pots and pans, kerosene lamps, and Batman capes and Ninja Turtle stick-ons for the kids. On these days, along with the jitneys, a number of *bendi*, or horse-drawn carts, also travel village roads and wait in front of the market for passengers. A *bendi* can carry two to six passengers and their produce and take them to the outlying hamlets where the jitneys do not go.

Most people are farmers but there are several small businesses in the community. In addition to the seven rice mills, there is a building supply company, a sand supply operation, and numerous small shops and food stalls. Taram boasts

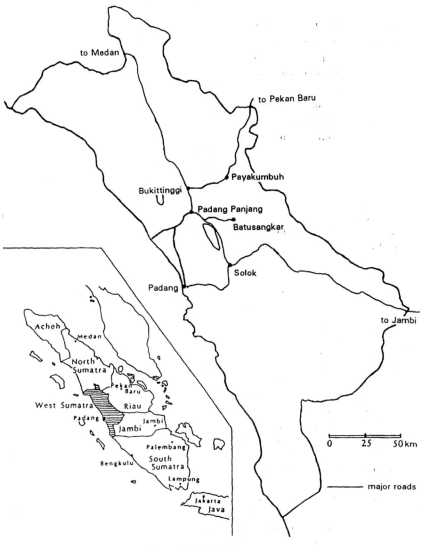

Map 2.1 West Sumatra

several village administration offices, each one topped with a stylized version of the peaked roof of the Minangkabau big house. There are also several schools and a state health clinic (PUSKESMAS, Pusat Kesehatan Masyarakat) that were constructed with state development funds during the 1970s. Water comes from large canals that crisscross the village and feed into numerous small ponds. Some ponds are used to keep fish and even smaller ones are used to wash clothes and bathe. Only a few houses have indoor wells or plumbing. Electricity was brought

Photo 2.1 Big house with an attached unit for daughter

to Taram in 1976, resulting in a constantly increasing number of electrical appli-
ances, televisions, sound systems, and satellite dishes throughout the village. Off
the main road, when nighttime arrives, people close and latch the shutters on
their houses, leaving the back paths in darkness.

Houses reflect inequalities of wealth in the village. They range from the magnificent Minangkabau big houses, or *rumah gadang*, made of wood with soaring
double-peaked metal roofs (see photo 2.1), to smaller brick and plaster houses
with flat metal roofs and cement floors, to one- or two-room wood or bamboo
dwellings with metal or palm-thatch roofs and wood or dirt floors (see photo
2.2). Most houses have small, neat yards that are swept daily. Some have grass
with low shrubs lining the yard; goats come in handy for keeping the grass
clipped or, for households with money, a man with a machete can be hired to trim
the lawn. People grow coconut, banana, or palm trees on their house land and sell
the extra produce. A few households have small gardens for vegetables but most
families buy their produce at the market.

Village routine is punctuated five times a day by the call to prayer blaring over
the loudspeakers at each prayer house (*surau*) and mosque in the village. People
stop their activities to observe the five obligatory prayer times (one of the Five
Pillars of Islam), which take about five to ten minutes, and then return to the
business at hand. Field laborers usually keep working during prayer times and
pray only upon their return home. On Fridays, many of the men in the village go

Photo 2.2 Wood-framed house

to the main mosque to pray. Some older women attend an Islamic study group led by a local woman. During the month of Ramadan, the Islamic fasting month, village routine slows during the day and refocuses on the evening meal after sundown. People turn their thoughts to preparations for the end of the month celebrations and gift-giving, the return of distant kin, and the visits with relatives and friends near and far.

MINANGKABAU VILLAGES AND THEIR HISTORIES

To begin to understand Taram and its particular configuration of geography, history, economy, and culture, it is necessary to look at how Minangkabau see themselves and their histories. Minangkabau identify all the area of West Sumatra as *Alam* Minangkabau, the Minangkabau World (see also Reenen 1996). In 1988 the population living in West Sumatra was approximately 3.9 million.[1] Minangkabau people claim a commonality of beliefs and practices—in their form of kinship, mythology, religion, and *adat*—that allows them to speak of a shared Minangkabau world. This insistence on a common identity is upheld by the Indonesian state, which views the Minangkabau as a single ethnic group. Outside of West Sumatra, Minangkabau are called "orang Padang," the people of Padang,

which is the main port town on the coast of West Sumatra. State and local muse-
ums also construct a unitary Minangkabau identity. Stylized peaked roofs adorn
state buildings throughout West Sumatra; those peaks also identify Minangkabau
businesses both within and outside of West Sumatra. Museum exhibits showcase
Minangkabau wedding costumes and big houses as "traditional" cultural symbols.

Although the Minangkabau claim a single identity, they make a distinction
between people of the *darek*, the three central provinces of Agam, Tanah Datar,
and Lima Puluh Kota, which are considered the cradle of Minangkabau culture,
and the *rantau*, the outlying districts that were settled as Minangkabau moved
outward (see also Kato 1982, Reenen 1996) (see map 2.2). The rantau includes
the south and the west or coastal region of West Sumatra. Culturally these areas
are not considered to have as strong an adat as the central provinces. The coastal
region, in particular, has been subject to a number of outside forces historically
that had less of an impact in the heartland.

Despite assertions regarding their common identity, there are many Minangkabau—many "fantasies" of Minangkabau ethnic identity, to paraphrase Sears
(1996)—that surpass even simple divisions between heartland and *rantau*, or villages and urban areas. Minangkabau people are urban, rural, educated, and
devout; they work as civil servants, farmers, day laborers, and entrepreneurs.
Within any one district or village, people have different levels of exposure to
media, state ideology, Western-oriented education, and religious fundamentalism, creating different orientations to social life and community. These differences are not just the product of a globalized world. Economically and historically there have been variations among districts and villages even in the
heartland of the Minangkabau; these variations have produced distinct cultural
differences.

Prior to Dutch colonization the major trade routes from West Sumatra led to
the east out of the province of Lima Puluh Kota. Once past the mountains, traders
used two rivers to carry trade goods across the island for destinations in the
Malay Peninsula.

> The people of L Kota [Lima Puluh Kota] were regarded as the merchants *par excel-
> lence* of Minangkabau, and for a considerable time they had been prospering by trad-
> ing with Penang [Malaysia] by way of the east coast rivers and later by sending their
> coffee to Singapore. Under Padri administration L Kota became even more prosper-
> ous. A Dutch traveller in 1833 found the *luhak* [district] full of large attractive
> houses and the roads and bridges well-maintained. (Dobbin 1974:341–432)

The fact that the Minangkabau were often called Malay attests to the significance
of their eastern orientation and their place in currents of the Malay world.[2]

The presence of major trade routes helped to create marked differences
between hill and plains villages in the 1700s. Christine Dobbin, a prominent his-
torian of the Minangkabau, described these differences:

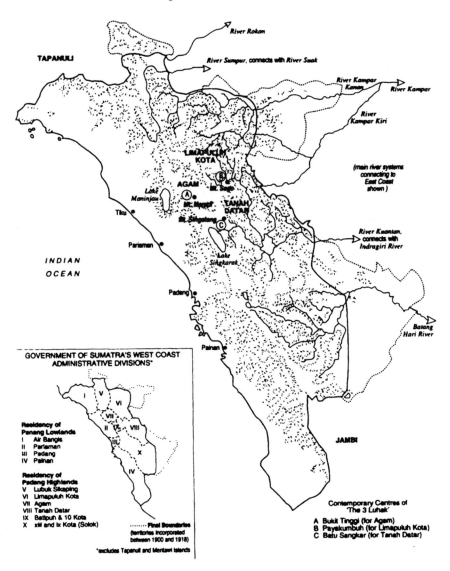

Map 2.2 West Sumatra: Topography of the "Minangkabau World" (Reprinted with permission from Ken Young, *Islamic Peasants and the State*, Yale University Southeast Asia Studies, 1994)

Economically the villages of the plains differed considerably from those of the hills. The work of the inhabitants of the former revolved around wet rice cultivation and the production of a marketable surplus, giving them a distinctive lifestyle of which lineage control and transmission of rice fields was an essential feature. Villages located in the hills, however, were forced through lack of much suitable rice land to turn to handicraft

or service industries, either in the form of manufactures such as weaving or by culti-
vating crops other than rice.... The dominant style of the hill villages was therefore that
of the artisan and the trader, occupations which provided opportunities for wealth to be
acquired by individuals rather than by the lineage as a whole. (Dobbin 1977:26)

The differences in location and types of resources these villages commanded
meant they were integrated in different ways into trade networks, commercial
ventures, colonial projects, and Islamic reform movements. Fluctuations in the
gold market, or in the demands for coffee or gambier, had serious impacts on hill
villages that depended on these resources. Villages dependent on manufacture or
commercial crops had quite different social orientations than those plains villages with ample rice fields. These distinct orientations produced different histories and practices that make any statements about "the" Minangkabau as a single
culture and society somewhat problematic.

Bachtiar's exemplary description of a village provides further evidence of the
differences among villages. Bachtiar states that,

> there is no such thing as a "typical" Minangkabau village community. Each territo-
> rially based community known as *negeri* has existed autonomously for a very long
> time, in some cases for four or five centuries. The inhabitants of each *negeri*
> reserved the right to regulate their own community affairs. They did not recognize
> any higher authority, except God, as holding the right to participate in their affairs
> without their consent.... Since each community existed independently, each devel-
> oped its own traditions, rules and regulations, and way of life. (1967:349)

The favorite expression used by villagers to express the differences from one village to the next is "different pond, different fish" (*lain lubuk, lain ikan*). Despite
the differences, villages did have certain structural similarities. A typical village
contains: "standardized measurements for dry and fluid goods, explicit norms,
hamlets, and a settlement center. It should also have a *balai* [council hall], a
mosque for Friday prayers, a court where cases can be tried, roads and pathways,
and bathing places" (Bachtiar 1967:362).

The distinctness of *adat* from one village to the next underscores the differences even among villages in the heartland. Recent scholarly work has attested
to the historical complexities of and transformations within Minangkabau culture
(Kahn 1993, Thomas and Benda-Beckmann 1985). These differences have been
shaped in varying ways by colonial and postcolonial processes. Rural Minangkabau villages have undergone profound economic transformations as a result of
colonial and state interventions and the world market in the past two hundred
years (see Dobbin 1983, Kahn 1976, 1980).

The earliest travelers to West Sumatra found its lush valleys already long since
turned over to rice cultivation. In his visit in 1818, Sir Thomas Raffles was
impressed with the "extensively populous and highly agricultural country" of the
Minangkabau highlands (Raffles 1835:432). The valley villages primarily grew

wet rice, while the higher elevations exported gambir, coffee, and gold, among other products, to the world market (Dobbin 1983). After the Dutch took control of the area in 1837, they forced the production of coffee in West Sumatra, while at the same time maintaining rice as a subsistence crop.

In the first decade of the 1900s the abolition of forced cultivation and removal of restrictions on rice as a commodity meant increased entry by Minangkabau farmers into commodity production. In the period between the 1930s and the 1960s, according to Kahn (1984), Minangkabau villages mainly grew rice for subsistence. Most of the rice harvest was stored in the family rice granary and used for home consumption. A money economy and subsistence economy existed side by side until the drive for agricultural development in the late 1960s and 1970s under the New Order state pushed rice almost completely into production for cash. In contrast to the situation in Negeri Sembilan, Malaysia, where women's rice crops remained in the subsistence sector (see Stivens 1996), rural Minangkabau women in villages like Taram turned their rice fields into cash crops. In the 1980s and 1990s West Sumatra was producing a rice surplus for a national and international market. Over the course of colonial and state interventions in agriculture, Minangkabau farmers changed from primarily subsistence rice producers with some access to cash through trade and cash cropping, to producers of rice for the market who now follow state mandates for agricultural production.

West Sumatra's location within national and international markets was aided by the Minangkabau practice of circular migration (*merantau*, literally meaning to go to the *rantau* or outlying territories of Minangkabau land). Naim (1971) estimated that as many Minangkabau live elsewhere as live in West Sumatra. These individuals are both long-term and temporary migrants, traveling to other areas of West Sumatra and Indonesia to seek employment or set up a business (Kahn 1980). Some have left the village permanently, lured by a vision of urban wealth or frustrated with the perceived constraints of the local system. Many migrants maintain close ties with their home village and return frequently, particularly during Ramadan, the Islamic fasting month, to bring their earnings to their kin and to catch up on home news. Some migrants disparage village attitudes as backwards but at the same time they eagerly lay claim to their own unique identity as Minangkabau (Sanday 1990). The constant flow of migrants between home villages and urban areas keeps Minangkabau villages closely integrated with national and international forces and influences. Returning migrants bring new ideas and perspectives that become part of the on-going discourse in the village.

MINANGKABAU AND ISLAM

The fact that the Minangkabau are Islamic and matrilineal has long intrigued scholars. Here I explore the history of Islam in West Sumatra as background for the practices and choices being made in Taram in the late twentieth century. Islam has maintained a presence in West Sumatra for over four hundred years, which partly accounts for its designation as "one of the most Islamized regions in Indonesia" (Abdullah 1966:1). Identified with the Sunni branch of Islam, the Minangkabau have been involved in several heated controversies in that time between different schools of Islamic thought. Although no records exist to date the arrival of Islam to Sumatra, the 1400s were most likely the period of first contact (see Dobbin 1983, Reid 1993). According to Andaya and Ishii, "existing evidence suggests that it was in northern Sumatra, closest to India and the Islamic heartlands, where Islam established its first beachheads" (1992:513). Acehnese traders carried their religion down both the east and west coasts of Sumatra and had control of the west coast of Sumatra to Pariaman by the end of the 1500s (Kahn 1980). The Dutch arrived on the west coast shortly thereafter and ended Acehnese control in 1666 (Kato 1982). Throughout the 1600s Islam's strong presence in the major trading ports on the west coast gave it considerable influence in the Minangkabau world (see Abdullah 1966, Reid 1993).

It was probably not until the late 1700s with the Islamic revivalist movement and later Padri movement that Islam consolidated its influence in the heartland of the Minangkabau world (Dobbin 1983). Before the Padri movement, the Minangkabau in the heartland (*darek*) had by no means been strong Muslims. This area was "relatively newly Islamized" in contrast to the conservative stronghold Islam had on the coast (Kato 1982:99). Islamic obligations such as the five daily prayers and the month of fasting were laxly observed and mosques were poorly attended (Dobbin 1974). A visitor to the region during the 1700s noted that the Minangkabau of the interior were "mostly pagan, or rather without religion, with the exception of the notables, who consider themselves Mahometans" (cited in Dobbin 1974: 327), suggesting the weakness of Islam in the highlands.

A moderate revivalist movement began in the late 1700s, led by Islamic men concerned with the practice of social vices in West Sumatra. Under the influence of the Padris, it became more radical and sought to abolish Minangkabau customs considered contrary to the Qur'an. According to Kato (1982), however, the Padri movement was not just an internal conflict between different sects of Islam. It became a means to unify and strengthen the Minangkabau world under Islam against colonial incursions. In this it was similar to political events in other areas of the Dutch East Indies in which Islam became an organizing force against colonial rule (Kipp 1993). The Dutch ultimately put an end to the Padri wars and gained control of West Sumatra in 1837.

The Padri movement and the consolidation of Islam in West Sumatra left a lasting impact on village *adat*. Following that period Islamic doctrine was explicitly assimilated into Minangkabau *adat* (Abdullah 1966, Kato 1982). The dominance of Islam over *adat* was reflected in a proverb concerning the origins of *adat*. The earlier version of the proverb stated that *adat* is based on appropriateness and propriety. Of the two later versions, the first states that *adat* is based on Islam and

Islam is based on *adat*, a version that is current in many villages. The second version states that *adat* stands on Islam and Islam stands on the Holy Book, signifying the dominance of Islam over *adat* (see Kato 1982).[3] As this version suggests, *adat*t changed to reflect more strongly the precepts of Islamic belief.[4]

Debates between traditionalist and modernist schools of Islam were focal points of change in the first two decades of the 1900s in West Sumatra. The Kaum Muda or Young Group of West Sumatra (usually labelled "modernist") advocated using Islam as a basis for modernization and emulation of Western civilization. The debates took place among Western-educated *perantau* (those living in the rantau), men of upper class, urban, colonial families in Padang who saw themselves as builders of a new nation. They pushed for a rational and more scriptural interpretation of Islam, seeking to eliminate non-Islamic practices from religious rites (Abdullah 1972). Based on their understanding of modernity, the Kaum Muda also argued that women should pursue higher education. They believed that women needed to be "free" of the Minangkabau family system and their role as guardian of the matrilineal family (Abdullah 1972:241). This sentiment was echoed throughout the following generations by both men and some women urban intellectuals, whose modern desires led them to argue against the constraints of marriage and yet blinded them to the privileges of matriliny for women (see also Hadler 1998).

Despite the clashes between matriliny and Islamic law (*syariah*), Minangkabau in the late twentieth century affirm that they have established a balance between *adat* and Islamic principles. According to Whalley, who studied Islam in West Sumatra, "The Minang are fond of stating that *adat* and Islam follow complementary paths in an inseparable unity.... Today, the Minang resolve that Islam and *adat* should stand side by side..." (1993:22). Many scholars and local experts agree that Minangkabau and Islamic traditions are not competing systems (see, for example, Hooker 1978, 1984). The two "systems are able to impose simultaneously their patterns of behavior and standards of value" (Abdullah 1966:1). For the Minangkabau, *adat* and Islam are pillars of one system (Kipp and Rodgers 1987). "The difference between *adat* and Islamic principle is not always known by peasants themselves, and certain local practices may be thought of as being part of Islamic law" (Ellen 1983:64–65). Consequently, in many ways village practices are Islamic *and* Minangkabau, the two closely interconnected in Minangkabau thought (F. and K. Benda-Beckmann 1988, Whalley 1993).

The correspondence between *adat* and Islamic law does not mean, however, that the two systems of belief reside compatibly beside each other without affecting the other. In fact Abdullah (1972) points out that Islamic doctrine prompted qualitative changes in *adat* (see also Kato 1982, F. and K. Benda-Beckman, 1985). The potential for change in Minangkabau ideas of gender was quite strong. Islamic gender ideology does not have a place for powerful senior women. With the coming of Islam to Southeast Asia, new sources of authority became available for men, as ritual specialists and Islamic leaders, that were not open to women (Reid 1993, Andaya 1994). In the 1900s urban adat experts reconciled the difference between Islamic ideology and Minangkabau adat by emphasizing men's authority in the lineages and villages of rural West Sumatra, while downplaying women's authority (see Blackwood n.d.).[5]

Rural Minangkabau under the Indonesian New Order continue to be strong adherents of the Islamic faith, participating in national and international Islamic forums. Many village activities in Taram support Islamic projects. For instance, state improvement funds are allocated primarily to the building, maintenance, and upgrading of neighborhood prayer houses. The end of Ramadan (Hari Idul Fitri) is celebrated village-wide in a prayer ceremony attended by members of most households in the village. Through speeches and prayers, villagers are continually reminded and called upon to apply the wisdom of Islamic principles to their own lives. Although it takes many forms in Indonesia (Geertz 1960, Noer 1973, Woodward 1989), Islamic discourse is another factor shaping meaning and identity in village life.

A VILLAGE HISTORY

The history and economy of the village of Taram secures its distinct character as a strongly lineage-based farming community. Taram, which sits in a fertile plain between the 5,000-foot-high Mount Sago and the Bukit Barisan, has a long history as a rice-producing community, a center of Islam, and a stronghold of matrilineal adat. A visitor to Taram in 1835 recorded the following: "This small district is extremely prosperous; the houses look very nice and are painted with flowers. There are considerable coffee gardens, an abundance of rice fields and well-stocked fishponds" (cited in Dobbin 1983:38). Taram's location at the head of the one of the trade routes to East Sumatra established it as a major market town with twice weekly markets. Although the route to East Sumatra no longer heads due east from Taram, Taram's proximity by road to nearby Payakumbuh, the main market and town (*kota madya*) of the district, has allowed it to maintain its position as one of several prominent markets in Lima Puluh Kota. The road between Payakumbuh and Taram is traversed by buses that run daily from early morning to dusk. Rice merchants come to Taram from towns throughout West Sumatra and points east to buy Taram rice.

During the late 1700s Taram was the site of a large Islamic brotherhood and school (*tarekat*) (Dobbin 1983). Although Taram was taken over by the Padri leader Tuanku nan Tua during the Padri Wars (Dobbin 1974), the proselytizing role of its *tarekat* during that period remains obscure. Lack of mention in historical records suggests it avoided serious involvement in the heated religious controversies of the period.

In addition to its renown as a rice producer, Taram is considered a stronghold of *adat*. Village life centers around its ceremonial activities. Ceremonial feasts are held for a variety of events, such as births, deaths, marriages, and circumcisions. Because feasts require the participation of many kin, most people are involved in these events at least once a month. Each event necessitates several deliberations as well as considerable labor by both women and men of the kin groups involved. Ceremonial events are circumscribed by *adat*; each ceremony involves a negotiation and a reworking of *adat*. Islamic practices are part of the ceremonial structure as well. Minangkabau in Taram consider their daily and ceremonial life to be congruent with the principles of Islam. At the level of everyday life, they tend not to make distinctions between *adat* and Islam. Islam is even woven into the matrilineal system. Each lineage has its own religious functionaries, the *imam*, or leader of congregational prayer, and the *khatib*, the person authorized to perform the marriage ceremony.

The vibrancy of adat in Taram is reflected in the centrality and strength of kin groups and their elders. Lineages in other villages have allowed many of their titles to lapse, either because there was no qualified or willing candidates to claim the title or because the costs associated with appointing a new penghulu were prohibitive. Taram lineages have maintained many of their titles. In 1990 there were 120 active titleholders out of a total of 164. Although in other villages a water buffalo must be butchered for the investiture of a penghulu, Taram elders circumvented the problem of costly investiture ceremonies by doing away with the requirement of a water buffalo.

Taram's population in 1989 was approximately 6,800. A few households of civil servants temporarily based in Taram were scattered throughout the village. Most of these were families from West Sumatra. The ethnic composition of Taram was almost exclusively Minangkabau. In the hamlet where I lived the only exceptions were the clinic doctor and his family, who were Chinese-Indonesians, several Javanese immigrants, and a large family of mixed Sulawesi and Minangkabau descent.

Prior to the creation of the Indonesian state Taram had six hamlets or residential areas surrounded by numerous rice fields owned by village inhabitants. Three hamlets clustered in the center of the village, forming the oldest sections, while the other three outlying hamlets were more recent additions developed as the village expanded. Under the Dutch system each village, or *nagari* as they are called in Minangkabau, had its own administrative head (*wali nagari*). In its efforts to manage its citizens, the Indonesian state imposed several different administrative boundaries on the local village system. The Village Law of 1979 reorganized village governance, creating village heads and councils at the *desa* (hamlet) level. This structure was designed to integrate village society more closely with the state "by linking it systematically into a coordinated and elaborate scheme for national development" (Watson 1987:57). Under this new system Taram's six hamlets each became a separate village (*desa*) unit with its own elected head (*kepala desa*) and appointed administrative officers.

Taram's prominence as an agricultural center has held fast. According to one of my informants born in the 1920s, Taram has produced cash crops since the last century. Taram women were known to generate some cash income from the surplus production of rice in the 1940s and 1950s. The Dutch built a dam in the 1920s on a small river along the eastern edge of Taram, providing irrigation for Taram's numerous rice fields. The dam and canals have been instrumental in the adoption of new technologies, allowing most farmers in Taram to grow crops year round. Since the late 1960s, farmers in Taram have been heavily involved in agricultural development. In Taram with its irrigated rice fields, farmers took advantage of state programs to increase the number of hectares under rice cultivation as well as overall rice production. By the late 1970s rice had been transformed into a major cash crop. Almost all farmers in Taram had switched to high-yielding varieties of rice and were raising at least two crops per year. In 1989, according to figures from the subdistrict (*kecamatan*) office for Harau, over 75 percent of all households in Taram were farm households; the total number of farmers and farm laborers exceeded 85 percent of the adult population.[6]

THE HAMLET OF TANJUNG BATANG

One hamlet in Taram, which I call Tanjung Batang, is the site of the main events in this book. During my fieldwork, I surveyed all 125 households in Tanjung Batang (see Map 2.3). According to my survey, 106 out of 115 are farm households that depend on income from farming for some or most of their household expenses. The remaining nine households (out of 115) have no income from land. Most of these are petty merchants or shop owners. Ten of the households in the hamlet are composed of civil service employees and their families. These include teachers at the local elementary school (*sekolah dasar*), several nurses and a doctor working at the state health clinic, and a police officer. Because these families are stationed temporarily in the village and lack permanent ties with village inhabitants, they appear only periodically in this book.

Of the 106 farm households, 83 percent own rice land. Many of these households also sharecrop land belonging to someone else for half of the harvest, or pawn in land, an arrangement in which they take land in pawn and work it, keeping all of the harvest. Only 17 percent of farm households in the hamlet are landless, their farm income coming from sharecropping or agricultural wage labor.[7] Most of the rice produced by farm households is sold as a cash crop to local millers, who transform the *padi* (unhusked rice) into husked rice and sell it to merchants throughout West Sumatra and beyond.

The large majority of farm households in Tanjung Batang are smallholders who own or rent small plots of land that they work themselves. Terms such as proletarianized or semi-proletarianized do not adequately convey a sense of the economic relations within the village. Proletarianization suggests a linear movement from peasant production, where peasants own the means of production, to wage labor, where households have only their labor to sell. Peasant households

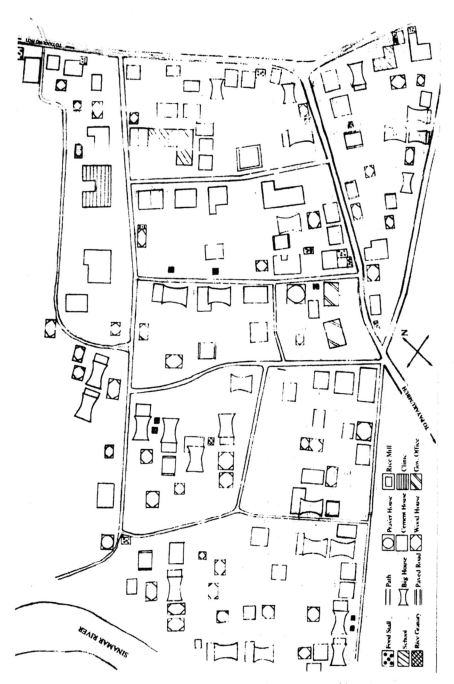

Map 2.3 Map of Tanjung Batang

tend to be involved in a range of production relations, not just one form (see, for comparison, Deere 1990, Stivens et al. 1994). A large number of farm households in Tanjung Batang draw on additional forms of income, including agricultural and nonagricultural wage labor, civil service, petty trade, petty commodities, and remittances from family members who have migrated to jobs in other areas. Where access to land is limited, households depend on non-farm wage labor or migrant labor, most notably by husbands and unmarried children, to provide sufficient income in addition to farm income.

VILLAGE ECONOMIC STRATIFICATION

Taram's integration into capitalist circuits through its rice production has produced shifts in people's income as well as their understanding of village social relations. I turn here briefly to an account of the economic stratification in the village because it underlies many of the tensions documented in this book. Due to differences in access to land among farm households, there is considerable variation in household wealth. Villagers speak of households as rich (*kaya*), average (*biasa*), or poor (*miskin*). Although the differences across these three categories are not large, particularly when compared to Indonesia's urban well-to-do (White 1989), they bear important implications for the opportunities that different households encounter and the ways they are valued by other villagers. I refer to the three categories as classes despite the fact that the term "class" is more typically used to convey a complex set of social relations entailing not only property ownership or productive capacity, but power and authority (Wolf 1992). I use it here in a narrow sense to identify differences in level of productive resources as determined primarily by access to or control of land. Although access to or control over land may be a somewhat narrow measure of class, it has proven in studies of rural Java to correlate highly with access to other material resources (Hart 1986; see also Hüsken and White 1989, White 1976).

I made a determination of class status in the following way. Drawing on White's (1976) calculations of household subsistence needs (basic minimum consumption requirements for rice and nonrice needs), I estimated that a household of five needs to produce 400 *gantang* of rice per harvest to meet the minimum daily expenses of household members. A *gantang* is a local measurement approximately equivalent to three liters of *padi*.[8] Then I used the amount of rice produced per harvest as a rough indicator of household income and wealth. Rice production rather than actual landholdings was a better indicator of household income in this study for several reasons. First, land ownership alone is not an accurate measure since many households produce rice on land they work or hold in pawn from others. Second, since land fertility is inconsistent throughout Taram, an equal area of land may produce very different amounts of rice and income from that rice. Third, it was often difficult to determine the actual amount of land a household owned or had access to. For all these reasons, I use rice production figures rather than size of landholdings to provide a better indicator of household income and class status.

Following villagers' categories, I separated households in the village into three classes based on rice production: poor, average, and well off.[9] These three categories reflect household ability to meet subsistence needs (see also Scott 1985, Wong 1987). Poor households do not produce enough rice on which to subsist (less than 400 *gantang* per harvest); average households produce enough (more than 400 and less than 1,000 *gantang* per harvest) to meet their subsistence needs, pay for their children's educational costs (usually through high school), and sometimes buy a few luxuries; and well-off households have ample income and produce a profit (more than 1,000 *gantang* per harvest).

Access to land and thus class status is closely correlated with power in Javanese peasant societies (Hart 1986), but for rural Minangkabau villages, I use it as only one factor to judge a family's influence and control in the village. I focus on the interrelations and implications of both class and kinship rank in my analysis. In this village wealth corresponds with kinship rank; changes in class status create conflicts between elites and their wealthy, subordinate kin, leading to shifts in local understandings of social relations. In chapter 7, I examine the consequences of rank and differential land access for agricultural relations.

MINANGKABAU *ADAT* AND THE IDEOLOGY OF RANK

Adat, like kinship, is a focal discourse in rural Minangkabau villages. *Adat* is a term used throughout Indonesia and Malaysia to refer to local customs. The meaning of the word, however, is much broader than the English words used to define it, such as custom, tradition, law, or values (Peletz 1996, Sanday 1990). It has been likened to the symbolic universe that orders the Minangkabau world (F. Benda-Beckmann 1979, see also Abdullah 1966). Sanday identifies adat as "a hegemonic ideology ... which legitimizes and structures political and ceremonial life in the villages" (1990:146). Her definition amply describes the encompassing nature of *adat* as an ideology. *Adat* is more than rules of kinship and behavior or prescriptions for ceremonies; it constitutes the foundational discourse for Minangkabau identity. As such, it provides the legitimation and justification for Minangkabau social practices. *Adat* provides the basic structure of social life but it is also constantly negotiated and reconstituted in light of changing historical and global conditions. It is a hegemonic ideology through which other discourses are filtered.

As the basic structure of village life, *adat* provides certain guidelines for behavior, including those concerning kinship relations in the village. *Adat* organizes kin relations into a coherent lineage system that constitutes the basis for all social relations in the village. The lineage system contains three levels of increasingly distant kin, the *suku* (clan), the *payuang* (M., lineage), and the *kaum* (sub-lineage). The *kaum* is the group that holds common rights to ancestral property (*harta pusaka*), which includes the house (*rumah gadang*), ancestral rice land, and title. This group includes all those related matrilineally to a common, known ancestress.[10] The house and lands pass down from mother to daughter, while the family title (*gelar*) is passed from mother's brother to sister's son (uncle to nephew within the woman's line). The title bearer is called a *penghulu*, which I refer to throughout the text as a titled man. The elders of the kin group include the titled man and the senior woman, who is called *Bundo Kanduang*. (Please refer to the appendix for further details on the lineage system.) *Bundo Kanduang* is also the name of a mythical queen of the Minangkabau. Although the Indonesian state has appropriated this term for use in a governmental organization geared toward women, people in Taram assert that they have always used the term to identify the senior woman of the kin group.

This basic structure of kinship transforms into an idiom for social relations throughout the village. The kin tie, which in Taram is referred to as *kamanakan* (M., lit., sister's children, but it also refers to all matrilineal relatives) is used to define all families in the community. Villagers identify three different types of kin or kamanakan, each with different rights and obligations depending on when and how they arrived in the village. These categories of kin are not distinct social classes such as those found in other areas of Southeast Asia with an aristocracy (Kato 1982). However, they do define distinct categories of people within the community. Because the various types of "relatives" are called *kamanakan* (sister's children), I refer to these social categories as kinship ranks.

The kinship ranks are composed of (1) *orang asli* (original inhabitants), who are all *kamanakan batali darah* (blood relatives; lit., sister's children tied by blood) and members of the original founding clans, (2) *orang datang* (*kamanakan dibawah pusat*, kin below the navel), newcomers or outsiders who arrived later and were adopted into the original clans, and (3) descendants of slaves (*kamanakan dibawah lutut*, kin below the knee), who were bought by and became members of the original clans (see also Bachtiar 1967:373).[11] Judging by the variety and even proliferation of these terms in villages throughout West Sumatra, these categories, like *adat* itself, are quite flexible, constructed anew by villagers to meet new conditions or create new boundaries between one group and another.

Members of the original founding clans (*suku*) of Taram claim to be descendants of individuals from the royal court at Pagarruyung in Tanah Datar province (near Batusangkar today). They are said to have "blue blood" (*darah biru*) and are considered nobles (*ningrat*) or high-ranking (*tinggi*). Because the original clans have higher status, I use the term "elite" to refer to them. This usage follows Bachtiar, who called members of the original clans "the elite" or "upper class" (1967:378). Only this group has the right to titles, lineage houses, land, and other privileges, such as certain types of ceremonial dress, that set them apart from the other kinship ranks.

The middle rank of the kinship hierarchy is composed of newcomers who arrived in Taram some time after the village was settled by the original seven clans. Newcomer families come from nearby towns or districts or even other islands. Most newcomers come looking for work or for land to sharecrop because they have no land to work in their own villages. If they decide to remain and become permanent members of the community, they align themselves with an elite sublineage who is willing to adopt them as members of their lineage. The process of adoption is called *bamamak*, to get a *mamak* (the term for the mother's brother of a sublineage but also used generically to refer to the entire elite family [Abdullah 1972]). Adopted kin are not allowed to hold titles but they may be given access to sublineage land to sharecrop. In earlier days, according to my consultant Dt. Rajo, a client family was given the use of the sublineage's house land, one plot of rice land, a fishpond, and garden land.

Although bracketed within kinship ideology, the relationship between elite and adopted kin is one of clientage, hence I use the term "client kin" when referring to adopted newcomer families. The practice of adoption brings unattached families under the authority of elite senior women and men of the sublineage. Client kin are expected to fulfill certain duties and obligations toward their elite kin, while elite kin provide guidance to their subordinate kin in matters concerning *adat*. Client families assist elite kin at all ceremonies hosted by the senior woman's house as well as those hosted by elite kin's affines. Clientage creates a network of people reliant and dependent on elite kin, a point I develop in chapter 6.

The third and lowest rank in the village belongs to descendants of slaves, or those who serve (*dayang*), in polite Minangkabau parlance. Before slavery was outlawed by the Dutch in 1860, people who became slaves were either unable to repay debts or were captured in war. During the Padri Wars in the early 1800s unbelievers were sometimes made slaves (Reenen 1996, Kato 1982). Debt bondage was not slavery but actually a type of serfdom in which the subject owed complete obligation and fealty to the patron. These subjects became junior and dependent members of the extended family (Reid 1983). In Taram, families descended from slaves, whom I refer to as servant kin, serve elite families and are incorporated into their elite's lineage. As with other cases in Southeast Asia, servant kin are considered subordinate members of their lineages. They are denied certain privileges, including the right to ancestral property, title, or lineage house, and are not permitted to attend certain ceremonies or marry outside their group. At ceremonies, servant kin help with preparations "downstairs," (*kerja dibawa*), that is, in the kitchen, or nonceremonial space on the ground level of the big house, and sometimes serve food and drink during the ceremony. In return for their assistance, servant kin are usually given the use of lineage rice fields and lineage land on which to build a house.

Since the formation of the Indonesian state and its declaration of the equality of all citizens, rank considerations have been muted in the village. Most people are reluctant to speak about rank to outsiders. During the first few months I was in the village, everyone I spoke to claimed to be elite (*asli*) either directly or indirectly. Terms of rank were not used in everyday conversation. One elite woman called her client kin *famili,* an Indonesian word meaning relatives. Another woman told me that no one uses the term *budak* (slave) anymore to refer to servant kin. Villagers assert that in everyday life there are few apparent differences among the kinship ranks.

Nevertheless, the ideology of kinship has important implications for people's lives. It encapsulates all social relations within the village and provides the basis for elite control. Elite clans are the dominant sociopolitical group in the village with power over their subordinate kin. As Bachtiar notes, the distinctions among the kin groups creates "unequal opportunities in the realm of political power and social prestige" (1967:378). The men and women of the lower ranks are expected to follow their elite elders in all matters concerning *adat*. The control of subordinate kin makes elite women powerful actors in the village, a point I develop in detail in chapter 6.

A QUESTION OF POWER

In order to begin to understand what constitutes power in the village, it is important to examine and deconstruct the "official" sphere of authority vested in titles. As noted in the last chapter, arguments about Minangkabau women's household authority or "formal" authority leave the definition of power uncontested. As an initial step in the exploration of power, I examine the dynamics of village-level authority to determine the factors that authorize men's power.

The dynamics of authority at the village level are somewhat different than the lineage and clan level. While men and women at the lineage and clan level work together to handle the affairs of their kin, at the village level in Taram, an *adat* council composed of the twenty-four top-ranking titled men (*penghulu*) presides over unresolved civil disputes. At council deliberations titled men take center stage as representatives of their lineages; women do not usually participate. The council is consulted in questions of land disputes or social breaches (although villagers can bypass the council and take such matters to the state court, whose jurisprudence is based on national law and not *adat*) (see Tanner 1971). At this level men have the authority to come to agreement on village-wide issues.

In explaining the authority of the *adat* council, Dt. Rajo said, "only a *penghulu* can represent a *penghulu*" at the village level.[12] This statement has its precursor in Dutch laws that established men as the sole representatives of their lineages. Dutch colonizers consistently underwrote men's power and ignored women. The Dutch plan of control in Indonesia was to bolster local authority figures who would then carry out the policies of the Dutch rulers. Dutch authorities in West Sumatra assumed that the titled man was the lineage chief and traditional authority of the Minangkabau (Kahn 1976, Sanday 1990, Schrieke 1955). In West

Sumatra they installed the highest-ranking titled man as village head in each village and used other titled men as assistants to the chief. In addition to appointing titled men as village heads, the Dutch also insisted on one representative for each lineage. The general policy of the Dutch colonial administration was to "establish a system of communal ownership in which one person, the formal representative, would be the person with whom the administration would deal in all its capacities.... [T]he administration preferred to have one male addressee for all purposes" (K. Benda-Beckmann 1990:102). The Dutch also bolstered men's authority through formal establishment of a court system in which only male lineage heads could represent a lineage in disputes; a woman could not represent herself (K. Benda-Beckmann 1984:56). By imposing a Western-oriented legal system, the Dutch sanctioned men's leadership and legitimated men's authority as heads of lineages. Following Indonesia's independence from the Dutch in 1945, the form of village administration changed, but the system set in place by the Dutch, in which men had representative authority, continued to be the model for village administration.

Because Minangkabau men are privileged as title holders in local and regional spheres of power, some scholars argue that they hold greater power and influence than women (see Krier 1994, and Peletz 1995 for the culturally similar people of Negeri Sembilan). In my view men are privileged as title holders where the state intervenes with its administrative organizations and offices, bringing to bear a gendered model of power that disadvantages women. And yet, while men's authority at the village level is substantiated by the state, within clan deliberations *adat*-inscribed notions of authority underwrite women's authority as senior women. I turn now to a clan deliberation as a way to explore the complexities of power in a rural Minangkabau village.

A CLAN DELIBERATION

Reliance on too-narrow definitions of power, such as those encapsulated in terms like "official" or "public" power, obscures the extent and meaning of women's power. For the anthropologist, power in small-scale communities is often most obvious and easily recognized in and attributed to individuals who occupy "formal" positions in politics and religion: the head of the clan, the village mayor, the religious expert. But power operates in many ways as humans create social relations.

The following story of a clan deliberation illustrates the subtleties of power in an apparently "traditional" formal setting presided over by a group of titled men. It is also a story that introduces Santi's family. The deliberation concerned the proposed marriage of the daughter of a servant family belonging to Santi's lineage. A large group of women and men representing the three lineages of the clan were present at the ceremony along with members and relatives of the servant family.[13]

The central figures in the deliberation are Santi and her nephew Dt. Mangkuto. They are heads of the lineage (*payung*) to which the servant family belongs. Santi is a strong-willed and opinionated woman in her mid-sixties. Like most older women, her long gray hair is knotted in a bun and always covered loosely with a simple drab scarf. She is the sole resident of her nicely kept big house, although she is rarely alone. Her children, grandchildren, and other young relatives frequently pass through the house. Dt. Mangkuto, who has butted heads several times with his forceful aunt, lives with his wife in a village about one hour by bus from Taram.

Members of the servant family include Mariam and her sister Rahmah, the mother of the young woman getting married. Both women have been to Mecca on the *haj*; despite their servant rank they are well regarded as devout Muslims. Mariam's family occupies a big house, although they do not own it. It belongs to their elite kin but there are no surviving women in the sublineage, making Santi their closest elite kinswoman. Rahmah's house is a small contemporary-style house. Neither woman is deferential or submissive in demeanor but they are careful to show respect to their elite kin.

Another key figure is Nurani, an elite representative of the second lineage in the clan. Nurani's mother Yenita lives next door to Santi; the two families work closely together in most clan affairs. Nurani, in her mid-forties, is a generation younger than Santi. Her business acumen and sociability make her a well-respected member of the community. Nurani has come to be the senior representative of her lineage as her aging mother retires from active involvement.

A number of questions were dealt with at the deliberation, the most important being the elaborateness of the ceremony, which villagers refer to as the level of *adat* to be used. Since the marriage was for a member of the servant rank, usually only a simple ceremony, considered "low" adat, would be conducted. A low-level ceremony involves only people within the hamlet and cannot be held in a big house. During the deliberation a dispute arose concerning what exact procedures would be allowed.

On the evening of September 13, I attended the deliberation with Nurani. We picked up Santi at her house, and then stopped to get Mariam, Rahmah's older sister. Mariam was slow in coming out of her house, so Santi yelled from the path for her to hurry up. Nurani looked a little embarrassed at the outburst and said, "Shh, Mak Santi," laughing. But Santi didn't want to wait any longer, so she yelled at Mariam once more, telling her to follow, and then we set off again, walking slowly. When we arrived at Rahmah's house, a couple of men were sitting in the front room, so we proceeded down the side of the house and entered through the kitchen to sit on the floor in the middle room. All the furniture had been removed from the front room and mats laid on the floor. Furniture had been moved aside in the middle room also and mats laid out. The walls of this room were lined with furniture, including a cupboard, television, and refrigerator.

Santi was told the titled men were still talking over at the big house next door. She insisted that she be included in the discussion, so she left the house to meet with the titled men. I was told to stay put, which I complained about, but I was informed that this was a family matter. Since there was some disagreement, they would be embarrassed for me to hear them arguing. After another ten minutes the titled men and Santi returned to Rahmah's house.

The men all settled themselves in the front room along the four walls. There were twenty men in all, not all of them titled. Among them was the titled man of Rahmah's sublineage and his brother; Dt. Mangkuto, the male head of the lineage; Santi's son; and two titled men of Nurani's lineage (her brother lives in Jakarta and was not there). We waited a good half an hour for the titled man who holds the highest title in the clan (*pucuk suku*). He never did come but sent someone to represent him, an older man with a big hooked nose and floppy cotton cap on his head. Dt. Mangkuto sat in the middle on one side. On the other side in the middle was his cousin, Santi's son. The representative of the male clan head sat against the wall farthest from the front door.

I bridged both rooms, having been told to sit with the men, but deciding to sit in the doorway between the front room and the middle room, where all the women sat. At least twenty women filled the middle room in several distinct groups. Among them were a group of elite kinswomen who came from a neighboring hamlet about a fifteen- to twenty-minute walk away; Rahmah, who was a nervous wreck, sitting with her relatives and daughter; and the three women I came with, Nurani, Santi, and Mariam, who sat next to me at the doorway between the two rooms.

As the senior man of Rahmah's lineage, Dt. Mangkuto opened the discussion with a few formal words of introduction. He then laid out the questions to be resolved. The ensuing discussion lasted about one and one-half hours. The men spoke in orderly fashion, rarely two of them talking at once. About seven men did most of the talking, mainly the titled men present; all the rest of the men sat and smoked and did not offer any comments. Most of the questions were directed at Dt. Mangkuto.

The meeting was going well. There was apparent agreement that the ceremony would be a small one, but that the big house belonging to the elite sublineage would be used for part of the ceremony. The men began discussing whom to invite; they asked the women if they agreed so far and who they thought should be included. A comment was made by one of the men that he didn't understand the women's part and that the women should just arrange it themselves, but some discussion between the two groups ensued about whom the women would be inviting.

During the discussion, Santi sat listening intently most of the time, and once or twice called out some information, or clarification, without being asked. Dt. Mangkuto called on Santi several times, asking her what the women were going to do. Sometimes she made decisions on her own, and sometimes she deferred to the women's group as a whole, asking for their opinion. Nurani also listened intently, but only spoke to the men when asked a question. The first time Nurani was asked a question about the local chapter of the PKK, she was sitting slightly behind Mariam. She tried to speak around her, but Mariam was quickly pulled back to sit behind Nurani, so Nurani had a clear view of the men.

After discussion about the invitations, Dt. Mangkuto asked the two senior women, "How about it? Is that all right? Have we come to a decision?" One replied: "We have, let's do the invitation then... especially the invitation to the hamlet folk." The other woman: "The proposal which Mangkuto has expressed has been accepted by us, we have agreed to it. That's it." First woman again, who was getting tired of the twists and turns of the discussion: "Let's not repeat this again. That's it." Another woman in the background seconded her statement.

Yet as the meeting progressed, the agreement concerning the use of the big house fell apart. Non-elites are not supposed to use the big house for their ceremonies. Using the big house for any part of the ceremony would increase the status of the ceremony, and by extension the servant family. Santi, the senior ranking women of the lineage, was adamantly opposed to using the big house. She argued forcefully with Dt. Mangkuto, declaring, "It's not going to be in the big house. Just here only [in Rahmah's own house]." Both men and women voiced reservations about its use and raised questions about what proper *adat* would be in this case. The titled man representing Rahmah's family supported the use of the big house. As Santi and others continued to assert their opposition, the consensus began to shift away from using the big house. Finally, the titled man of Rahmah's family stopped the meeting to consult with Rahmah, the mother of the bride. More questions were raised, more statements in opposition. After much more discussion among the men, with women voicing their opinions in the middle room, Dt. Mangkuto summed up the situation: "So, we decide it that way then. That is, we are not going to use that big house; we will do the celebration right here then."

Near the end of the meeting, the women started talking among themselves to iron out the different things that they needed to take care: who would deliver invitations, who would be asked to contribute trays, and so forth. Their discussion was not orderly. Several women would talk at once, or in small groups, and then Santi would accept or pronounce the decisions.

In the front room the men were trying to wrap up their discussion. One of the men summed up the process: "We are done then. We were divided before we sat down [for our deliberation]. Now, after we sit together, we are becoming one!" A few minutes later another man commented, "While we are finishing up, I should express one thing, just like polishing, to make everything smoother. Is there anyone who feels hurt? Because we are looking for a clear solution." A check to see if there were any hurt feelings allowed any remaining disagreement to be voiced. When none were expressed, Dt. Mangkuto responded: "We have solved it by our deliberations, so we should put it behind us."

When it was clear the issues were settled, the men decided to hold the next meeting to inform the hamlet on Monday, the seventeenth. The women agreed and said they would get together on Sunday to start making preparations. Then the men started talking about some meetings they wanted to have to discuss adat. But Santi interjected, "We have called it done, right? So it's done, it's done. Let's go home then." At that, everyone rose to leave.

In this story there are a number of twists and turns that prevent a simple reading of power. In Minangkabau deliberations the various elements of seating and speaking seemingly privilege men. Seating arrangement at deliberations vary, but men and women always sit separately. In this case the men sat on the floor in the front room of the house while the women sat in a separate group in the next room closer to the kitchen. At smaller deliberations and in smaller houses men and women sit in the same room but always with men nearer the door and women nearer the kitchen.

The spatial orientation of people in this deliberation can be read as putting men in the superior, public space while confining women to the rear (kitchen), inferior space. A closer look at the topography of Minangkabau houses, however, helps to unsettle the assocation of men/superior, women/inferior. Seating for all meetings is based on the model of the big house, where men sit in the outer space of the open hall and women sit toward the inner space nearer the central post. The central post of the house is located between the hall and the entryway or veranda (*pangkalan*, meaning base, beginning, or origin), a space usually lower than the hall that also contains the kitchen (Ng 1993). The central post is the "ritual attractor" of the house, which in Austronesian houses means it "represents, in concentrated form, the house as a whole" (Fox 1993:1). Minangkabau proverbs refer to women metaphorically as the Center Pillar of the Big House [the lineage house] and Holder of the Key to the Chest [lineage property] (Reenen 1996).[14] In discussing the gendering of space in Austronesian houses, Waterson suggests that "rather than a division between 'back' and 'front' portions of the house, in a number of cases the more meaningful contrast would appear to be between 'inner' and 'outer' parts, women often being associated with the womb-like 'inner' portion of the house—the source of life, fertility and nourishment" (1993:227). Waterson notes ironically that "rather than women being 'confined' to the back of the house, it is men who are 'confined' to the front—a dubious honour at best" (1993:229).

The association of Minangkabau women with the symbolic source of power in the big house provides a different reading of seating arrangements. Men sit in the respected but outer part of the house, reflecting their transient relation to it, while women sit at the heart of the house, reflecting their place as the enduring and permanent core of the lineage. The easy association between power and public falls apart in this reading, replaced by a more complex relation between gender and power.

Looking more closely at the process of speaking during deliberation also helps to unsettle simple readings of power. In the story above, men lead the deliberation and do most of the talking. In this case Dt. Mangkuto, as the highest-ranking man in the lineage involved, takes the lead in opening the discussion and moving it along, although the representative from the clan (*suku*) is present. The women appear to speak from the sidelines only in response to questions asked. In addition, men's and women's styles of speaking differ. In this discussion men tend to rely on obscure metaphors and proverbs, while the women are more direct and to the point when they speak (see also Tanner 1971). But although titled men are the main speakers at this deliberation, what does this process tell about the nature of authority?

Throughout the deliberation the men check with the women to see if they are in agreement. At first they ask them questions about the women's part of the celebration, wanting to know who of the women in the village should be invited and what civic organizations should be contacted for help. The women seem anxious to move the meeting along with their ready agreement ("that's it, that's it"). But once the problem is raised anew about the use of the big house, the senior woman Santi is quick to jump in and voice her opinion. In fact, the meeting next door before the deliberation was supposed to have brought agreement among those present, so that in this public setting, no one would have to argue about where to have the ceremony, which would be humiliating to the Rahmah's family. With Santi adamant about her position, the men try to find a way to agree without hurting people's feelings. Nothing is finalized until it appears everyone is in agreement; then Dt. Mangkuto states the agreement for everyone to hear.

THE *ADAT* OF CONSENSUS

This process reflects the key to decision-making in all lineage matters: deliberation and consensus. Decision-making within the lineages is based on the process of consensus (*mupakat*) among all adult members of the lineage. In this case the elders of the lineage, those most knowledgeable about *adat*, meet to work out an arrangement. Younger kin are not present except the bride-to-be, who does not offer any opinion. A well-known Minangkabau adat proverb expresses the process in the following way:

> The nieces and nephews are subject to the mother's brother,
> The mother's brother is subject to the titled man,
> The titled man is subject to consensus,
> Consensus is subject to the power of reasoning,
> The power of reasoning is subject to what is proper and possible,
> What is proper and possible is subject to truth,
> It is truth which becomes king.[15]

This proverb articulates both a hierarchical and egalitarian principle followed in Minangkabau decision-making (K. Benda-Beckmann 1984, see also Prindiville 1981). Senior men are identified as the chain of formal authority, but the final authority rests in unanimous agreement (consensus) among all members of a sublineage or lineage, that is, both men and women. These are contradictory principles that appear to give men authority while at the same time basing that authority on a process of consensus.

The consensus process is based on the principle that everyone has an equal voice (*hak suara sama*). It should be noted, however, that the principle of "equal voice" is tempered by the principle of seniority, or respect for elders. This principle grants greater wisdom and influence to the elder generation. It also grants greater influence to those of elite rank, making a subordinate kinswoman like Rahmah somewhat fearful of going against the desires of Santi. I was told that young people, including the newly married, have to learn from their elders; they have no opinion of their own yet. Even those with children may not have enough "wisdom." Though no decisions are made without full agreement in the consensus process, the opinions of senior men and women hold more weight. They can thus shape the opinions of others or prevent others from making a decision to which they are opposed.

How then to interpret a formal meeting in which titled men are the speakers and senior women sit on the sidelines? Are titled men the power brokers? Do their titles give them the final say in decision-making? In the case above, Santi's position was the one that eventually prevailed. Although some of the men tried to finesse the situation by allowing certain privileges (by using the big house for part of the ceremony only), Santi was able to prevent any concessions. Sanday (1990) argues that a forceful senior woman, which clearly Santi is, has equivalent power to a senior man. But this process provides more than equivalence. In the context of deliberations, the consensus process reallocates power along several vectors between men and women.

It is apparent from the deliberations above that the duties of a titled man are more cooperative than controlling: they are to confer, discuss, and help solve or settle issues and problems. On this point the *adat* writings of Hakimy provide substantiation: "The leadership (*pimpinan*) of a penghulu does not mean to be in charge of (*mengepalai*), but includes matters of the inner self and the outer world, the intellectual and spiritual..." (1994a:18, see also Kato 1982:46). The authority vested in titled men gives them power to speak but not to act independently within the lineage. As Tanner and Thomas (1985) point out, Minangkabau men's authority does not give them the power to hand down decisions on their own; their major role is to arbitrate disputes. Based on her assessment of ceremonial processes, Pak comes to a similar conclusion. She states that titled men do not constitute a political apparatus but an administrative body that executes collective decisions (1986:266). Titled men are not heads or "chiefs" but part of the power structure.

These discussion leaders are not in fact the ultimate authority separate from and above that of the group. Elite women equated the senior woman's responsibilities with those of the titled man. According to one elite woman, "The senior woman [*Bundo Kanduang*] is the same as the men elders [*ninik-mamak*], one can't make a decision without the other agreeing." Dt. Rajo, one of my male consultants, agreed that neither can make decisions alone. Both men and women lineage elders must be in agreement. "If the men elders [*ninik-mamak*] allow something, and the senior woman [*Bundo Kanduang*] doesn't, they must discuss it first. If both of them approve, then okay. If just one side approves, it's not okay. They have to be in accord first." According to Dt. Rajo, "as with the division of labor in the rice field, senior women [*Bundo Kanduang*] and senior men [*ninik-mamak*] each have their own responsibilities."[16] These statements provide evidence that both women elders and men elders have authority in matters of *adat*. They are like two sides of a coin. Each has their own responsibilities and together they see to it that lineage affairs are carried out. The authority of the titled man is more diffuse than the term "leader" or "head" would suggest.

On closer examination, men's authority is not the dominant force within the village. Though they voice the final decision, that decision is a result of group consensus and cannot be made unless the group is in agreement. Deconstructing men's power as "heads" of lineages in an "official" context of lineage deliberations reveals the complex processes at work in rural villages.

Minangkabau village relations are much more complex than a simplified picture of men's public authority and women's domestic authority. In terms of the Minangkabau it is insufficient to assume that authority and power resides with those who hold titles. Narratives of power that privilege any singular point of authority (head, clan chief, titled man) or any singular structure (lineage system, public venues) do not tell the whole story. For the Minangkabau, power—even in the official, public settings of lineage deliberations—operates through consensus, thus reallocating authority throughout the ranks of senior elite men and women. Although within state-sponsored structures men are privileged as leaders and voices of authority, that privileging has less significance in local social relations organized on the basis of kinship. Within the village, women's authority as elders in their kinship groups ensures that they are powerful actors in the deliberative process.

In this chapter I have provided an overview of Minangkabau identities in West Sumatra, emphasizing the differences among places and people in order to make sense of the particular configurations that shape the village of Taram. As the clan deliberation illustrates, the webs of power within the village are complex, encompassing notions of *adat*, gender, rank, and title. Having positioned women as powerful actors despite a long history of colonial and postcolonial support for men's authority, I turn now to examine why it is that women's voices cannot be silenced nor their authority ignored.

NOTES

1. The population of West Sumatra in 1988 was 3,943,363 (Kantor Statistik 1989). Of that number the great majority are Minangkabau, but since the Indonesian state does not compile census figures by ethnic group, the exact figure is not known.

2. Drakard notes that prior to Dutch colonization the boundaries of the Malay and Minangkabau worlds were "amorphous and mobile frontiers not mutually exclusive" (1990:12).

3. "Adat basandi syarak, syarak basandi Kitabullah" (Hakimy 1994b).

4. Interestingly, following the consolidation of Islamic belief in Minangkabau, the conversion of two neighboring ethnic groups by Minangkabau proselytizers resulted in a switch not only to Islam but to matriliny (Kato 1982:101, n. 30), a fact that underscores the importance of both matriliny and Islam to the Minangkabau of that period.

5. Whether rural Minangkabau uphold the Islamic ideology of gender asymmetry contained in the concepts of *akal* and *nafsu* is another question. According to Islamic interpretation, men are thought to possess *akal*, or reason, in greater degree than women, while women are said to have greater passion, or *nafsu*, than men (see Peletz 1995). This Islamic principle was not mentioned in Minangkabau village studies by Reenen (1996) or Whalley (1993), whose work focused on an Islamic center for women, although Krier (1994) asserts that rural villagers in Sidiam adhere to this Muslim principle. This principle was not apparent in the interviews I conducted in Taram.

6. Comparison with Stivens's (1985, 1992, 1996) work on rural women in Rembau, Negeri Sembilan, is instructive. Due to the shift to and then decline in rubber production, the recent demise of rice production, and the pull of wage labor in Rembau, women's land is providing little income and forcing increased dependence on remittances from working husbands and children. In Rembau agricultural transformations have weakened women's position in their households, whereas in rural West Sumatra, the viability of rice as a cash crop provides ample income to women landowners. In fact, the number of hectares under elite women's control has increased.

7. Tanjung Batang is not representative of all hamlets in Taram. In one other hamlet that I surveyed, 50 percent of the households are landless and depend on sharecropping for access to land. The difference is due to that fact that most landowning families live in three central hamlets, while the outlying hamlets are comprised of a greater percentage of client families.

8. Unhusked rice (*padi*) is taken to the mill where it is hulled. Milled or hulled rice (*beras*) is measured by weight. One kilogram of husked rice is produced from 1.66 *gantang* of unhusked rice.

9. I also took into account other sources of household income, including wage labor, petty trade, etc., in determining class status, but did not have exact figures for these sources.

10. This description of the lineage system is essentially consistent with that of Kato (1982:49–50), who labels the three levels *suku*, *payung*, and *paruik* (*saparuik*, of one womb). *Paruik* in his usage refers to the smallest group of people sharing one title. Bachtiar (1967) notes that *paruik* and *kaum* are comparable terms in Taram: "descendants of a maternal ancestor connected with a particular ancestral house (*rumah gadang*) form a *sabuah parui* (out-of-one-womb), a matrilocal extended family that in reality may well be identical with the *kaum* group" (1967:370–71). Kahn (1980) describes a slightly different system of lineages for Sungai Puar, reflecting that village's particular *adat*.

11. The terms and number of categories vary from village to village. Other terms used include *kamanakan dibawah dagu* (relatives below the chin, the "real" kin) and *kamanakan dibawah pinggang* (relatives below the waist, for descendants of slaves). For further discussion of these categories, see Bachtiar 1967, Junus 1964, Kato 1982, Reenen

1996, and Swift 1971. The three categories I use are based on the terms used in Taram.
(See Appendix for further elaboration.)

12. In a nearby village, however, a woman can represent her lineage when there is no
qualified man.

13. The following account is based on my observations before and during the deliberation as well as the audio tape of the deliberation, which was transcribed and translated
from the Minangkabau language into English by Sjamsir Sjarif. I thank him for his excellent rendering of a difficult tape.

14. The Minangkabau phrases are: *Limpapeh Rumah nan Gadang, Umbun Puruak
Pegangan Kunci.*

15. *Kamanakan barajo ka mamak/Mamak barajo ka panghulu/Panghulu barajo kemu-
pakat/Mufakat barajo ka alua/Alua barajo kepatuik jo mungkin/Patuik jo mungkin barajo
kapado bana/Bana itulah nan manjadi rajo* (LKAAM 1987:116. Translation follows K.
Benda-Beckmann 1984:1).

16. As can be seen in these statements, the terms *ninik-mamak* and *Bundo Kanduang*
represent two sides of village authority, men elders and women elders. The term *ninik-
mamak* defined by Echols and Shadily (1989) as "village elders," however, has no specific gender identification. According to Junus (1964), the Minangkabau term *niniek* (variant spelling) means grandmother or female ancestor. In combination with *mamak*, the
term *ninik-mamak* should refer to both men and women elders. It is possible that this term
has been masculinized in line with "*modernisasi*" and the state insistence on men's
authority.

3

✛

Senior Women and Their Houses

In this chapter and the next I examine a familiar location for studies of women: the house. It is a familiar location because of the strong association in scholarly literature between women and houses. If women are found anywhere in ethnographies, it is certainly in houses. But my purpose in starting with houses is to destabilize common assumptions about houses and households, in particular rural matrilineal households. I do this by viewing the household not simply as a set of interior events and domestic tasks but as the very center of kinship and community relations. In particular, I explore the centrality of the mother-daughter relationship to rural households as well as the implications of men's relations to both their affinal and natal households. By paying attention to women as both mothers and daughters, I reveal a dynamic often obscured in household studies. The differences and conflicts between mothers and daughters that arise as they move through the life cycle from junior to senior women help to uncover the way women negotiate and reconstitute matrilineal practices in rural households.

HOUSEHOLD CONNECTIONS

Households have been used as a standard if at times unwieldy tool in the study of rural life.[1] In peasant studies households are the primary means used to analyze agrarian change. Equally useful to analysis is the physical structure of the houses themselves. Drawing on Levi-Strauss, cultural studies of the "house" in Southeast Asia are used as a way to circumvent rigid analyses of kinship based on lineage structure. Although Levi-Strauss's concept of "house societies" is limited more or less to hierarchical, lineage-based societies, it has

51

proved a fertile concept for thinking about the relations between buildings, people, and ideas in Southeast Asia (Fox 1993, Carsten and Hugh-Jones 1995). The "house" can refer to physical structures as well as cultural categories, cosmological order, or kin groupings.

Houses in some Indonesian societies are one of the most salient categories for talking about social groupings (see Fox 1980), a fact especially true for the Minangkabau, a lineage-based society. The Minangkabau big house embodies kinship, gender, and rank. The big house contains the smallest segment of the lineage; the size and splendor of the house attest to the rank and status of that lineage. In her wonderfully detailed description of the "traditional" Minangkabau house, Ng (1993) notes that the Minangkabau house is not only a symbol of lineage identity but, more importantly, it is identified with a core group of women (see also Reenen 1996). The Minangkabau house contains a group of closely related kinswomen, who from one generation to the next "move through the house reproducing lineage continuity" (Fox 1993:3).

I follow Ng in viewing Minangkabau big houses as the embodiment of the centrality of women to the household and lineage, but as I explore in this chapter and the next, big houses and their contemporary-style replacements are more than templates for living or sites for social reproduction.[2] Houses are the connection between kin/families and the social processes they embody. Rural Minangkabau families may be contained within one structure for several generations, or they may split into several single-family houses as daughters move out. Variations in house structure and household composition reflect social divisions and tensions within and between kin groups, genders, and generations. Although mothers, daughters, and sisters are the "source of continuity" in houses, their relationship is not simply reproduced from one generation to the next. It must be continually negotiated in each generation in response to changing conditions to ensure both the future of the house and the lineage. In the drama of houses mothers and daughters figure prominently and powerfully.

I explore two sets of relations in households, those oriented around production and those oriented around gender. The two overlap in many instances since household production is gendered. For the Minangkabau, *adat* prescribes particular duties, rights, and privileges to each member of households based on gender and kinship. It sets the foundation for individuals' actions within and between households. In this chapter I emphasize household economic relations (particularly access to land and control of resources), not because I believe these are the only significant household relations, but because for rural villagers in Taram, land and its ownership are intimately tied up with definitions of households and kin groups. Land and households are also intimately connected with state and global processes of agricultural development. As I go through this analysis, I explore how matrilineal practices and state and global discourses intersect in Minangkabau households.

HOUSES AND MATRILINY

Rural Minangkabau households reflect and speak to matrilineal kinship in their physical structure. Big houses are impressive buildings constructed of wood planks and a minimum of twenty-five posts covered with a peaked zinc roof and decorative wood siding (see photo 3.1). The roofs of older big houses were made from black, palm-fiber thatch. Big houses constitute just 20 percent of houses in the hamlet of Tanjung Batang. The small number of big houses is somewhat misleading, since it seems to suggest the decline of big houses in this village, but only elite families have the right to build big houses. Of the twenty titled sublineages in Tanjung Batang, 75 percent currently own and maintain a big house.[3] In fact, two new big houses have been built since 1976 in Tanjung Batang to replace collapsed structures. Other elite families have invested money in renovating or improving their big houses.

The big house is the structural representation not only of the elite status of the sublineage that owns it but of the matrilineal relations within it. It usually contains an extended family of three to four generations, including a senior woman, her daughter(s), their husbands, and children. Compartments lining the back and one end of the big house are designated for mother and daughters, while the front half of the house is an open space or hall (*ruang*) for public

Photo 3.1 Close-up of a big house in Tanjung Batang

gatherings and lineage ceremonies (see figure 3.1). The central post of the house is located between the hall and the entryway or veranda (*pangkalan*, meaning base, beginning, or origin). The entryway is lower than the hall and contains the kitchen (Ng 1993). As noted in the previous chapter, the central post, or "ritual attractor" of the house (Fox 1993:1), is identified with the senior woman; she is called *limpapeh rumah nan gadang*, the central pillar of the big house (Reenan 1996).

At marriage a daughter moves into the annex or end compartment (*anjuang*) farthest from the central post and entrance to the big house; her husband resides with her there. Older married sisters (if they are living at home) move down the row of sleeping compartments toward the central post. In Tanjung Batang the eldest women or grandmother may sleep in a compartment attached to the entryway. Some big houses have annexes on the veranda end of the big house for older married daughters. Because a son leaves the house at marriage (and usually well before), one room next to the kitchen end of the house may be designated as the

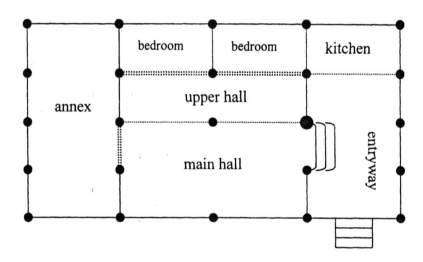

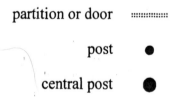

Figure 3.1 Floor plan of a big house

men's room. Should a son or brother be divorced or widowed and forced to return home, he may use that room, but kinsmen in such a situation usually prefer to sleep at the nearby *surau*. The big house represents the "ideal" Minangkabau household, its structure signifying the preference for keeping daughters at home (matrilocal postmarital residence).

The division of the house into an interior part, containing sleeping compartments and the kitchen, and a front, public space where ceremonies are held is typical in many houses in Southeast Asia. As noted in the last chapter, a number of observers suggest that this inner/outer division corresponds with a simple division between female/male, domestic/public, and inferior/superior. Waterson, however, cautions against such associations of house and space (see Waterson 1993). As the symbolism of the central post and the progression of daughters through the house suggests, Minangkabau women are identified with houses, not as the inferior part but the core and continuity of the house. In fact, women dominate the house both in daily life and during ceremonies (see also Pak 1986). Men, because they marry out, are not part of the daily life in the big house and only take center stage temporarily during ceremonies. Even husbands spend most of their time away from the house working, particularly those who have found paid labor elsewhere, and only return in the evening (see also Ng 1993).[4] The close association of Minangkabau women with the big house highlights the importance of women to the lineage, not simply as its reproducers but as its pre-eminent figures, its source, and its power.

MOTHERS, DAUGHTERS, AND MATRIHOUSES

Minangkabau *adat* contains two key principles that support women's dominance in rural households, particularly elite households. The first, matrilineal inheritance of property, means that ancestral property is passed from mothers to daughters. The second, matrilocal residence, means that married couples reside with the wife's family. For rural Minangkabau these principles substantiate women's control of houses and married daughters' right to live with their mothers, while requiring brothers and sons to move out to wives' houses. In terms of land, matrilineal inheritance underscores women's rights as heirs to and controllers of matrilineal property. Daughters inherit the rights to land and its disposition; sons may be given use rights if land is available and their mothers are willing to help them out, but they cannot pass on matrilineal land to their children. These principles inform people's practice of household relations.

For the purposes of analyzing household relations, I distinguish between three groups: the sublineage (which I also call matrikin), the matrilineal unit, and the conjugal unit. Although men and women of the sublineage differ in their relations to the house, these differences are often overlooked when the two are treated as a single group. The sublineage, which is the smallest group of living kin of a common ancestress (usually three to four generations), holds common interest in land, house, and title, but mothers and daughters have different rights in land and houses than sons and brothers. Further, the sublineage is not the same as the group of kin living in the house since kinsmen reside elsewhere for most of their lives. I use the term "matrilineal" unit to refer to kinswomen, usually mothers, sisters, and daughters, who live together in an extended household or in other ways share family resources. The conjugal unit is a subsidiary unit within the matrilineal unit in the extended household.

In order to distinguish between different types of households in the village, I refer to the extended households of mothers and daughters as "matrihouses." This term is not used locally or in the literature but I feel it is a useful way to highlight the female generations, in particular the mother-daughter relationship, in these households.[5] A matrihouse is distinct from other households in the village by the presence of two or more generations of married, adult women. It may be a big house, an extended household living in a contemporary house, or even a two-generation household with a recently married daughter.

Portrait of a Matrihouse

The histories of matrihouses (like the genealogies of sublineages) are constructed around the bond between mothers and daughters and the movement of daughters and granddaughters within or out of houses. Matrihouses persist from generation to generation as daughters are born, marry and bear children, and eventually achieve the position of senior women themselves. Over the generations matrihouses may develop into a cluster of houses (*kampung*) of related kinswomen as descendants of daughters split and establish their own houses. The following story of Hartati's family provides an excellent example of relations in a matrihouse.

> This four-generation family, one of the wealthiest elite families in the village, lives in a lively, bustling big house. It includes Hartati's elderly mother; the senior woman Hartati, who is widowed; her younger sister Siti and her husband (no children); one married daughter, Yetri, with her husband and two children; and an unmarried daughter. Another married daughter left the village and lives with her husband and children in Jakarta. Hartati has three brothers; the titleholder is Dt. Rajo.
>
> The big house has been extended on both ends to add extra bedrooms. Hartati's room is upstairs in the big house near the door to the entryway, while her elderly mother (now widowed) and Siti and her husband live downstairs in the other addition they built on the house when Yetri got married. Yetri, the only married daughter at home, has the prestigious end room (*anjuang*). Regarding the relationships within the household, Yetri commented to me, "We all get along well. That's why we all live here."

Hartati, the senior woman, has been given control of the big house by her mother, who is in her eighties. Siti never had any children, so Hartati, who is in her early sixties, was the logical choice to take over as senior woman. Fortunately, Hartati, like her mother before her, is well suited to the position. Hartati married an elite titled man belonging to Yonalis's lineage; his title was considered the highest-ranking title in the village. Outgoing and sure of herself, Hartati is keenly interested in maintaining the reputation and standing of her family. Her interest in improving her family's position in the village is signified by the fifth peak on her big house (all other big houses have two or four peaks). She and her family were successful in negotiating for the right to build the additional peak, a sign of the prosperity and status of the family. For her daughters' weddings, she threw extravagant ceremonies, the lavishness signifying their wealth and importance. Hartati also takes an active interest in the affairs of her lineage. She not only oversees the affairs of her kin, she can also be found helping with preparations for their ceremonial festivities.

Possessing a number of sizable rice fields, Hartati's family is one of the top producers of rice in the village, producing over 2,000 *gantang* per harvest.[6] No one in Hartati's family actually works in their rice fields. Hartati hires workers to do the planting, weeding, and harvesting in some of the fields. For other more distant fields, she has sharecroppers who do the work and return half of the harvest to the family. Hartati uses the income from the rice harvest for herself, her mother, and her unmarried daughter. Siti has a plot of land that is farmed for her; she keeps the income from the harvest for herself. Her husband also brings in a small amount of money from the sale of cattle he owns.

Yetri, the married daughter, has two small children that she stays home to care for. As the daughter who stayed home, she is most likely the one to take over when her mother is too old to manage the affairs of the family. She says she will be the next senior woman and is already learning about lineage affairs from her mother. A stylish woman with shoulder-length black hair, Yetri seems content with her place in the house and the expectations about her future. Although she works closely with her mother, she also has her own income from her husband. Like her mother, Yetri married a titled man, who is from the same lineage as her father (she married into her *bako*). Her husband works as a civil servant in the nearby town; the income he gives his wife goes to the expenses of raising their children. In addition Yetri also has a plot of rice land given to her temporarily by her husband's mother. Because of her family's wealth, Yetri does not work the land herself but hires someone to sharecrop it for her.

Although the women in the household have individual incomes and receive further income from their husbands, Yetri described their house as a "collective household" (*rumah bersama*). They operate separately and collectively. The family is collective because they share the same interests and pool their resources to maintain and improve the common assets, the house and land. The ancestral property (*harto pusako*) belongs to all of them and links the generations of mothers and daughters. Yetri told me, "My mother and I each have our own rice fields that we use for our own needs and desires. There are also other fields that are used for all of us. The produce from those fields is brought home for food for all of us, mother, daughters and children." Big occasions like wedding ceremonies are also handled together. Hartati and Siti discuss what they need first and then ask for help from the others, including husbands. But the family is also separate because married daughters build up their own resources in order to have a separate income that they can control themselves.

This rather idyllic portrait of relations in a matrihouse would seem to suggest that the transfer of houses and land moves smoothly from mother to daughters. Franz von Benda-Beckmann (1979) argues just that point, stating that questions of inheritance and property relations are unproblematic for women because they uniformly benefit from the matrilineal system. Contrary to his idea, the discussion below illustrates that mothers and daughters develop their relationships through a lifetime of negotiation and contestation. It also illustrates men's more marginal relationship to the matrihouse as sons, husbands, and brothers.

MOTHER-DAUGHTER RELATIONS

To take a closer look at relations in matrihouses, I examine the households in Tanjung Batang with mothers and married daughters resident. In 1990, twenty-eight households in the hamlet (out of 125) were composed of the matrilineal unit of mother and married daughter or daughters.[7] Many mothers have more than one daughter, but in only a few cases was there more than one married adult daughter living in a matrihouse (with her husband and children). These households represent all ranks within the community: fifteen were elite (27 percent of all elite households), ten were commoner (22 percent of all commoner households), and three were servant households (21 percent of all servant households). The consistency in number of matrihouses across ranks is significant. It shows that matrilineal ideology is not something upheld and practiced by elite families only but is a shared practice throughout the village.

In seventeen of the twenty-eight matrihouses (61 percent) mother and daughter operate as a single unit in relation to land. Daughters in these households do not have their own land. Fitriani's family falls into that category:

Fitriani, a heavy-set woman with an easy laugh who is just approaching fifty years old, is the highest-ranking senior woman in her clan (*suku*). A well-respected leader and shrewd manager of her lineage, Fitriani has fallen on hard times. The expenses of education for her five children, weddings for her daughters, and the costs of maintaining an old big house forced Fitriani to pawn some of her land, leaving only one small piece of land that she works herself. Her husband left several years ago so there is no additional income from him anymore.

In Fitriani's house is her recently widowed eldest daughter Wira and her three small children, as well as Fitriani's youngest daughter who is still in school. Fitriani's second daughter, Lina, who is married and a farmer, lives nearby. Wira had been living in the town of Bukittinggi with her husband and children, supported by her husband's earnings. Now Wira shares her mother's income from her rice field but has also started working as an agricultural laborer to make some additional money. She does weeding and harvesting for other farmers. Fitriani said she and her daughters are one household. "What we get is one, it's not divided, the produce from the rice field is not divided. In the morning we eat together, our spending money is the same, we cook together. Everything is together."

In matrihouses like Fitriani's, mother and daughters share the produce of undivided rice fields. In some cases daughters may also have access to their own income, either from their husbands, through their own labor, or from small-scale businesses.

In the other eleven households (39 percent), the daughter controls some of her own land as well as her own earnings. Hartati's household fits that category: her daughter Yetri has her own land and income, but Yetri sets some money aside for household expenses, including paying for repairs or additions to the house and hosting ceremonies. Consequently, some of her "own" income is used for the benefit of the whole household. Married daughters need to inform their mother, and mother's brother, if necessary, about particular actions they are taking. Yetri said that if she wants to take a trip, for instance, to visit her sister in Jakarta, she would ask, "*Mak* [mother], I want to go to Jakarta, can I or not?" Or if she wanted to buy something for the house, like the new couch set she recently purchased, she would tell her mother first. Daughters in matrihouses cannot make decisions on their own when it concerns the whole household; they have to check with the senior woman first.

Trying to distinguish between mother's and daughter's interests in a matrihouse is difficult, however, not only because some individual income is used for joint projects but also because ultimately the house and land will belong to the daughter. The senior woman controls the rice land and uses the income to pay for common household needs. Daughters have separate income that gives them a degree of independence from their mothers. They have access to land from several sources, but on average for all matrihouses mother's land produces over three times as much rice as daughter's land (69 percent to 31 percent) (see table 3.1). Although mothers and daughters have their own land and income, women insisted that mother and daughters in a matrihouse are one. As one woman told me, "As long as a daughter lives with her mother, she gets a lot. It is still one house and food and daily expenses are one."

Table 3.1 Sources of Land and Total Rice Production (per Harvest) in Matrihouses (N=28)

Source of Land	Daughter (%)		Mother (%)	
		percent of total		percent of total
Mother	46	14	—	—
Self	5	1	77	53
Husband	8	3	23	16
Father	13	4	—	—
Titled man	28	9	—	—
Total %	100	31	100	69
Total production of rice (average: 821 *gantang* per house)		5,450 gt.		17,550 gt.

Mutual Cooperation in Matrihouses

The sharing of resources in a matrihouse points to a value common to village Southeast Asia: mutual cooperation and assistance among kin (*tolong-meno-long*). In a matrihouse all members provide some form of (unpaid) labor or contribute cash to the household. Household and farm tasks are gender-segregated but everyone is expected to help out. Both boys and girls help to watch over younger siblings, while mothers may leave very small children with a variety of adults, including grandmother, aunts, uncles, or husbands. Girls help their mothers with sweeping dirt out of the house and washing clothes, while boys tend small animals owned by the family, such as goats. Unmarried daughters, who are not yet adept at planting, help the family by weeding the rice fields, while adult daughters will plant, weed, and harvest rice on the family land.[8]

Unmarried sons help with the harvest, usually by carrying the sacks of unhusked rice (*padi*) to the miller. Fitriani's son Efran told me that during his early teens he did a variety of agricultural tasks for his mother: clearing the stalks from harvested fields, carrying bags of fertilizer from home to the field, planting seed beds, and preparing the seedlings for planting. He also tended the family cows and chickens and worked in his mother's corn garden.

Family members are expected to assist with household concerns but no one demands absolute obedience, giving rural household relations a decidedly non-authoritarian cast. And yet the expectation of cooperation is buttressed by the "rule" of the elder (senior woman or senior generation). As in other Southeast Asian cultures, respect for elders means that younger members generally defer to the needs and decisions of the elder generation. For their part senior women feel that their children lack experience and need to be guided, even as adults, to learn the best way to handle things.

Child care arrangements in matrihouses are quite flexible. A married daughter with young children can choose to stay at home while her mother works. Likewise, if the mother is getting older, she may decide to stay at home and look after her grandchildren while her daughter works. In fact, senior women are proud to be seen carrying a grandchild around while their daughters are busy with other things. This arrangement works quite well when either mother or daughter is only absent temporarily, for instance, to go supervise a harvest or go to the market. It is more difficult when daughters have full-time jobs because childcare then takes up much more of the grandmother's time. The following story of Nurani's household illustrates the group effort put into childcare.

Nurani, a well-off farmer and one of Yenita's three daughters, lives in her own spacious contemporary-style house, which she built near her mother's big house. Nurani's one daughter Reni married several years ago and, after a brief stint living in the city with her husband Ahmad, moved back home with Ahmad and their two children. They occupy one of Nurani's four bedrooms, another is Nurani's, the third is saved for Nurani's son when he is home (and is otherwise a utility room), and the fourth belongs to Reni's first child, a young girl. Reni, in her mid-twenties, is very much a modern daughter, with her civil service job and her own opinions about marriage and child-rearing.

When Reni moved back home after her second child, she continued to work as a civil servant in a nearby town, returning home around 1:30 on workdays. During work both children are under the care of their grandmother Nurani, who manages several rice fields for herself and her mother Yenita. Usually Nurani finds enough work in the house to keep her busy while she watches the children. Besides, her two sisters live nearby in Yenita's big house, quite handy for emergencies. One day I came home to find Reni's infant son in the arms of his great aunt (Nurani's sister Dela), not in his grandmother's arms. Nurani had been called to her rice field to measure the rice harvest and pay the workers. She couldn't wait for her daughter to get home from work and so dropped the baby off next door.

Another time a teething and fussy infant grandson had used up Nurani's last bit of patience. She wanted to go to the market for supplies for an upcoming ceremony and neither of her sisters were home at the big house to do babysitting. Her daughter was late getting home from work. The buses she took to and from work were not always reliably on time. Nurani kept watching the path for her daughter. As soon as she saw Reni coming down the path, she changed clothes and was out the door heading to the market before Reni was in the door herself. Nurani said later that she did not mind staying home to help Reni but she got restless and wanted to be doing other things that childcare didn't allow her to do.

As senior women get older, the responsibilities of managing the household fall more and more to their daughters. Women who have been involved in agricultural work retire in their fifties or sixties if they have a daughter who can manage or work the fields themselves. Elderly women no longer actively participate in household work but let their daughters take over. Nurani's mother Yenita keeps herself busy weeding around her big house and doing some cooking, but she no longer pays attention to daily affairs or goes out to her rice fields. According to Nurani, Yenita doesn't even worry about the harvest because her daughter is able to take care of it for her.

The ideal of mutual cooperation so important in Southeast Asian communities serves to emphasize the equality and distinctness of each household member as well as the importance of working together. Households are joint efforts based on consultation, consensus, and cooperation. Relations in matrihouses reflect two other beliefs typical in Southeast Asia: one, that women are productive individuals, and two, that whoever brings in the money to the household has the right of disposal over it (Rudie 1993). Rural Minangkabau women expect to earn or produce their own income. They also expect and depend on resources and assistance from other family members. As senior women, they control those resources for the interests of the matrihouse and sublineage.

SONS AND MOTHER'S BROTHERS

> He does not really have a house or a place he can call his own.... From the day of his departure to a surau [prayer house], a man ceases to be physically "in" the *adat* house, even if he still belongs to it.... The house itself is for his mothers and sisters. (Kato 1982:61)

Married sons are not present in the daily life of the matrihouse, but they remain kinsmen of the house with certain responsibilities and obligations. My reading of men's relations to their kinswomen suggests that they maintain a strong interest in and support for their natal kin group. Men's relations as sons and brothers vary considerably depending on their age and rank. A son is under constraint to cooperate with his mother in order to ensure her continued support of his interests. "A son feels he must not hurt his mother who has cared for him so faithfully, patiently, and sacrificially and who he expects to provide him with an emotional refuge and substantial aid during crises in his adult life" (Tanner 1971:52). I heard similar sentiments from several men in Tanjung Batang. I asked one of my male consultants, Hartati's brother Dt. Rajo, who lives in his wife's house, about his duties to their mother. He replied: "I help her out whenever she needs it. If I don't help her, our relationship would be ruined. It would make my life very difficult. Later, if I divorce or my wife dies, I will not be received at my mother's house; she won't take me back. She might take back the rice land that she has given me, if I don't help her, or I won't be able to come home." His statement articulates the importance of cooperation with his mother and the expectation of assistance from her.

As members of the matrilineage, sons are encouraged to be hard-working and generous for their mother's family. A good son brings honor and good fortune to the sublineage. In the past sons were expected to migrate (*merantau*) to other areas before marriage to seek their fortunes. Once they were successful, they could return home with their wealth and then have a marriage arranged for them. Many young men from Taram currently work seasonal or temporary jobs in other areas of West Sumatra and Indonesia; some are construction workers on road projects, others are petty traders. Unmarried men usually send some of their wages home to their mothers.

Fitriani's nephew, whom she raised after her sister died, is an unmarried man in his early twenties. He works as a day laborer on road or building construction crews. This young man told me, "The money I earn goes to buy clothes and cigarettes for myself and the rest to help Bu Fitriani. I usually give her about half of what I earn. When the economic situation of her household is not good, I have to look for work to help them out." This help also includes doing work for Wira, Fitriani's eldest daughter. Although Wira tried her hand at farm work, she was not too keen on agricultural labor, so she decided to open a small shop next door to her mother's big house as an alternative source of income for herself and her small children. Her married brother, Efran, and her cousin together built the shop for her out of bamboo and saplings that they cut down in the woods. They also worked on building a new house for her with the material that she bought.

The obligations of a son to his mother and other kinswomen persist throughout his lifetime. A married man, a farmer and the eldest son of a widowed client woman, talked about the work that he does on his mother's rice field: "I use my water buffalo to smooth my mother's wet rice field after it has been plowed, usually every planting season, about once every four months. I also help with the harvest [with his wife and her family]. The edges of the wet rice field and the canal I repair, if needed, and check on her rice field whenever I'm in the area to see if everything is okay. If there is a serious problem, I let her know." When I asked him if he was paid for helping his mother, he laughed and said, "Why should a mother pay her child? When I go to her house, I am given food and drink. That is enough." Not all sons provide labor; those who are well off may give their mothers money to hire labor to do agricultural tasks. An industrious son is also expected to help increase family rice lands either by buying new land with his earnings or by turning uncultivated lineage land into rice land (*taruko*) through his labor.

The relationship between mothers and sons reflects the sense of mutual cooperation and kin group solidarity so important to rural kin groups. A son maintains strong ties with his natal kin and shares with them an expectation of mutual assistance throughout his lifetime. He remains part of the family with an equal voice in family matters and growing influence if he has shown himself to be a reliable and supportive member of the kin group. Although a son has room to make his own decisions, he must always remember his matrikin and his duties to them. As a son, he remains under the influence and control of his mother. She is the one who can lend him land and provide financial assistance.

TITLED MEN AS KINSMEN

The men who carry the family titles maintain a somewhat different position than other sons. As the carriers of family titles, they assume positions of influence in lineage affairs as well as greater responsibility for the property and affairs of the sublineage than other sons. (See the appendix for more information on titles.) Despite the greater prestige of their position, titled men have the same obligations to their mothers and sisters as other sons. They are expected to help maintain the status and reputation of the sublineage and assist their kinswomen in lineage affairs. The potential heir to a title is under some constraint to remain closer to home because of the value of the position for family prestige. A few titled men live in outlying districts or areas of Indonesia (*rantau*), but as a consequence have little effect on lineage affairs. In Fitriani's case she saw to it that the titled man in her family remained close to home.

> Fitriani had no brothers, so her older sister's son was given the family title of Dt. Sango at a young age. As the boy was growing up, both his mother and another aunt passed away, leaving Fitriani the only surviving sibling in her sublineage. Showing early evidence of her cleverness and skill in negotiation, Fitriani arranged a marriage for the young Dt. Sango. He was married to a woman from a nearby hamlet in Taram, ensuring that he would remain in the village near her and under her control.

As titled men, their role is similar to that of the senior woman. As with the senior women, they need to be informed about the activities of the sublineage and have to give their consent before certain things can be done, such as pawning land or holding major ceremonies. For titled men who live in the same village as their mothers, "supervision" of their sisters' children means dropping by to see how things are going. According to Fitriani, her nephew "comes by and asks us how things are. He asks if we have enough or not. If he can help us out, he will." When there is a marriage in the family, the senior woman and the titled man consult on the suitability of the prospective spouse and must come to agreement before any arrangements can be made.

Titled men are often referred to as mother's brother (*mamak*). This usage is somewhat misleading to outsiders since it suggests that the titled man is a kinsman in a senior position to the eldest woman (mother) and thus has more authority. As noted above, however, a titled man like Dt. Sango may actually be junior to the senior woman. Fitriani told me that although her nephew Dt. Sango is the titled man (with the highest-ranked title in the clan), he does not have enough experience or knowledge about the proper conduct of lineage affairs, so she consults with another titled man in her lineage if serious problems arise. The authority or influence of a particular titled man depends on his age and experience in relation to others in the lineage. Although the position holds some influence, young titled men have to prove their ability and wisdom in dealing with kin group affairs. Like daughters of senior women, titled men have to learn their role before they can be trusted to provide adequate guidance to the sublineage.

Men as sons and brothers play an important role in the matrihouse. Men have certain rights and duties to the matrihouse, including the right to return after a divorce and the duty to maintain its status and reputation through their hard work and exemplary behavior. As members of the matrilineage, they join in deliberations concerning affairs that involve the sublineage and have an equal voice in those affairs. As titled men, they serve as elders in conjunction with senior women. Men have a different and more limited set of rights in the matrihouse, however, in comparison to women. Although their lives are oriented to its needs, men are marginal members of the matrihouse. They do not reside in nor manage it and interact only periodically with their kinswomen. It is these different sets of rights and responsibilities in relation to the matrihouse that allow me to distinguish between the matrilineal unit of mother and daughter who reside in the house and the kinsmen who are outside of it yet part of the sublineage.

HUSBANDS AND SONS-IN-LAW IN MATRIHOUSES

Matrihouses also include in-married men, sons-in-law who marry into and reside with their wives' families. Men as husbands and sons-in-law are present in 86 percent of the twenty-eight matrihouses in Tanjung Batang. According to many sources, in former days a son-in-law was only a temporary resident in his wife's family house. He visited at night and then returned to his mother's house in the morning.[9] A husband is now a more permanent member of his wife's house, though he "remains an honored (but relatively insecure) guest in his wife's house" (Tanner 1971:34). As "guest" residents, husbands provide additional labor, land, or income to the household. A husband does not have a decision-making role in the affairs of his wife's sublineage, however. He is called on to attend ceremonial deliberations as *urang sumando* (in-married man), which he does out of respect for his wife's family. At these deliberations he can voice his opinion, particularly as it concerns any help he might provide or any experience he may have in the matter, but he is not directly involved in the decisions made.

Husbands are expected to have their own source of income, which usually is used for the expenses associated with raising their children. Several older men stated that more of the husband's income goes to his children than in the past. In discussing the changes in husband's duties, Dt. Rajo said, "Before, husbands just gave money to their wives once in a while and they helped in the rice fields. Now things have changed. Husbands have more responsibility. Before, the children were the mother's responsibility. Back then, if the husband gave his wife money on market days, that was great! Thursdays and Mondays [the market days in Taram], that was it." With the increased expectations about rights to husbands' income, husbands are looked to as another source of income for the family. This income remains under the husband's control, but how a husband uses his money is influenced by the expectations of both in-laws and kinswomen.

Men have discretion in how they spend their income, but they are subject to strong pressure to be a good provider for their wives' families. According to Dt. Sati, if a husband is spending his money frivolously (for instance, by gambling it away) and not helping his wife out enough, a wife can complain to the senior woman of her husband's lineage. "She'll say, 'My husband doesn't come home until late, he doesn't do anything. I need your help.' The senior woman will have a talk with the husband, try to get him to do the work, try to get him to change. Of course it depends on the husband's willingness to change." Young married men in the village in particular garner complaints from their in-laws for not helping out enough in their wives' households. Husbands in general are thought to be "notorious for their unreliability and irresponsibility" (Prindiville 1981:29). One reason for this attribution is that as husbands, men are not part of the kin group even when they live in the same house. Because a husband is from another lineage, affines are more likely to be suspicious of him and to believe that he is less reliable than their own kin.

The experiences of Nurani with her young son-in-law Ahmad, who has been living in her house now for one year, reveals some of the problems and expectations:

Ahmad, who married Nurani's daughter Reni, is from another town. Although still in his twenties, he is an industrious and capable person with his own brick-making factory. He spends much of his time away from his mother-in-law's house supervising his business, leaving in the early morning and returning most evenings in time for dinner. When asked about her son-in-law, Nurani replied: "Ahmad gives money to help pay the electricity bill every month. He also gave me 20,000 rupiah ($7 US) and said to get some more fish for the pond. I'm glad he gave me the money. But he never gives enough to pay for things outright, I always have to add my own money. He never helps around the house, either. He doesn't offer to do anything, even chop weeds. But I can't say anything to him, it wouldn't be good."

Her complaints about her son-in-law suggest that he is not living up to her expectations. Ahmad provides as much as he can for his wife but he is not (yet) as invested in taking care of his mother-in-law's house. As this story suggests, a son-in-law is given respect in his wife's house and is not directly approached about perceived failings, although it is noted.

If husbands are farmers, they are expected to provide labor on the household's rice fields (clearing, plowing, and harvesting), whether it is the mother's or daughter's land. Farm labor is not recompensed but is considered a contribution to the household. In addition to farm labor, men provide supplemental income to the household through agricultural labor, such as for plowing, or through salaried or wage labor jobs outside the village, including civil service employment, petty trade, contracting, and road or building construction. This supplemental cash income in some cases may be a significant amount of income, particularly where husbands are contractors or have their own business, or in cases where wives have very little land.

An elite husband who farms with his wife may ask for access to or sharecropping rights in some of his mother's rice land as a way to provide additional income to his wife's family. His ability to gain access to land depends on his relations with his kinswomen and their financial condition. His mother will try to help him out, if she can, and if he is a responsible, industrious farmer. Such assistance speaks to the wealth and generosity of his mother's family. Income from that land is usually split between his wife's family and his mother. But this arrangement depends on the situation. If the mother is well off and the son's family in financial straits, the mother may let him keep all the harvest for his family's needs. Or, as in Yetri's case, although her family was not poor, she was allowed to keep all the produce from her husband's mother's land. In contrast, a husband from a poor elite family may be unable to bring any land to his wife, even if she has little herself. Thus, a husband's ability to bring any land to his marriage depends on his mother or other senior kinswomen, who have prior rights to land.

On a more concrete level, actual contributions of land by husbands (including both mothers' and daughters' husbands) in matrihouses averages out to less than one-fifth (19 percent) of all the land that these households have access to. Most of that land comes through the mother's husband (78 percent) (see Table 3.1). Although husbands provide some access to land for their wives' households, the primary source of income is from the land owned by the matrihouse, which women control. In client matrihouses, however, fathers tend to provide greater access to land than mothers (44 percent compared to 26 percent), in several cases providing the only source of land the family has access to. In these cases the fathers were elite men with use rights in land. A few matrihouses are joint households in which both members of the senior couple make significant contributions to household resources. In only one case did the mother's husband provide all the income for the family since all the mother's ancestral property had been pawned.

The duty of a man to provide material assistance to both his matrilineage and his wife's family creates tensions for men between their responsibilities as husbands and sons (see also Prindiville 1985). Because a man has some discretion in how his earned income is spent, he is sometimes torn between assisting his natal household or his wife's household. Both kinswomen (mothers and sisters) and wives feel that they have a right to make claims to a man's income. There are no set rules for dividing income between kin and wife. Kin who feel they are owed more assistance try to persuade their kinsmen by raising questions about his loyalty to his lineage. One elite man described their attitude as follows: "A husband who doesn't help out his mother is said to think only about his wife, not his mother or his sister's children (*kamanakan*)."

Under the influence of the Indonesian state with its emphasis on the nuclear family and the responsibility of husbands to wives and children, many people express the idea that husbands should take care of their wives first. Dt. Sango, Fitriani's nephew, explained how he handles his dual obligations: "My income is for my children's and wife's needs. If there is enough left over, I give it to my mother or sister. When I am making money, maybe once a week, I will give it to my mother, but it's not regular. My mother doesn't demand it. My responsibility is to my wife, to give her money if I have it. If I can't help my wife, she has her own rice lands to fall back on." Wira, who as noted above received substantial assistance from her brother Efran in building her shop, explained the delicate balance that her brother has to maintain between assisting his kinswomen and assisting his wife. "If he has extra money, he gives us some, but if not, he doesn't. His wife would be upset if he gave his mother money when he didn't have enough for his wife. So we can't ask him for money, or she'll get upset. If there's extra, then his wife won't be upset if he gives us some." When I asked Dt. Sati, who is married to Nurani's sister Dela, what would happen if a husband did not give his wife money, he said, "It can't be. There wouldn't be any use in such a husband."

The complexity of men's relations with their affines and matrikin are illustrated in the following incident involving Yenita's second daughter Dela, her husband Dt. Sati, and her sister-in-law Fina:

Dt. Sati, a congenial man who has spent his life in the village, married Dela in the late 1970s. Dela is doing quite well living at her mother's big house. She has her own income from rice land her father gave her and from some of Dt. Sati's rice land. When their two sons were small, Dt. Sati quite often took care of them while Dela was busy at her food stall. He would bring them to Nurani's house, where there was an indoor well, for their morning and evening baths. When the youngest son got upset, he was as likely to call out for his father as his mother, long wails of *ayaaaah* [father] or *ibuuuu* [mother], resonating through the house.

Trouble started when Dt. Sati's sister Fina, who lives in her own big house, decided she wanted to build an addition to the kitchen. Dt. Sati owns a rice mill with his two siblings: his sister Fina and a brother who does not live in the village. Because the three siblings together control their ancestral property (their mother is deceased), Fina asked her brother for permission to pawn some of their rice land; failing that, she wanted an advance on profits from their shared business to pay for the improvements. Dt. Sati thought both suggestions were bad ideas. He told Fina that there wasn't enough cash right now from the rice mill. They still needed to pay off the loan, so she should wait until there was more money to make the renovations. He also mentioned that since she has children in middle school, she should worry about their expenses first before she makes more improvements to the house.

Fina was irritated by her brother's refusal to agree with her plan. When he didn't show up at her house for several days, she decided to seek him out to pursue the matter further. So she came to Dela's house looking for her brother. Dela told her he was away working, buying *padi*, and she didn't know when he'd be home. Feeling frustrated, Fina got upset at that point. According to Nurani, who happened to be at her sister's house when this interchange occurred, Fina implied that Dela was spending all Dt. Sati's profits so there was none left for Fina to use. Fina seemed to think that the things Dela buys all come from Dt. Sati's money. She told Dela that something bad would happen (*hukum karma*) for the way she had been spending Dt. Sati's money. Nurani thought Fina was just resentful of Dela's wealth. Dela's money doesn't come from the profits at the rice mill; Dela buys things with the money she makes on her rice harvests. Both Nurani and Dela were upset by the accusations and said that Fina should have been talking to Dt. Sati about it, not to his wife.

In this incident, no one thought that Fina was out of line for expecting her brother's assistance. The problem was that she did not resolve it with her brother but made accusations against his wife for spending money that didn't belong to her.

The capital for the rice mill came from a loan taken against the ancestral property of the three siblings. Consequently, all have equal shares in the profits and have to agree on business matters. Dt. Sati interpreted his sister's anger in the following way, "She thinks I'm not giving her or her children enough attention even though she has money for her expenses from the rice land and other things that she owns. She thinks all the profits from the milling business I take to my wife. That often happens in families. It's difficult to weigh what to do."

This case underscores the responsibilities that men have to both their wives and their matrikin. Dt. Sati later told me that because his wife's economic situation is good, she does not ask for much from him. If, on the other hand, his situation was good and his wife had little income, then she could expect his part of the profits. Now he usually splits his income about three-quarters to his children and one-quarter to his sister's children.

As this incident shows, men remain strongly involved with their matrikin; they assist with family needs while also providing income for their wives' families. Men like Dt. Sati do not object to having to give money to their sister's children, but to the difficulties of working out complicated relationships. As husbands and fathers, men also maintain enduring ties with their children, ties that remain even after divorce, remarriage, or death. F. Benda-Beckmann (1979) states that men are more interested in their own children and passing on their income to them. But the evidence from Taram suggests otherwise. A generous husband is expected to want to help out his children, even when he no longer lives with them. In Reni's case, although her father has long been divorced from her mother, he has not forgotten his children. He gives spending money to his son who is away at college; he also bought a water buffalo in Reni's name, so that profits from its sale or off-spring go to Reni.

As husbands, men are valued for the labor and income they provide, as well as their reproductive capabilities, but they maintain a subordinate position in the matrihouse for several reasons. Although a senior woman does not control her son-in-law's movements, he must show her respect by working hard for her household. Any failings on his part can affect his marriage and the relations between his mother and his mother-in-law's kin groups. A husband's income is considered supplemental in the great majority of matrihouses because the pri-mary resource base is the senior women's land. Finally, the concerns of the household are viewed as kin concerns, which include in-married husbands only peripherally. Consequently, the conjugal unit constitutes an important but sub-sidiary unit within the matrihouse.

Concern for the "plight" of in-married men has been a recurring theme in mainstream anthropological studies of the Minangkabau and peoples of Negeri Sembilan. Imbued in Western narratives of men's authority over wives, anthro-pologists were perplexed and confounded by the status of husbands in rural Minangkabau households. An in-married man, especially a young husband who has yet to prove himself, may be uncomfortable in his wife's house (Krier 1994, Stivens 1996). In the New Order period of the Indonesian state, his discomfort may be a result of state support for a man's authority over his wife. But in my reading of men's statements, rural Minangkabau men feel pride in their value to both affines and kinswomen; they stress the importance of their relations with both their wives' families and their mothers' lineages. Although men are more closely connected with their wives' households than in the past, men in these households remain committed to matrilineal practices that situate them as sub-sidiary members in their wives' households.

INHERITANCE AND MOTHER'S CONTROL OF LAND

The ancestral land (*harto pusako*) that senior women have in their possession passes from mother to daughters. However, as I noted in the last chapter, con-trol over lineage matters and ancestral land was said to reside in the mother's brother (Hakimy 1994b), while kinswomen, it seemed, simply used the land to grow their crops on. As with other statements about Minangkabau gender relations, this interpretation is somewhat misleading. In this section I focus on the question of control over land. By exploring the dynamics of land transfers from mothers to daughters, a clearer picture of senior women's control of land emerges.

In an effort to understand Minangkabau land ownership and determine where rights to land lay, attention has been directed to property disputes among the

Minangkabau (see, for instance, F. Benda-Beckmann 1979, Krier 1995). Dispute processes, however, differ from the land transfers that occur within the matrilineal unit. Cases involving property disputes arise when the history of pawning and redeeming of land over generations is poorly remembered or when genealogically distant kin seek to gain access to land that has no direct female heirs. In some cases the last living member of a sublineage pawned land or gave use rights to another family, who then claimed that land as theirs. Once the original landholders are gone, no one knows for sure whose land it is. Such cases in Taram are handled by the *adat* council but have been known to drag on for years while the titled men try to arrange a compromise among the lineage members of the two disputing sides. Higher-ranking and more influential titled men may have a better chance of swinging the case in their favor.

Because scholars assumed that land moved unproblematically from mothers to daughters, intergenerational land transfers have received little attention. The everyday practice of land inheritance from one generation of women to the next, however, constitutes the core of land transfers. Stories of inheritance processes underscore the control that senior women have over land. Daughters speak of getting rice land from their mothers after marriage. Several women told me that when they got married, they were given rice land by their mothers, not by the lineage or the titled man. Dt. Rajo described the process as follows: "Sometimes a mother may want to let go a piece of rice land so her children can stand on their own. She will say, 'Here's a piece of land [*piring sawah*], work it. You can have the produce from it.'" In his recounting, the mother acts on her own to give some of the ancestral land to her child. She probably informs the titled man that she has done so, but his permission is not needed. Once daughters receive land from their mothers after marriage, it is under their control. They decide how to manage it and what to do with the produce. They do not have the right to pawn it, however, without the mother's permission. If a daughter or someone in her family is sick and they need money to cover medical bills, she can ask both her mother and the titled man if she can pawn some land for cash and will probably get their agreement. But in less serious cases, a mother has been known to refuse her daughter's request to pawn land.

The timing of land inheritance depends on the senior woman and the situation of her family. Some mothers keep the land in their own hands as long as they are alive. Some senior women disperse all their lands to their daughter(s) before they pass on, as Hartati's mother did. When the senior woman is ready to pass on her land permanently to her daughters, she consults with the titled man. Dt. Rajo explained, "Usually, when the mother is old, and she doesn't need the rice land for anything anymore, she will say, 'Here, this is for you, and you.' The one who decides is the mother in deliberation with her kinsmen. But only with her *datuk*, not any other." In this case, it is the two lineage elders who confer, the senior woman and the titled man. The titled man acts an advisor but the senior woman has the controlling interest.

One well-known case in the village illustrates the irrevocable nature of a senior woman's decision:

A senior woman in Santi's clan who had no heirs and outlived all the members of her sublineage decided to give her land to a client kinswoman who had cared for her in her old age. Her decision created much shock and dismay for Santi and her family because they had expected to get that land, but neither the titled men nor the senior women of her lineage could negate that decision after her death. For a long time a lot of people were unhappy about the turn of events because they had hoped to inherit, or at least get something. It was like a little war, according to one consultant. The ancestral property was given to people with no relationship to the family, no "blue" blood. They were not real blood kin (*kamanakan batali darah*), only client kin (*bamamak*). When I asked Dt. Rajo how that happened, he said emphatically, because this is a matrilineal system (*karena matriarchaat, namanya*).

His final statement I took to mean that because Minangkabau *adat* is matrilineal, the senior woman has the last say. His analysis differs from most *adat* interpretations. Land is usually said to belong to the sublineage as a whole, and by extension the lineage; once the senior woman dies, her elite kin take possession of that land. In contrast, the fact that in this case elite kin were unable and unwilling to counter the senior woman's wishes suggests that no one can interfere with or alter a senior woman's decisions regarding land use and disposition.

The question of the role of titled men and brothers in generational land transfers when the senior woman does not make any specific provisions is more complicated than in the examples above. In some cases the titled man acts as mediator to ensure that each of his sisters receives her fair share after their mother dies. In other cases when the oldest heir is still a young girl, an uncle might take temporary control of land. In one case that I was told about, the titled man took responsibility for the land after his sister died but refused to return the land to his niece once she was married. The niece felt that she had prior rights to that land as her mother's heir and that it was her uncle's duty to return it to her. Out of respect for her elder, however, she never openly contested his possession of the land, waiting instead until the uncle died before she claimed the land. In yet another response to the question, other elite women were unequivocal. One woman simply stated that the daughters and not the sons receive the mother's land. The reason given: "Minangkabau *adat*."

Another more detailed explanation of this process was given by Wira, Fitriani's eldest daughter. She explained to me that when her mother dies, the rights to their rice land will go to herself, her younger sisters, and her younger brother Efran. Then she clarified, "If he asks, I will let him use some (*dipinjam*). It is not his to keep. If he doesn't ask, then it is for me only. Usually it goes to the females. If my brother wants to use some, whether or not it is enough for me, I will give him some. Whether or not we give permission, he can always ask. But my younger brother is fond of me and doesn't ask for rice land." Her explanation highlights sharing of land between siblings—an expectation of cooperation and generosity contained in the Minangkabau ideal of mutual assistance (*tolong-menolong*)—that draws on certain Minangkabau notions of gender. According to Minangkabau folk stories (*tambo*), sons are expected to go out (*merantau*) and earn a living on their own, often with the financial assistance of their mothers. A son (or brother) that has to ask for land from his kinswoman will be considered a lazy, unresourceful, and unambitious man who has failed to earn his own income. This moral tale suggests that land use is negotiable, but as Wira sees it, a caring (resourceful) brother will not wish to hurt his sister by asking for land if she does not have enough for her own family. A brother can take land if he wants to, but if his sister is in need, such action would reveal him to have a base and stingy heart with no respect or concern for his family.

Dt. Rajo explained inheritance by offspring in somewhat different and contradictory terms, emphasizing the rights of the eldest to take land:

> If the mother dies and she still has her own rice land, it goes automatically to the eldest child, either a son or a daughter. If the son doesn't have any rice land, he will control it first because he is the oldest. The thing is the oldest gets it first. But if he doesn't need it, he can give it to his younger sibling. Whoever is in the worse situation economically. But that is only a use right, not ownership, because they all hold it together.

Dt. Rajo emphasizes the right of the sublineage over land as well as its negotiability based on economic need. But when I questioned him further about both sons and daughters inheriting, he clarified the process:"Actually, mostly the ones who control the rice land are the daughters. Sons can usually find other kinds of income; we won't take the rice land. Our responsibility is just to supervise rice land." Here he first suggests a rule of primogeniture, rather than matriliny, that allows an eldest son to gain first use rights to land. But on further questioning it appears that daughters usually get land regardless if the son is eldest. Then he reiterates the statement found in adat writings that as mother's brother (*mamak*), men's responsibility is to supervise the land. This statement suggests that men have to determine who needs land. But Dt. Rajo goes on to suggest that the ethic of land use gives priority to the daughter. This ethic is similar to the one mentioned by Wira, but Dt. Rajo provides a slightly different reason why daughters should get land instead of sons: sons have better opportunities to find wage labor than daughters and so do not ask for land.[10]

Simple questions about who has rights to land produce a seemingly endless variety of responses. Dt. Rajo's statement plays on the idea that women have greater need for land than men. It provides a reason for Minangkabau land transfers that resonates with the state image of a "domestic" economy (see chapter 4) where men get jobs and women stay home to care for children. In contrast

Wira calls on the Minangkabau ideal of mutual assistance (*tolong-menolong*) to explain why brothers do not ask for rice land.

DISCOURSES ON LAND RIGHTS

The different opinions on the matter of land inheritance point to a number of distinct discourses, each of which are mutually implicated. On one level is Minangkabau *adat*, which privileges women as controllers of land. This ideal is usually taken for granted and so left unsaid; but when individuals are pushed to clarify the process, they state the obvious: women's right to land is based on *adat*. The second level is the negotiability of land use. Granted women's control, what appears most obvious in daily practice is a process of negotiation for rights to use land. For instance, with adequate land, sons may be given land to use; without adequate land, all requests are denied. At this level, several discourses operate: the adat of mutual assistance and notions of properly gendered sibling behavior, which favors women's claims (mentioned by Wira), as well as the capitalist ideals of a gendered wage market in which men work and dependent women stay home (mentioned by Dt. Rajo). In the second version, women need to be protected because of their greater vulnerability than men. All these become claims for getting access but not rights to land.

The third level of discourse imbricated in claims to land comes from the historical processes of religious, colonial, and postcolonial intervention in rural Minangkabau land practices. These processes, which have privileged men as landbrokers and supervisors of lineage land, entail three different discourses: Islamic reformism, Dutch legal policies, and Indonesian land laws. As I mentioned in chapter 2, Islamic reformists influenced Minangkabau *adat*, including the pattern of matrilineal inheritance (Oki 1977). Under Islamic inheritance laws, fathers pass on property to their children. Minangkabau attempts to reconcile the two resulted in a division of property types. Minangkabau recognize two types of property: (1) ancestral property (*harto pusakŏ*), which includes land, houses, and title, and (2) acquired property (*harto pancarian*), property bought with earned income. Where a son's property in the past went to his sister's children, changes in inheritance practices have established a son's right to pass on earned income (*harto pancarian*) to his children rather than his sister's children (see F. Benda-Beckmann 1979, Kato 1982).

Dutch legal policies that favored men as representatives of lineages, as noted in chapter 2, also favored their control of land. According to K. Benda-Beckmann, "the rights of members of a sub-lineage, and especially those of the older women, were undermined step by step and over a long period of time by colonial decrees and laws" (1990:101). In 1853 the Dutch recognized women's land rights by "providing for registration of immovable property in the name of the oldest living female of the descent group; after her death the names of her daughters were to be entered as new owners and heiresses" (1990:101). Later laws that established the man as the formal representative of the group gave him exclusive rights of registration, distribution, and management of communal property. Although these laws had little impact because few people bothered to register their lands, over time they gave men greater advantage in dealing with the colonial administration (K. Benda-Beckmann 1990).

These practices were continued under the Indonesian state. The Basic Agrarian Law of 1960 provided an avenue to convert traditional land titles into individual ownership by the formal representative, whom the state assumed was the male representative in accordance with previous Dutch practice (K. Benda-Beckmann 1990). Minangkabau women resisted land registration programs, fearing the loss of their land to the "formal" representative (K. Benda-Beckmann 1990). In Taram, women chose not to participate in land registration programs unless all members of the sublineage were listed as owners (thus preventing individual claims). In some cases, if they all agreed to it, they would register the land under the name of the woman who owned it. Due to the costs of land registration, however, most family land in Taram remains unregistered.

State assumptions about land ownership also affected agricultural policies. In the early years of development, state agricultural officers in West Sumatra worked predominantly with male farmers, who were thought to be the landowners. State agricultural extension programs, such as BIMAS (Mass Guidance Project), which sought to encourage and assist farmers in applying new farming techniques (Tinker and Walker 1973, Rieffel 1969), were aimed solely at men, an approach typical of agricultural development projects in Southeast Asia and the world. In West Sumatra, state agricultural extension programs were introduced to Minangkabau farmers through meetings between agricultural extension officers and male village elders and religious leaders (*ulama*) (Esmara 1974). Even state-sponsored research projects studying the impact of agricultural development used only male farmers as subjects (see, for example, Sadanoer 1976). The neglect of women as farmers meant that primarily men took advantage of early cooperative farm programs. A cooperative farm program (*Koperasi Unit Desa*) set up in 1967 in Taram started with fifty-seven members, of whom only one-quarter were women. Half of the women registered with the program identified their occupations as housewives, and only four were listed as farmers.[11] By 1972 nearly as many women as men were involved, but most of the officers remained titled men of elite families. Despite the neglect of female farmers, women's dominance in agriculture meant that they eventually got access to the information and technology offered. As with the farm cooperatives, women became more involved when they saw that it would further their own interests. They had to rely on their kinsmen, however, to get credit and loans because these had to be in men's names. Consequently, despite colonial and postcolonial support for men's control of land, elite women landowners in Taram continue to maintain control of valuable rice land.[12]

These various discourses help to explain the claims people make in the village about who has rights to land. The fact that hegemonic discourse encourages men to claim land explains why some titled men have held onto land themselves. Dutch and Indonesian laws signal to Minangkabau people that their land practices run "contrary" to others in the nation and the world. It therefore allows some men to feel justified in making claims to land despite family expectations about mutual cooperation and generosity. It also explains why other justifications have arisen to reinforce women's rights to land.

Despite state efforts to the contrary, the control of land and its passage from mother to daughter is the core understanding and practice of land rights in the village. When confronted with new claims that try to assert men's rights to land, women reestablish their rights by revising the claims they make ("my brother is fond of me"). Even changes in some inheritance practices that pass men's earned income to children are being recouped to the matrilineage. Houses built with father's income or land gained with father's help eventually becomes the daughter's. Earned income passed on in this way to daughters is reconstituted within matrilineal practice. A titled man may pass his land to his children for the term of the child's life but his kinswomen will eventually recall that land to their own sublineage, invoking *adat's* principle of women's right to that land.

The movement of land from generation to generation—for the life of the *kampung*—reveals that land use rights are flexible, as Minangkabau *adat* is flexible, but ultimately controlled by senior women, not mother's brothers. Although Krier (1995) argues that titled men work against their sisters and kinswomen to gain land, the discussion above does not support her interpretation. Titled men are given the duty of "protecting" ancestral property, a duty that enjoins them to "look after" their kinswomen's holdings, but does not give them the right of disposition of land. Men's relationship to land needs to be understood in light of their dual concerns for both their children and their *kamanakan*, their kinswomen. Because men are enjoined to protect their *kamanakan*, they work with their sisters to ensure that lineage land stays within their lineage. As members of that lineage, they gain no advantage by giving land to their children if it diminishes the stature of their own lineage. Further, a titled man weakens his own position as elder and disrupts the cohesion of the sublineage when he puts his own interests above that of his kinswomen. Rather than seeing men's and women's interests at odds, land practices in the village speak to the investment in matrilineal ideology that both women and men share.

MOTHERS TO DAUGHTERS

Having demonstrated that the practice of matrilineal inheritance gives women control of land, I want to return to mothers and daughters. Despite the fact that land and houses pass from mothers to daughters, it is possible for daughters to lose access to ancestral property. Not every daughter is able to inherit rights to land and move into a position of dominance in the matrihouse. Land does not move unproblematically; it is contested and negotiated between mothers and daughters in an ongoing process throughout their lives. As in other households, authority and power are constantly being negotiated and reworked (see Hart 1992, Moore 1992), in this case between mothers and daughters over who will become the next senior woman.

A daughter represents the prestige and good fortunes of the lineage. As Tanner (1971) notes, a daughter feels constrained to follow her mother's will. Daughters do not want to disagree with their mothers because they stand in danger of losing their inheritance. And yet, because a daughter is the heir and future of the lineage, she may try to contest her mother's will (Tanner 1971). The situation between mother and daughter is more complicated even than this rendering suggests because most families have more than one daughter. Although the eldest is usually the most likely candidate to take over for her mother, ascension to status of senior woman is not necessarily easy or direct.

There are many factors that shape the dealings between mothers and daughters. A woman takes into consideration her daughter's capabilities and interest in managing the affairs of the sublineage, as well as her choice of husband and her ability to produce her own heir. For the daughter's part, the generosity and fairness of her mother play a role in her decision to follow her mother's will, stay with her mother after marriage or build her own house, or leave the village altogether in search of other opportunities.

The question of marriage plays an important role in a daughter's future. Although a daughter's marriage does not significantly alter relations between mother and daughter in the Minangkabau matrihouse, marriage is crucial not only to the continuation of the sublineage but to its continued prestige and rank. Individuals, whether male or female, are not considered adult until they have married. Everyone is expected and strongly encouraged (in some cases forced) to marry, an expectation generally true throughout Indonesia and Southeast Asia as a whole. While this imperative is one of the commonplaces of most cultures, its significance goes beyond the mere requirement to reproduce. Marriage constructs an extended network of kin and affines that forms the basis of social life in the village. For rural Minangkabau women the continuation and expansion of this matrilineal kinship network through marriage and children is critical to their own standing and influence both in the kin group and in the community.

Marriage establishes two categories of affines: *bako*, the matrikin of daughter's husband (husband givers), who are considered of higher status, and the matrikin of son's wife (husband receivers).[13] Each group has certain responsibilities and roles in ceremonies that mark life-cycle events for the sublineage. As in other areas of Southeast Asia, a sign of status is the large numbers of people that provide assistance or attend ceremonies. A sublineage with large numbers of kin through marriage ties has greater status because they command more labor and more loyal kin.

Because the future viability of the sublineage rests with the women, senior women (and elder brothers) carefully watch young women and make efforts to keep them within easy reach. Unmarried daughters are expected to be chaste, decorous, and modest, ideals encapsulated in the term *malu*. This expectation reflects Islamicist and *adat* ideals for young women (see Hakimy 1994a). A young woman should follow the advice of her maternal kin regarding marriage and her future, learn how to be a proper wife, and learn how to protect the interests of her family. At this stage of a woman's life, she has less power than she will as a mature woman, when she assumes increasing control of herself and her household (see also Whalley 1991). The restrictions on young women's movements has been interpreted by some scholars as a limitation and disadvantage in comparison to men's greater mobility. From the point of view of the woman's lineage, however, the greater loss would be to the lineage and the woman herself as heir and future senior woman.

A son's marriage does not produce lineage heirs, making men peripheral to lineage reproduction. Nevertheless, a son's marriage is important because of the network of kin it too creates. As husband givers, the matrikin of the groom stand in higher status to the matrikin of the bride and will receive place of honor at ceremonies. Husbands are highly respected as the provider of seed for the next generation. Prindiville notes that "families are at considerable pains to obtain the best possible *urang sumando* [husband], and a 'good catch' is much sought after..." (1981:29). Men become good candidates by proving their worth on the *rantau*, if they are not from wealthy families, but the first consideration, particularly for elite women, is the rank of the candidate's family. Men from high-ranking lineages are very desirable because they ensure the continued high rank of the family they marry into (see also Krier 1994). In the past such men usually had several wives over a lifetime. I asked an elderly elite woman why she had married one of her husbands, who was a titled man and had had several wives. She did not hesitate but responded immediately, "Because he had good blood!" In the past and sometimes still today, a high-ranking family is paid a groomprice at their son's marriage, although the amount today has more symbolic than actual value.

In this society a woman's marriage to a lower-ranked husband can effectively diminish the sublineage standing in future generations. Husbands who are considered poor candidates are men from commoner or servant families, men from outside the community, or men who are not Minangkabau and hence of unknown rank. Although children of an elite woman and a client man are still considered elites, the chances of their offspring gaining rights to the house or title will not be as good as their matrilineal cousins whose fathers are elite. Alternatively, marriage to an equal or higher-ranked man can improve the sublineage standing, for instance, through gaining access to rice land.

An unmarried or childless daughter cannot develop the necessary kin networks to support a position of dominance, risking the future integrity and status of her sublineage. This is not an insignificant concern for women since status and property are at risk, a point that was driven home in a conversation I had with Reni, Yenita's granddaughter.

Reni was in turmoil over whether to have another child. She is the sole granddaughter and heir to Yenita's big house and substantial rice fields. Reni's first child was a girl, but her daughter is not a strong child. Reni worries that she should try to have another daughter to ensure the continuation of her sublineage. But she is also conflicted about having more children, since she already has two, the second one a boy. According to state policy, two children are sufficient for a family.

A woman without heirs, as she ages, becomes more peripheral and less influential in her lineage and in the community. Everyone feels extremely sorry for such a woman because she faces the loss of her lineage through extinction. Her kin will begin to maneuver to gain control of her land when she passes on. Consequently, senior women are invested in controlling young women both to avoid the risk of a bad marriage or no marriage at all and to maintain and strengthen their lineage standing.

The dangers of displeasing one's mother through a bad marriage are demonstrated in the following case concerning Yonalis's family:

Yonalis, the aging senior woman of a very wealthy elite family, had three daughters and one son. The son carried the family title and married Hartati. Ema, the eldest daughter, defied Yonalis's wishes to have her marry an elite man from the same village and instead married a non-Minangkabau man. Now in her fifties, Ema has spent most of her married life with her husband in places outside of West Sumatra. She is an energetic and sociable woman, yet the burden of her marriage continues to haunt her. Throughout her marriage Ema received little support financially from her mother. After her husband retired, Ema and her four children returned to Yonalis's house to live. Yonalis had abandoned the family's deteriorating big house and lived in a contemporary-style house with several rooms. Although sharing the same house with her mother, which would usually mean being allowed to share income from her mother's rice fields, Ema has to rely on her husband's pension. She told me she is poor and feels like a boarder (*penumpang*) in her mother's house. But others in the village say that Yonalis was very hurt by her daughter's decision to marry an outsider. It threatened the continuation of the "good blood" of her sublineage.

Yonalis's youngest daughter did not make the same mistake and followed her mother's wishes, marrying a well-positioned elite man. She was rewarded with a big wedding, the highest *adat* wedding in recent memory, but she then left the village with her husband, who worked in East Sumatra. That left the second daughter, Nurma, whose own marriage was not of the highest caliber, as the only one to stay in the village with her mother.

Nurma slowly built up her own assets and reputation with help from her mother and her husband's civil service income. Together with her husband she built a new house next door to her mother's, a spacious one-floor, ground-level dwelling constructed from plaster and brick with concrete floors. The large sitting room has several expensive couches, chairs, and a coffee table; the floor is covered with rugs. By the time her mother retired from active participation in lineage affairs, Nurma was well-respected in the community. A strong, determined woman who takes her rank very seriously, sometimes to the point of haughtiness, Nurma took over for her mother as family representative and manager of her mother's lands. She claims that her family are direct descendants from royal lineage, although not all elites agree with that claim. Nurma told me several times that the titled man in her family is the *raja* (king) of Taram. When her mother died, Nurma, who was then only fifty, became the senior woman even though her older sister occupied their mother's house.

What will happen in the future is unclear but Ema has suffered her whole adult life because her mother did not approve of her marriage partner. Ema's decision to defy her mother weakened the link between herself and her mother. While Ema and her family remain living in the mother's house, she and Nurma will probably share most of the mother's land. But given Nurma's greater responsibilities as senior woman, Nurma may ultimately have more control than her older sister over family land and affairs.

This case not only reveals the problems caused by a bad marriage but also illustrates the power that a mother has over her daughters. Although Yonalis did not stop Ema's marriage, she made it unpleasant for her daughter throughout her life. When Ema finally returned home, she had no prospects of becoming senior woman and faced her mother's continued disdain and unwillingness to help support Ema's four children. Such actions by daughters have ripple effects over the generations, as one daughter's line loses access to land and eventually may disappear if her descendants decide to move out of the village in search of better opportunities.

Conflicts in the relationship between senior women and daughters reflect the power that senior women hold. Senior women's interests are at stake in reproducing and building up the membership and influence of the sublineage. It is their daughters who will inherit and must be controlled in order to assure that status is not squandered in the future through bad marriages or poor management of land. Consequently, senior women are mothers but they are also elders with a vested interest in their kin group and authority over their children.

CONCLUSION

Minangkabau adat privileges rural women, in particular senior women, as heads of households and controllers of land and labor. In this chapter, relations in extended households underscore women's dominance in everyday political practices. Analysis of the complex power dynamics within matrilineal extended households suggests that land ownership and control reinforced by *adat* serve as the basis for women's claims to authority over other individuals. The senior woman's control of land and house enables her to control both sons' and daughters' labor and to make claims to husband's labor and earned income. Although there are differences across rank and income, women invoke matrilineal ideology to maintain their dominance.

Mother and daughter constitute the core relationship in the matrihouse because they share ongoing rights in the house and the land, which provides the primary source of income in these farm households. House and land do not move automatically to the daughter, however, resulting in ongoing negotiations between mothers and daughters over rights to land and resources. The marital couple is subsidiary to the matrilineal unit. The subsidiary nature of the conjugal unit has been of long standing (see also Tanner 1971). Bachtiar notes that "as a part of the *kaum* group, customarily residing at an ancestral house, a nuclear family tends to be dominated by the interests of the *kaum* group as a whole and is thus not able to exert its identity as a distinct group" (1967:367). The marital couple constitutes the reproductive unit of the household, but only in the strict sense of procreation since other household members are also involved in child rearing.

In contrast to the more common patriarchal households that dominate anthropological texts, in rural Minangkabau matrihouses mother and daughter are the controlling members. Although Western feminists have remained rightly suspicious of the inequalities of household labor, arguing that domestic duties are subject to men's control, in rural Minangkabau households senior women are in control of their own labor (they labor for their own interests) and that of their families. While a woman shows her husband and his kinfolk a great deal of respect, she is not subordinate to her spouse. Women are reproducers of the lineage but they are reproducing their own kin group, not that of their husbands (or their brothers). It is senior women's interests at stake as well as brothers' in reproducing and building up the membership and influence of the sublineage. In this matrilineal system, men are not the primary ones controlling women through marriage; it is female heads of lineages who desire their daughters (and their sons) to marry well and have children. Although they are indeed mothers, they are powerful women that head matrihouses and control ancestral land.

NOTES

1. A number of excellent works critiquing the concept of households as bounded and undifferentiated units exist, including Donham 1990, Dwyer and Bruce 1988, Folbre 1988, Guyer 1986, Guyer and Peters 1987, Hart 1992, and Moore 1992.

2. Contemporary-style houses are usually built with plaster and brick walls, cement floors, and flat (that is, not peaked) corrugated metal (zinc) roofs. In some cases these houses model the floor plan of a big house, but most do not.

3. Some client families have been allowed to build smaller versions of a big house. These houses have less posts, and so, despite their appearance, are not considered "true" big houses.

4. This pattern is typical for other Southeast Asian societies as well, including the Acehnese (Dall 1982) and the Langkawi of Malaysia (Carsten 1997). According to Carsten, Langkawi women dominate the house space with their presence and activities, while men are nearly absent. The impression that women are more or less restricted to the back of the house is highly misleading, applying only when male strangers are present and even then mainly for young women.

5. See also Lea (1995), who uses the term "matri-House" for a group in central Brazil.

6. A local measurement, a *gantang* equals approximately three liters of unhusked rice (*padi*).

7. This group of twenty-eight households includes both two-generation families in which the daughter has just married but not yet had children and three-generation (extended) families. A few extended households in the village were composed of a mother (and her husband), a married son and his offspring. I excluded these households from my analysis of matrihouses since no daughter was present. The discussion in chapter 4 explains more fully why only one-fifth of households in the hamlet are matrihouses.

8. For more information on gender differences, see Blackwood 1998.

9. According to Josselin de Jong (1952), the Minangkabau had duolocal residence in the past, by which he meant that a man had two residences, his wife's and his mother's. Duolocal residence would not, however, apply to women.

10. The greater availability of wage labor for men is partly true, at least in manual labor. Many young men can find unskilled jobs, such as road or building construction, that are unavailable to women. However, with improved education rates, women's ability to find nonagricultural work, particularly in civil service, with its concentration of teachers, nurses, and low-level administrators, has increased.

11. Several state programs and offices belatedly directed efforts toward strengthening women's economic position (Royal Netherlands Embassy 1987, Sjahrir 1985).

12. It may even be that women are coming to view land as their own property. Several women told me that if they redeem any ancestral land, they do not have to share it with their mothers or sisters. In these cases daughters are treating redeemed land as an early receipt of ancestral property that will belong to the daughter's direct heirs alone. Kassim (1988) suggests a similar thing is happening in Negeri Sembilan.

13. There is a stated preference for cross-cousin marriage: marriage to father's sister's son is called *pulang ka bako* (returning home to the bako). Though cross-cousin marriage is preferred, it is not the most frequent type of marriage (Ng 1987). Marriages of other types are approved for a number of ideological reasons. Note here the gender inversion of Levi-Strauss's marriage exchange. It is husbands who are links to other lineages through their exchange. See Krier, forthcoming and Peletz 1987 for further discussion of groom exchange.

4

National Discourses
and Daughters' Desires

In this chapter I maintain my focus on household and mother-daughter relations but I look here at the relation of state and global processes to daughters' desires for their own households. Where extended families were the model for an older generation of women, many daughters born since the formation of the Indonesian state in 1945 have set up their own households separate from their mothers. This younger generation has a different set of identities to choose from. Where senior women born before Indonesian statehood produced themselves in relation to Dutch colonial, nationalist, and capitalist processes, their daughters intercept and reconstitute state and transnational discourses of modernity and development, selfhood and family, that emphasize women's domesticity. Differences between the generations, and the way it is refracted by rank, reflect the impossibility of speaking of "Minangkabau women" as a unitary group (see Sears 1996).

RECONFIGURING DAUGHTERS' DESIRES

National and global processes open a space for rural Minangkabau women who grew up in the postindependence era to reconstitute their identities in ways not before possible nor imaginable in rural villages. In the following I explore a number of discourses promoted through education, state programming for women, the media, and Islamic fundamentalism to show how they create a hegemonic ideology of domesticity for Minangkabau women. In order to document how these discourses have changed daughters' desires, I examine the differences between women in the village who were born in the 1920s and 1930s and women born in the 1950s and 1960s.[1]

Education

Since Indonesian independence, the state has sought to improve education by building elementary and middle schools in local villages. For women born in West Sumatra in the 1920s and 1930s the only education generally available was a three-year elementary program (*Sekolah Rakayat*). Education beyond that level required moving to and boarding at schools in the district capital. Over 85 percent of women born in those years had only an elementary school education or less, reflecting in part the reluctance of senior women to allow their daughters to leave the village. Many rural Minangkabau girls were not allowed to pursue higher education (see table 4.1). An elite women, who in the 1950s was the first of her generation to go to university, said,

> Girls were not allowed to go to school if it meant going far away, or leaving the village. Before, Taram did not have a middle school [SMP], and students had to go to Payakumbuh if they wanted to continue school [which meant they had to board in town because there was no fast transportation]. Parents were afraid to let their daughters leave home for two reasons. First, they were afraid their daughters would marry husbands from outside the village, and second, that they might not marry at all.

As education became more accessible in the 1950s and 1960s, attitudes toward daughters leaving home for further schooling began to shift. Over 40 percent of daughters born in the 1950s and 1960s graduated from high school (SMA) versus only 2 percent in the earlier generation (see table 4.2). A number of these women attended secondary schools located in towns away from the village.

Table 4.1 Education Levels for Women Born in the 1920s–1930s

	None	Some SD	SD	SMP	SMA	Total
Elite	2	7	5	2	0	16
Client	3	4	4	2	1	14
Servant	0	7	1	0	0	8
Total	5	18	10	4	1	38

Table 4.2 Education Levels for Women Born in the 1950s–1960s

	None	Some SD	SD	SMP	SMA	Some Univ.	Univ.	Total
Elite	0	0	13	7	25	3	1	49
Client	1	2	18	7	9	0	0	37
Servant	1	0	6	0	7	1	0	15
Total	2	2	37	14	41	4	1	101

Ironically, the woman who was the first of her generation to attend university was the daughter of the opinionated and conservative Santi.

Irwati, who was born in the mid-1940s, was Santi's eldest daughter. The family's ample rice lands had ensured that Irwati could attend school as far as she wanted. But in her generation moving to the coastal town of Padang to attend college was still not a good choice for a woman. I asked Irwati how she was able to go to college. She said, "I was stubborn and insisted that I be allowed to go. My mother was very fond of me, she couldn't say no, and so she let me go. But my mother's decision made a lot of people in the village angry. At that time they still felt it was not right for a daughter to be so far from the village because of the concern that we would not return home."

Irwati's choices after college proved those concerns to be well founded. She took an administrative job in Padang after graduation, then married and raised her family in that town instead of returning home.

The shift in education rates reflects a shift in attitudes toward the value of education for daughters. Many families make sacrifices in order to put their children through high school. People articulate the belief that education is a key to obtaining a salaried job with a guaranteed income and pension. Villagers recognize the potential economic benefits of higher education and urban careers for women, especially when successful educated daughters use their income to help out the family. For example, one elite daughter who worked in Jakarta for six years was able to save enough money so that she could build her mother a new house in the village. Consequently, families are more willing to risk a daughter's move to the city.

Rates of education for women vary somewhat across the kinship ranks. Half of the elite women born in the 1950s and 1960s in the village graduated from high school. Client kin have the lowest rates of education for girls, with less than a quarter receiving a secondary school (SMA) education. Since client families tend to be poorer than elite families, the difference between the education of women in the two groups is probably due to family income.

Education levels for men born in the same generation (1950s and 1960s) show some differences from women (see table 4.3). Across all ranks men's graduation

Table 4.3 Education Levels for Men Born in the 1950s–1960s						
	Some SD	*SD*	*SMP*	*SMA*	*Some Univ.*	*Univ.*	*Total*
Elite	0	6	1	20	7	0	34
Client	0	15	3	10	0	1	29
Servant	1	3	2	2	2	0	10
Total	1	24	6	32	9	1	73

rates from high school were only slightly higher than women's (44 percent to 41 percent), but three times as many men than women attained at least some university training. The majority of men with university training came from elite and servant families.

The higher rates of university education for men suggest that young women's movements remain a concern for families. As Dt. Rajo explained, "Now, one or two daughters might become teachers, but their families want them to stay close. If there are lots of daughters, it's okay. But the daughter is more important than the son, especially if there is only one. Otherwise, who will continue the lineage? With sons, it doesn't matter." Although recognizing the importance of education for their children, rural Minangkabau are less willing to risk sending their daughters away to school than their sons. Yet the change in education rates between the two generations shows that, despite these concerns, daughters have been successful in contesting restrictions on their movement. They have gained much greater access to higher education than was possible for an earlier generation.

While education for girls has become a desirable goal, education has served state interests in promoting national models of gender and modernity. The "modern" school system provides little state validation for matrilineal practices or the values of rural life. School girls learn "proper" gender roles and are indoctrinated into the importance of becoming wives who serve their husband's needs. Schoolchildren wear uniforms that model the national dress code and reinforce gender difference: girls in skirts and blouses, boys in pants and shirts. On Fridays high school students wear more formal attire. Young women don woven sarongs and dress blouses while young men wear jackets and (sometimes) ties, modeling the image of parents they are soon expected to be.

In addition to promoting a particular gender ideology through the schools, the state promotes education as a way out of the village and a means to better, higher status, salaried jobs. At an elementary school graduation ceremony I attended, the superintendent of schools encouraged the students to be successful. His idea of success was oriented toward the goals of change and development (*kemajuan*) that the state espouses. The village, he said, was changing but just beginning to be modern. He encouraged students to adopt "modern" values and strive for careers and jobs, which in the context of rural life means looking beyond the village for the source of success.

Marriage Rights

The right to choose when and whom they will marry has been another important issue for many women. Women of an earlier generation married according to their mother's will, even though they did not know or like their marriage partner. When I asked one woman what would have happened if she had refused the candidate her parents chose for her, she replied, "I would have had to leave the house, even leave the village. I probably wouldn't have been given any rice fields." Between the generations of women born in the 1920s and 1930s and those born in the 1950s and 1960s, the age at marriage has increased from seventeen to nineteen-and-a-half years old. Part of the reason for the change is the increased number of years of schooling women are receiving (average age at graduation from secondary school is nineteen). As long as young women are in school, most families do not pressure them to marry. Some women wait until they have secured a permanent job before they marry, particularly those seeking civil service jobs, which may add another two to three years before they start considering marriage.

Sentiment in the village has shifted somewhat with these changes. Where the older generation is concerned that their daughters marry good men of titled families, younger women's attitudes about marriage partners have been influenced by discourses of modernity. Reni, Nurani's only daughter, is a good example of the complexities of young women's expectations and beliefs about marriage.

After Reni graduated from high school, she had wanted to attend college like several of her friends, but Nurani was unable to pay for both her son and daughter to attend college at the same time. Reni applied for a civil service job instead and sometimes took trips to visit her friends at the university. During this time, her attitude toward marriage was that she should choose her own husband. "Later on, parents die, and then we are left with their choices. If we follow them, who is happy? If you follow their choice and later divorce, and are unhappy, that's no good. We have to make ourselves happy first, we can't please our parents." She was not without long-term priorities, however. Reni felt that it was important to marry an educated man with initiative and desire to work, even if he was not elite. Echoing a modern individualism, Reni felt that her own happiness was more important than following the wishes and customs of the senior generation—of marrying a husband with a title and blue blood.

Around the time she married, Reni's ideas began to fall more in line with her mother's concerns. She told me how she finally decided on her husband. Nurani wanted her to marry a man who belonged to her father's lineage [*bako*], but Reni was never interested in him. For a time she was interested in a young man from Java, but her mother was adamantly opposed to him, so Reni eventually decided against pursuing that relationship. As she approached the age of twenty-five, an age which is considered old for an unmarried woman, a woman friend suggested that her brother might be a good match. Within a couple months, Reni decided to marry him, although he was from another village. Her choice was not the best one according to her family, but one that was acceptable because they were able to verify that he was of elite rank.

The "romance" model of marriage has strong appeal for young women, but many daughters remain committed to the importance of "good" marriages for the future of their kin group. Consequently, many marry within the village or make accommodations to their kin's wishes. With the greater likelihood of daughters leaving the village for education and meeting men from outside the village, elite elders have had to loosen restrictions about marriage partners. In Reni's case marrying an elite man from outside the village accommodated some of the concerns of her mother. Such a partner would not diminish the standing of their sub-lineage.[2] The senior generation in their turn have ceded ground and allowed daughters more room to marry the ones they choose.

MODELS OF DOMESTICITY

Many young women grow up believing they are better off today under the patriarchal New Order because they can seek their own jobs and choose their own husbands. Trained in the importance of education, the opportunities of urban life, and the drawbacks of rural life—the lack of access to luxury goods and well-paying jobs—these young women find the older generation old-fashioned in many ways. With the increased availability of education, civil service, and other wage labor jobs, young women have demanded the right to pursue higher education and careers in urban areas.

Access to these options has also exposed the younger generation of women to different models of family and household than those of the rural village. The Indonesian state, echoing Western development planners, has long trumpeted the importance of the nuclear family, women's role as housewives and mothers, and men's role as heads of families. State programs promote the importance of motherhood and the idea that women are primarily responsible for their children and their family's health, care, and education.[3] All state family policies are oriented around a nuclear family defined as a husband, wife, and children, a definition of family that disregards the many forms of family found within the borders of Indonesia.

According to the state directive, a woman has five major duties (*panca dharma wanita*): (1) to be loyal backstop and supporter of her husband, (2) to be caretaker of the household, (3) to produce future generations, (4) to raise her children properly, and (5) to be a good citizen (Sullivan 1983:148). Statements by high state officials (among others, the minister for education and culture and the minister for social welfare) reiterate the importance of women's role as housewife. In a speech to wives of government officials, Mrs. Tien Suharto, wife of then-President Suharto, declared, "A harmonious and orderly household is a great contribution to the smooth running of development efforts.... It is the duty of the wife to see to it that her household is in order so that when her husband comes home from a busy day he will find peace and harmony at home. The children, too, will be happier and healthier" (quoted in Manderson 1980:83). This statement underscores the idea that within the domestic sphere women have primary responsibility for children and household concerns.

Programs instituted for women by the state after 1966 implemented this new view of womanhood, focusing solely on women's role in the family. Dharma Wanita, instituted in 1974, is the organization of wives of civil servants. (Dharma Pertiwi is the organization for wives of members of the armed forces.) All wives are expected to participate. In the early days of this organization, a wife was expected to participate in Dharma Wanita according to the rank of her husband, even if she was a civil servant herself. In line with the above stated directives, this group attended exclusively to domestic issues. As this group grew, earlier women's organizations active in the struggle for independence and for women's rights began to disappear or were reoriented to follow the new national directives for women (Wieringa 1985).

Another women's organization, PKK (Pembinaan Kesejahteraan Keluarga, or Family Welfare Organization), established in 1973, has had the most far-reaching effect. PKK is a voluntary organization and is the main channel used by the government to reach women at the grass roots level (Royal Netherlands Embassy 1987). PKK's leaders come from the wives of government officials. These women hold offices according to the rank of their husbands and are not elected or remunerated for their duties. Although they are under heavy pressure to take on these duties as good wives, their participation is considered voluntary. Both PKK and Dharma Wanita are strictly controlled by the government and follow the dictates of the government regarding their structure and programs. Their members are kept busy with cooking and etiquette demonstrations and courses for sewing and flower arrangement, family planning, health, and nutrition. Dharma Wanita regularly hosts events promoting different kinds of products that it wants women to buy, such as cosmetics, baby food, and clothes, among other things. Even though some of the information provided is useful, these organizations propagate a middle-class ideology of womanhood and create a desire for items that reflect a middle-class status. They work together with state pronouncements about women's essential role as wives and mothers to reinforce the idea of women's domesticity within the nuclear household (Tiwon 1996).

In addition to state policies and propaganda, women are inundated through national media with representations of urban, middle-class women. Advertisements in women's magazines and on television bombard women with the most fashionable clothes and skin care and health care products necessary to make them successful women. Avon, Revlon, and Pond's are some of the non-Indonesian companies promoting this vision of femininity. The national dress code reflects this ideal of femininity—dresses, skirts, jewelry, and makeup are the only acceptable attire for women at work. Television shows also pick up the domestic theme. On a popular television series produced by a government-owned television station, one of the themes of the series is that the good woman is a domestic person (Aripurnami 1996, Sen 1993).

Minangkabau newspapers published in West Sumatra for local readers are another source of the discourse on femininity and domesticity for women.

Singgalang, a daily paper out of Padang, contains a women's section devoted to health, beauty tips, and heterosexuality. A columnist advises women not to worry if they are not beautiful; there are other characteristics they can develop that will still be attractive to men. Another column claims that men and women need each other; each sex is incomplete without the other. "Although it's not impossible for a woman to find meaning without a man," advised Fadlillah, "it gives women's lives new meaning when a man is there" (1996:3, my translation). Another article admonishes women to be modest (*malu*), which is seen as the proper trait for a Minangkabau woman, and warns against too modern an attitude, "modern" here referring to the supposed "loosened" values and morals of those in the cities.

Islamic fundamentalism in Indonesia is another principal agent in the discourse of domesticity. Islamic leaders in Indonesia as elsewhere have interpreted a woman's primary role to be wife and mother. They assert that motherhood is the natural role for women and the one they were born to. In an article on the status of women in Islam, an Indonesian Muslim scholar and intellectual of the modernist school of Islam developed this line of thought further: "Man is suited to face the hard struggles of life on account of his stronger physique. Woman is suited to bring up the children because of the preponderance of the quality of love in her. [W]hile the duty of breadwinning must be generally left to the man[,] the duty of the management of the home and bringing up of the children belongs to the women" (Raliby 1985:36). This view of woman closely corresponds to the one fostered by the Indonesian state. In fact, Islamic scholars and prominent Muslim women have interpreted the Qur'an to accommodate state ideology regarding women. Statements by Indonesian Muslim women who are highly placed in government and those who are leaders of women's organizations support state policy on women. In an article on "Women and Career in Islam," the author, an Indonesian businesswoman, finds no contradiction between development directives for women and the Islamic emphasis on wifely duties. She states, "[T]he main duties of women are ... family affairs, including the children's education matters. [O]ther duties, such as social and professional roles, are additional depending upon the condition of respective families" (Pramono 1990:73). This statement suggests that woman's duty is primarily to her family and only secondarily to her community. It echoes the terms of the state directive on women to educate the children and provide support for their husbands. Support for women's careers "outside the household" is contingent on women's ability to maintain their families and homes in proper order (see Pramono 1990). Throughout the "modern" Indonesian state women are imagined and represented as models of domesticity.

CONTRADICTORY HOUSEWIVES

The images of womanhood that are familiar to rural Minangkabau women in the 1990s underscore the values of modernity, domesticity, and the nuclear family.

Rural Minangkabau women understand that in the "modern" world, staying home and taking care of the children represents the good life and accords with state philosophy about women's lives. The power of these images sometimes brought surprising answers to my questions about women's lives as rural farmers. Several women told me it was better to be a housewife and not have to work. Among them was Lina, Fitriani's second daughter, who has been farming both for her mother and as a laborer on other peoples' fields for several years. Lina said, "If you do other work, it's difficult. Your rice fields get less attention, your children get looked after less. If you sell things [at the market], then you're not often at home. You get home at night and that's tiring. If your husband is responsible, then the mother can be the housewife [*ibu rumah tangga*]." Some local women, who were busy farmers or active in community affairs, declared that it was more important to stay home and take care of the children. Ironically, none of these women who claimed to be housewives (*ibu rumah tangga*) fit the stay-at-home housewife model. Each of them had work that took them outside the household and each had income from that work. Some of them were well-to-do farmers who did not have to do field labor (see also Hart 1991). These women for the most part were owner/overseers, women who hired others to work their fields or let their fields out on a sharecrop basis.[4] One woman owned a prosperous rice mill and another was a rice merchant with her husband. The rice merchant told me her husband does all the work, but when I pressed her about her business, she revealed that she buys the rice at harvest from her clients and has it brought to the mill where her husband handles the processing and sale of rice. Women in the village who could actually be labelled housewives were mostly young married women who did not have their own source of income and stayed at home taking care of their small children. Even these women did not fit the (Western) model of housewife since most of them were supported by their extended families and their husbands, not their husbands alone.

The claim to housewife status reflected several processes at work: the devaluation of farming, the official representation of women as housewives, and the notion of "work" as paid labor. In terms of the larger society, farming was seen as a low-status occupation; middle-class status was associated with a working husband and stay-at-home wife. Many women admired the image of the middle-class housewife found in cosmopolitan magazines and advertisements; her life seemed preferable to work in the mud of the rice fields. By asserting that they did not work, these women invoked the "modern" definition of work as something for which one gets paid, such as a job or career. Their assertion also laid claim to a higher status than farming. And, by accentuating their domesticity, these women aligned themselves with the state model for women as housewives.

Yet claiming the status of housewife was not simply a desire for higher status or a response to a state model. Many of these women maintained their own sense of what a "housewife" means. Like Lina above, several women included their rice fields as part of being a housewife, a move which, on the one hand, made their management and control of land and income invisible to the larger society, but on the other, created a new definition of housewife. As Lina explained about being a housewife, "Of course you go to your rice fields. But you don't have to leave the house for so long. To the rice fields in the morning and return home in the afternoon." Rural Minangkabau women incorporated their control of and labor on their rice fields into their sense of themselves as "housewives." Although some women claimed to be housewives, they were not the housewives of state ideology.

MODERNITY AND SMALL HOUSES

The availability of nonagricultural labor for women in a "modern" global economy models alternatives to life in a "backwards" rural household. Younger married women do not want their daughters to have to work in the rice fields because they see farm work as a dead-end, low-status job. Postcolonial discourses promote images of family and happiness that threaten extended family households and their control over a daughter's future. The discourse of modernity and the market, with its emphasis on individualism and consumerism, promotes a model of self-earned income for the earner's use alone, not for the extended family (see also Stivens 1996). Through advertising, the market urges the satisfaction of personal pleasures and the attainment of individual goals, such as higher status associated with the possession of consumer goods such as televisions, stereos, and automobiles. Given these images, a daughter may have less incentive to live with and work for her mother and more incentive to focus her own interest and income on her own family.

Several Minangkabau scholars have argued that the processes of capitalism and a global economy have resulted in a trend in Minangkabau households toward nuclearization and a decline in the extended family form (Kato 1982, Naim 1985). The size of houses in Tanjung Kubang does seem to support that suggestion. There appears to have been a transition over time from big houses with extended families to smaller single-family units. Although older studies do not specify actual numbers of extended family households in rural Minangkabau villages, they do state that the typical household residence was an extended family living in a big house (Maretin 1961, Schrieke 1955). The prevalence of big houses in Taram is supported by Bachtiar's 1962 study (1967). He notes that the *rumah gadang* was the dominant style of house in the village. According to his description, most people at that time probably lived in extended family groupings.

Based on information from women of the senior generation in Tanjung Batang, most women born before 1940 lived with their extended family (84 percent), the great majority of which were housed in big houses (80 percent). Elite women remained in their family's big house after marriage. Interestingly, women of client and servant families also told me they lived in big houses, suggesting that it was a common practice at that time to house adopted members of the sub-lineage in the big house. These adopted kin probably lived in small rooms attached to the big house and worked for their elite kinsfolk. Those who lived in single-family houses (5 percent) were newcomers to the village or women whose mothers deceased at an early age.

The numbers of big houses reported by the senior generation may be somewhat inflated, however. Very few of the client and servant women I surveyed even mentioned the type of house they lived in unless it was a big house. Not living in a big house was a good indication of lower rank, something most people preferred not to discuss. Some older women mentioned specifically when they built their own house, which suggested to me that before that time they had lived with their extended family. Whether or not these women all lived in big houses, it seems fairly clear that most women lived with their families in extended households.

Household composition in 1989 provides quite a difference picture. The composition of the 115 households in Tanjung Batang in 1989 varied widely within a range of single generation to extended family units.[5] Based on my survey of households (here meaning the group living in one residence), I found that two-generation families comprise 64 percent of households in Tanjung Batang (see table 4.4). Three- and four-generation families, the extended households or matrihouses, comprise 26 percent (in contrast to 84 percent for women born before 1940). Nuclear households, those composed of a wife, husband, and children, comprise 55 percent of two-generation households, or only 36 percent of all households. The remaining households are comprised of a single generation, usually elderly (10 percent). Although actual nuclear households are not in the majority, clearly more families are living in single family households than in extended families and many more are doing so than in an earlier generation of families in the village.

The number of two-generation households may be suggestive of a pattern found in other rural areas where smaller households become more prevalent as peasant families are integrated into wage and commodity markets (see, for example, Collins 1986, Kandiyoti 1990, Wilk 1989). Since the development of rice as a major cash crop in the early 1970s, farm households have had greater access to cash, making

Table 4.4 Household Composition

| | Number of Generations | | | | |
	One	Two	Three	Four	Total
Elite	4	35	13	3	55
Client	5	31	9	1	46
Servant	2	8	2	2	14
Total	11	74	24	6	115

the building of individual houses by daughters more feasible. The older client and servant women above who reported building new houses did so mostly after 1970, which is consistent with the greater availability of cash in the village.

If the extended family household reflects the matrilineal "ideal" constituted around a core unit of a mother and her married daughter(s), why are a number of daughters living in their own households? What encourages a daughter's desire for a house of her own apart from her mother's? Is this a trend toward nuclearization, and if it is, what is prompting it? Due to the fact that explicit historical data on relations in extended households were unavailable, in the following discussion I am less concerned with the increases or decreases in types of households than in the differences in contemporary extended and single-family households.

Households and Life-Cycle Variation

Part of the reason for the number of single-family households can be attributed to the vagaries of the life cycle. As was true for households of the older generation, a number of one- and two-generation households in 1990 were due either to the early death of the senior generation or to the arrival of new families to the village. In nearly one-third of these cases, the senior woman had died relatively early in life, leaving her daughters with small children at home. In all likelihood, some of these households will become extended households in the next generation. Another reason for the variation was due to failure to bear daughters. In households of this type, sons moved out at marriage to live with their wives, leaving the senior generation alone in the house. In a few of these cases, a son returned home to live with his elderly mother after divorce or sent his young daughter to live with her grandmother and assist in domestic work.

Migrating in search of jobs or business is another significant factor in the number of one- and two-generation households. Nearly one in four daughters leave the village on temporary migration, usually elder daughters. In some cases there are no daughters left at home, accounting for 16 percent of one- and two-generation households (see table 4.5). As noted in chapter two, migration is a common occurrence and long-standing tradition in West Sumatra. Many individuals

Table 4.5 Reasons for One- and Two-Generation Households (N=85)					
	Daughter Moved Out	*Mother Deceased*	*Migrant Daughter(s)*	*No Daughter*	*Recent Arrival*	*Total Households*
Elite	16	13	5	5	0	39
Client	12	12	5	3	4	36
Servant	4	2	4	0	0	10
Total	32	27	14	8	4	85

migrate on a temporary basis, while others return to the village permanently only after they have retired from work.

Although most of the scholarly attention to migration has focused on men, judging from family genealogies in Taram and the numbers of women who migrated from the village in the 1920s and 1930s (7 percent), it was not uncommon for daughters as well as sons to migrate to a different locale.[6] Daughters might decide to leave due to lack of land to farm or unwillingness to farm, overcrowded housing, or tensions at home. This pattern is still common today as migrants search for better opportunities elsewhere. The change from the earlier generation is in the larger percentage of women who migrate, reflecting the greater availability of jobs for women outside the village than in the past. Villagers say that a wife should follow her husband if he has a good job elsewhere, or prospects of greater income than his wife, but many of the women migrants are educated, unmarried women who have gotten permanent jobs elsewhere. As with sons, *merantau* siphons off additional daughters who are not needed at home and would cause too great a burden on ancestral land if they stayed to make claims to it (see Naim 1985). Daughters who migrate out have much weaker claims to lineage property. If they or their husband are successful in making a living, they are expected to refuse any claims on produce from ancestral property, leaving it to the sister who lives in the village and manages the house and lands.

Residence and Matriliny

Some argue that the increase in nuclear families for rural Minangkabau reflects a weakening of matrilineal kinship (see Maretin 1961). Residence patterns after marriage, however, offer strong evidence of a continued commitment to matrilineal practice. Most daughters do not move out immediately after marriage but wait until their younger sisters have married, spending the intervening years in the matrihouse. The average length of stay at home after marriage is almost ten years for those daughters in Tanjung Batang whose mothers are still alive and living in the village.

Based on the residences of eighty-one adult married women born in Tanjung Batang after 1945, nearly 73 percent live matrilocally[7] (see table 4.6). This figure

Table 4.6 Daughters' Residences (N=81)				
	Matrilocal			Patrilocal
Mother's house	Own house	Other female kin	Neolocal	(with father's or husband's kin)
46%	26%	1%	9%	18%

Note: Data pertain to all married daughters born in Tanjung Batang who reside within the village of Taram. "Own house" refers to daughters' own house.

Photo 4.1 Daughter's new house next to her mother's big house

includes those who live with the mother and those who live nearby on matrilineal property or with matrikin. In fact some women do not even move farther than the front yard of the mother's big house (see photo 4.1). Another 18 percent live patrilocally with the father's or husband's family and 9 percent live neolocally in the village on land that is purchased by daughter and husband together.

The cases of daughters living patrilocally (with husbands on affines' matrilineal land, or near their fathers) are due in some cases to the poverty of the mother's family or, in other cases, to the lack of a daughter in the husband's mother's household. If a husband has access to land or kin connections with wealthy elites, then the daughter might decide to live with her husband's relatives. In fact, most of the daughters who live with their husbands in Tanjung Batang come from client or low-income households. Tisra, who married a man belonging to Santi's servant family, lived with her husband in a tiny house on Yenita's property. Her own parents, six sisters, and two brothers lived in another village about an hour away. Since she was from another village, I did not know if her family had any land, but the fact that she had six sisters meant there would be very little, if any, land to go around, making a move to her husband's village more desireable. Daughters who live patrilocally resist the practice of matrilocal residence for the sake of better economic opportunities. Their actions do not portend the beginning of patriliny, however, because in other ways they maintain matrilineal practices.

Clearly not all daughters remain at home in extended families but matrilineal practice in the form of matrilocal residence continues to be the primary organizer of residence for those who live in the village. Daughters draw on rights to land to build houses nearby mothers' houses, maintaining a strong connection with matrilineal kin. State ideology may be fueling daughters' desires to have their own separate households, but most do not move out precipitously or very far away.

DAUGHTERS WHO LEAVE

To gain a better understanding of the pressures, conflicts, and ideologies at work in the lives of the younger generation of rural Minangkabau women, I explore households of daughters and mothers living separately in the village. These households are of particular interest because the daughters purposely chose to move out of their mothers' houses. The number of these houses totaled thirty-six, of which twenty were daughter households and sixteen were mother households.[8] All daughter households in this group are nuclear (with a resident husband), except for two households where the husband is absent or divorced and one household where there are no children. Mothers' households include all types of households from single-woman-only to nuclear to extended households with other daughters resident.

Despite the nearness of daughters' houses in many cases, mother and daughter households maintain separate resources and income. Almost none of the mothers

Photo 4.2 Mother (left) and daughter in front of daughter's house

contribute income to their daughters on a regular basis, although there may be land sharing and some exchange of labor. In one case, a daughter with her own household sharecrops her mother's land and splits the produce with her mother— shared land provides income for both of them. In most other cases, the daughter manages her own household and relies on her own land and income along with her husband's land and income to support the household. In the following discussion I ask, first, what claims do daughters make about their reasons for moving out and, second, what influence husbands have in these households.

Daughters' Claims

Daughters point to a number of reasons for wanting to live in their own houses, most of which center around tensions in the mother-daughter relationship. Lack of generosity by a mother toward her daughters is one reason given by daughters for moving out of mothers' houses. This claim draws on notions of mutual assistance (*tolong-menolong*) between family members for its validation. A mother who is perceived as ungenerous or unwilling to help out each of her daughters equally may create a rift in the relationship that causes a daughter to leave as soon as she is able to support herself.

> Nurani, who lives in her own house near her mother Yenita's big house, expressed resentment over the way her mother has treated her. Yenita's income from ample rice lands enabled each of her three daughters to receive a high school education, but Yenita was very strict about whom they married. Nurani, who was forced to marry a man she was not interested in and later divorced, lived in her mother's house along with her siblings and their families for many years. She complains that her mother is stingy and never helps her as much as she does her younger sisters. According to Nurani, Yenita spoils the youngest daughter, who is a teacher with her own salary. This daughter lives and eats with her mother and doesn't even have to cook. Even though she has her own salary and can buy whatever she wants to buy, she gets money for shopping from her mother. And still Yenita gives her things. After the last harvest, Yenita bought a necklace but now the youngest daughter is wearing it. Nurani complained that she couldn't get any land from Yenita for her children, and still wouldn't have any if her father hadn't felt sorry for her and lent her some of his rice land [he was the last of his lineage]. For all these reasons, Nurani said, she worked hard and saved enough money from that rice land to build her own house down the street from her mother.

In contrast to the stories of daughters who disappointed their mothers (in the previous chapter), Nurani's story highlights the problems of a generation of daughters who feel they have been treated unfairly despite being loyal and helpful to their mothers.

Some younger elite women give a different cast to their stories of relationships with their mothers. They emphasize their desire to get out from under their mother's supervision after marriage, perceiving their mother's control as an intrusion in what they feel is their own affair.

Lina, Fitriani's second daughter, lived in the big house with Fitriani after she got married until she and her husband saved money to build a house for themselves and their two children. Their house is just steps away from Fitriani's big house. In talking about her relationship with her mother, Lina stresses her independence from her mother and desire to be on her own. She told me, "It's nice. Because I don't depend on my mother or ask for help, she can't mix in my affairs. She can't tell me how to or how not to spend money. She can't ask, 'Why are you sleeping? What, no work to do, then come help me!' We would argue frequently if we were too close. So I earn my own money, I don't ask my mother. I'm on my own. If I wasn't, maybe my own house wouldn't have been built yet." Lina's statement implies that if she was still under her mother's supervision, she would not always get what she wanted. The money she earns working for the farm collective allows her to buy things for herself. By living in her own house Lina can manage her own money and does not have to negotiate with her mother over how to spend it.

Reni, Nurani's daughter, had similar views about the desireability of living in her own house, although she has not yet been able to remain living on her own.

Reni spent her childhood living with her mother and brother, her two aunts, and their families in Yenita's big house. It was not until Reni was a teenager that her mother had her own house. Before Reni married, she told me that she would prefer going with her husband once she was married because she wanted to be on her own. She also remarked that according to Islam, a good wife must submit to the wishes of her husband, a religious sentiment that handily justifies her desire to move out of her mother's house. Not surprisingly, once Reni married, she moved with her husband to a town nearer her civil service job and his business.

They lived in an apartment building where, according to Reni, everyone worked and no one had any time to visit. She told me she liked living there without interference from other people. With the birth of her second child, however, she and her family moved back home with her mother again, a situation which has both good and bad aspects to it, she said. "When I lived in town, I was busy all the time and tired. I got up early and cooked, swept, washed clothes, bathed, all before going to work, worked all day and then came home to cook some more, take care of my daughter, do more washing. Then I would just collapse early because I was so tired." But when they lived in town, she was able to raise her daughter the way she wanted. At her mother's house, she said, although she gets help with taking care of her children, she can't control what goes on in the house. Her daughter gets spoiled but Reni does not argue with Nurani over how to deal with her. To Reni, living in her own apartment was advantageous because she could run things as she wanted. Under her mother's roof, she defers to her mother.

Younger women such as Reni and Lina express a desire for independence and separation from the extended family, a desire that reflects in part state ideology about the nuclear family and that woman's primary duty to her husband and family. Further, the state view that village life is backward supports young women in their resistance to the ideas of the older generation. In conversations with Reni, for instance, it was clear that she thought the older generation old-fashioned; she disagreed with their ideas about the relations between the sexes and also disapproved of the way her family treated her daughter. These points of difference encourage young married women to see their own small family units as something that they, as wives and mothers, should be in control of, rather than their mothers, the senior women. Their attitude toward their kin group reflects the idea that the "modern" housewife should manage *her* household and *her* family on her own.

In each of these cases the tensions between mother and daughter over the mother's control of the household echo in claims about unfair use of household resources or unwanted supervision over daughter's family. Nurani, who was born in the mid-1940s, represents the first generation educated after Indonesian independence. Her desire to be on her own tends to reflect more of the local ideas about mutual assistance and generosity. For Reni and Lina, two younger women born in the 1960s, their desire to have their own households reflects more strongly state ideology about marriage and family.

HUSBANDS IN DAUGHTER HOUSEHOLDS

The second question I explore about daughter's single-family households is the relationship between the husband and wife. Under the laws of the Indonesian state, husbands are empowered as heads of households. The Indonesian Marriage Law of 1974 states that "the husband is the head of the family and the wife is the mother of the household" (Salyo 1985:20). As noted earlier, state policy recognizes nuclear households as the primary household type. These twin dogmas about households reach into rural villages not only through state education but through a variety of other processes, some of which were discussed earlier.

State registration laws are one example of the way in which the state ideology of family is directly imposed on rural households. According to state law, all households must be registered with the village administrative office. Household registration forms contain the categories of household head (*kepala keluarga*), wife (*isteri*), and children (*anak-anak*), a system that imposes a nuclear family form and predetermines the positions of the married couple. According to the form, household heads are men. Only women who are divorced or widowed can be listed as head of household. School children's notion of family is also influenced by state practices. School registration forms ask for the name of a parent (*orang tua*) and parent's occupation. Only one parent is needed on the form and that parent is the father. Information on the mother is nowhere included on the form. School children are required to get their parent's signature on the form and thus are encouraged to think of their father as the central person in the family.

When I asked people to identify the household head in their family, using the Indonesian term *kepala keluarga* (the Minangkabau do not use the same term in their language), almost everyone responded with the name of a husband or male in-law, suggesting widespread recognition of the idea that men are heads of families. By identifying the nuclear unit with the household, the state in effect validates and prioritizes that unit at the same time that it diminishes the importance of the larger kin unit, the matrilineal unit, that is the basis of rural life.

The tendency of people to name a man as household head, however, has more to do with compliance to state directives than with a wholesale reconceptualization of family form. *Kepala keluarga* is, after all, an Indonesian term, not a cultural category for the Minangkabau.[9] When I asked one woman why the husband is said to be the head of the household, she replied, "He is responsible for support, for providing sustenance for the family. He guides the children and takes care of the wife." This response was from a very wealthy woman whose husband has never been able to do more than help manage the family projects. In a way, she was correct; husbands do provide support, but so do wives! Another woman was more candid. After stating that the husband is the head, she said, "When we go to the village office [*kantor desa*] [to register their household], they ask who is the head of the household. The answer is, the husband, not the woman." Another young woman told me with a laugh, "My husband is only home now and again. But in the book [referring to the village registry], the husband is the head of household. It's forced on us [*terpaksa*]." Given a category that does not fit with Minangkabau practice, people are willing to pay lip service to state ideology, but in so doing they are not necessarily representing their household relations accurately or acquiescing to state dictates.

THE DOMESTIC REVISIONED BY DAUGHTERS

The shift in rural Minangkabau men's responsibilities from their sister's children to their own children noted in the previous chapter reflects the influence of colonial and state ideology and "modern" education. Does state support for men as heads of households translate into husband's control over nuclear households? Have matrilineal practices also changed? To answer these questions, I first examine access to resources within the twenty daughter households that are separate from mother's houses in the village and then I look more broadly at all nuclear households in the village.

A comparison of the amounts of land available to matrihouses versus the amount of land daughters control in their own houses highlights some interesting differences. As discussed in the last chapter, the mother produces over three times as much rice as the daughter alone in matrihouses. In contrast, for daughters who live in their own households, their mothers produce 61 percent of the amount their daughters produce (see table 4.7). Daughters in their own households have access to more land than do their mothers.

Where is this land coming from? Daughters draw from a range of kin to gain access to land in both matrihouses and single-family houses. For single-family houses, husbands bring in more land to their wives than husbands of daughters in matrihouses (15 percent as opposed to 8 percent). Fathers are an equally important source of land in daughter households (15 percent). Additionally, small amounts of land come from kinsmen (5 percent). All told, kinsmen and male affines contribute land providing 35 percent of rice production in daughter households, yet this figure is lower than such contributions to daughters in matrihouses, which account for nearly 50 percent of land for daughters' rice production. Mothers' land constitutes the largest contribution of land to daughters in separate households (38 percent), probably accounting somewhat for the decline in their own

Table 4.7 Sources of Land for Daughters Living Separately (N=20 households)

Source of Land	Daughter Households (%)
Mother	38
Self	23
Husband	15
Father	15
Titled man	5
Joint	4
Total	100

Rice production	
Total	12,975 gt.
Average	648 gt/house

Rice production in mother households	
Total (N=17)	7,950 gt.
Average	467 gt/house

land. In addition to the land they received from their mothers, daughters have their own holdings (gained through savings and husbands' incomes) accounting for 23 percent of the land available for rice production. Another 4 percent of land comes from land deals that wife and husband arranged together. Land redeemed with the husband's assistance, however, belongs to the wife.

> In Lina's case, most of her family's ancestral land had been pawned by her mother Fitriani, leaving Lina with no land of her own except that which she shared with her mother. Both she and her husband are farmers and have worked together as sharecroppers and agricultural laborers for several years. They saved enough money in that time to redeem land that belonged to Fitriani's sublineage. Though her husband's labor and income was needed to allow them to save money, the land they redeemed belongs to Lina.

As long as a woman controls that land, produce from it is hers. In terms of land, her husband's contribution supplements the daughter's own land, but it appears that daughters who establish their own households wait until they have enough of their own land before they move, thus avoiding dependence on the husband's land contribution. Overall, the land a wife controls is on average five times greater than that provided by her husband. Consequently, although husbands provide more land in daughter households than in matrihouses, the larger amount of land that wives control maintains their dominance in single-family households even with husband present.

The foregoing illustrates that a daughter establishes her own farm household primarily when she has access to enough land of her own. Conversely, the ability of some households to hold onto daughters is closely related to the amount of land the mother controls. This pattern has interesting parallels in rural societies with patriarchal or patrilocal extended households. As a number of studies have shown, access to wage labor or cash income produces conflicts that loosen customary obligations within extended family households and leads offspring to form their own nuclear households. As money becomes more important in peasant households, it undercuts existing concepts of equivalence or exchange (Kandiyoti 1990, Wilk 1989). In this case, since mothers have less land than daughters already have access to, daughters have less incentive to stay at home under their mother's control and more incentive to live separately where they can make their own decisions.

RECONSTITUTING SINGLE-FAMILY HOUSEHOLDS

So far, these statements apply to the households of daughters whose mothers live in the village. It might make sense that such women with matrikin close by are not challenged about their rights to land. A look at all other single-family houses

Table 4.8 Contributions to Rice Production in Single-Family Households (N=62)		
	Gantang	%
Wife	21,890	64
Husband	7,700	23
Joint	4,550	13
Total	34,140	100

shows some slight differences. I examined the sixty-two single-family house-holds (one- or two-generation) in the village in which a husband was present to compare wife's versus husband's contributions of land (see table 4.8). House-holds of divorced or widowed women were excluded from this number. Hus-bands in all nuclear households contribute 23 percent of land, compared to 8 per-cent in matrihouses and 15 percent in households of daughters living separately. Further, an additional 13 percent of the land was held in common in these house-holds by wife and husband, meaning that they had purchased it together out of pooled or joint income. Men thus provide greater access to land in nuclear house-holds than in the other types. Yet for all nuclear households, women own or have access to 64 percent of household land, indicating that even where men are con-tributing more land, women's greater control of land and its income assures them greater rights to productive income within the household than their husbands.

A focus on land resources for all nuclear households provides one angle on household resources but is not the complete picture. Husbands also contribute cash income to their households, which may be used for daily expenses or to help secure access to more land or build new houses.[10] Nonancestral land that is bought or pawned-in through the efforts of both husband and wife is joint land during their lifetime. But even this land is reconstituted as matrilineal land at death and passed on to daughters. Where wife and husband both contribute sig-nificant amounts of income and share some land in common, I designated such households as joint households. As I use the term, "joint households" means that household subsistence is based on the productive income and labor of both spouses. Typically in such households, the house was built almost wholly from the husband's contribution or on the husband's family land. Joint households constituted 43 percent of all single-family households (husband present) in Tan-jung Batang (23 percent of all households). Among elite single-family house-holds, only a quarter are joint, while over half of client single-family households are joint households.

The difference in numbers of joint single-family households for client families in comparison to elite families relates to their control of resources. Husbands' contributions become more significant in households in which women have little or no access to land. Client kin with no land of their own rely on the resources of both husband and wife. In addition to farming to make ends meet, they depend on petty trade, remittances from offspring, and the husband's wage labor. In many of these households, both wife and husband work the land jointly. In others, husbands' earned income provides additional, often crucial, support for these farm families. If a landless family is able to get land in pawn, the wife has no prior rights to the land, in contrast to Lina, who redeemed family land. This land is a product of their joint labor and income and constitutes a joint resource that they temporarily share. Among all nuclear households of client families, the husband's land contribution was nearly identical with the village average. The difference was in the land held in common by both wife and husband. This figure came to 28 percent, more than double the average for all single-family households, although still not overtaking the resources that the daughter has access to. Consequently, client and low-income households are more likely to be cooperatively organized households than those of elite families, a pattern noticed by Deere (1990) among poorer peasant households in Peru.

In single-family households, husbands are more central and make a greater contribution than in matrihouses, which are under the rule of the senior woman. The husband's greater prominence in single-family households, however, does not give him control over these households. In these households, both wife and husband contribute to household resources. Some of the land they have access to is joint, but both partners also have separate income or land resources, which they control themselves. Should jointly held or pawned-in land remain in their possession past their lifetime, it will be the daughter who takes over control of the land. In like manner, whether their house is built by the husband or from joint earnings, the house is said to be for the wife or the daughter and will be passed on to the daughter. In addition, a wife has a right to her husband's income but the husband does not have the same right in his wife's income. He has to turn to his family if he needs financial assistance. In the typical rural single-family household, each spouse has his or her own resources and income. Though poorer families have less resources, the resources they do have are passed on to daughters.

Although state efforts to prop up men as breadwinners and heads of households are well known to the Minangkabau, these single-family households remain firmly invested in matrilineal ideology. Husbands do not assert claims to their wives' land nor to land that is redeemed through joint effort. Nor do they articulate a right to new houses that they help build with their earned income. Women assert rights to jointly built, single-family houses, maintain control of their own resources, and claim land for their matrilines that was gained with their husbands' help. Some of these single-family households may even become matrihouses in their turn if a married daughter stays at home to raise her family. In the process of creating their own small households, women reinstantiate matrilineality by incorporating new types of houses and new resources within matrilineal practice.

Although in some cases a husband provides the majority of household income, the control he thereby gains operates within a nexus of matrilineal practices that empower women to appropriate land and resources to their matriline. Even if fathers pass on permanent rights to land to their daughters (for instance, in the case of land purchased by the father), this practice does not instantiate patrilineality because such land is absorbed into the matriline. Labeling husbands as household heads and women as subordinate in the way the state does conveniently ignores local relations without erasing its complexity. In this village matrilineal iedology empowers women to configure new houses to their advantage.

ACROSS HOUSEHOLDS

Having demonstrated that single-family households remain firmly within matrilineal practice, the final question I want to consider is how the separation between mothers and daughters affects the matrilineal unit. Does the matrilineal bond break down between mothers and their daughters who live in single-family households? As I stated earlier, daughters who maintain separate households from their mothers have separate land and income, but there are many ways in which households of matrikin remain connected. Relations of mutual assistance are not only important within extended family households but across households of related kin. Daughters, sisters, and mothers continue to help each other financially or provide labor if a particular need or problem arises. According to Dt. Rajo, daily life is separate, but for life's continuation, it is one. Although they may live apart, matrikin still share the same interests in relation to ceremonies and rice land.

The following example shows the depth of a daughter's responsibility to her mother despite the fact that they live under separate roofs. The example involves Nurani, who lives in her own house, and her mother Yenita, the senior woman who lives in the big house.

> On one occasion Yenita found out that her only remaining son, who lived in Jakarta with his wife and children, had fallen ill unexpectedly. Her family gathered on the steps of Santi's big house next door to decide who should go to Jakarta to attend the son during his illness. Yenita listened to the discussion as everyone present, including grown grandchildren, offered suggestions or excuses. Nurani complained passionately that she should not have to go because she had to take care of her business. Dela, the second daughter, could not go, she said, because she had young children to attend to and it would be hard to travel with them. The youngest daughter teaches elementary school and could not take a leave. In the end Yenita decided that she and Nurani should go, despite Nurani's protests. Although Nurani complained to me afterwards that her business would suffer, she felt she had no choice but

to go along with her mother's decision. Even though Nurani lives in her own house, she feels obligated to respect her mother's request.

This family meeting illustrates the strength of the bond between mothers and daughters and the power mothers have as senior women to exert control over their offspring even when they no longer live together in extended households.

With each exchange, kinswomen renew and strengthen their kinship ties, erasing the division between households. Daughters may move out and establish their own households but they remain committed to their matrilineal kin. The move is not an attempt to sever matrilineal ties. In the long run, breaking that tie would be devastating to a daughter's future rights in her mother's property as well as to the status of the sublineage. Instead, the move is an attempt to build a space apart from the mother in which the daughter can operate more freely. The matrilineal unit remains viable but has been reconfigured across households.

CONCLUSION

Minangkabau women have "a multiplicity of feminine identities in Indonesia" (Sears 1996) to choose from and indeed all these representations operate to help produce a daughter's desire to leave her mother's house. As Grewal and Kaplan (1994) note, however, local subjects are not just passive recipients of transnational discourse; each infiltrates the other. Despite the dominance of the ideology of femininity and motherhood at the national level, state ideology is not hegemonic in creating a particular type of Minangkabau woman. Their lack of subjugation to national discourses is evidenced in their control of households, the very site that the state imagines women to be most submissive. Although there is some increase in a husband's contributions and responsibilities toward his wife's family, rural Minangkabau husbands do not gain control of their wives in single-family households. Daughters have not become the housewives and mothers of national fantasy, even when some of them claim to be. Rather than falling subject to husbands' wishes, they are reworking matrilineal practices to create new "houses" and maintain their rights over land and resources. This reworking positions husbands, not wives, as subordinate within the matrilineal household.

State discourse and popular representations of family are not hegemonic in women's lives, but they do provide a means for daughters to challenge their mother's control of family interests. A daughter's desire to move out speaks to the extent of a mother's power over her household and offspring. Through her position as senior woman of her kin group, the mother has the right to control family interests. She is the authority that a daughter must follow until the time that she takes over for her mother. Yet a daughter's desire for her own household is not just about a desire for independence; it reflects state and capitalist discourses about individualism and nuclear families. Without subverting matrilineal ideology, daughters assert the importance of their "own" nuclear families (husband and children) as a way to resist a mother's claims to their labor and income.

Because daughters continue matrilineal practices (of land and house ownership, inheritance, and matrilocal residence) and ultimately maintain strong kin ties across household boundaries, the "nuclearization" of rural Minangkabau households does not portend the imminent collapse of matriliny or its replacement by state-imposed ideologies of kinship and family. Rather the changes in household form suggest that mothers and daughters are engaged in the production and reworking of matrilineal practices under current historical conditions to sustain their own material and ideological advantages within kin groups and community.

NOTES

1. I focus on these two groups of women because those born in the 1920s and 1930s were the last group educated, if at all, under the old system, while women born in the 1950s and 1960s were the first group educated under the new educational system of the Indonesian state.

2. Even these marriages are sometimes risky, though, as Krier (1994) notes. Families in other villages may make claims to higher rank than they actually hold. If discovered after the marriage, it can cause problems for the sublineage in the future.

3. See, for example, Brenner 1998, Djajadiningrat-Nieuwenhuis 1987, Manderson 1980, Suryakusuma 1996, Sullivan 1983, and Wieringa 1985, 1992.

4. Not all women who were owner/overseers considered themselves housewives, however. And women who were owner/operators generally considered themselves farmers, although in some cases they called themselves "just farmers" (*petani aja*).

5. Categorizing households according to kinship relations among members results in an assortment of household types too numerous to list so I identify households by the number of generations in each. The most common types of two-generation households were nuclear (55 percent) and mother only with children (19 percent). The ten nuclear households of civil servants temporarily residing in Tanjung Batang are not included in the figures.

6. The figure is probably higher than 7 percent since people did not always tell me about kin who no longer lived in the village. In many cases I learned about older migrants only through casual conversation.

7. I exclude from this figure the women who have migrated to other areas of Indonesia. Having left the village altogether, their situation is somewhat different than women who remain in the village after marriage.

8. A number of daughters who were born in the village are not included in this analysis. In order to make a comparison between the two types of households, I excluded daughters' households whose mothers are no longer living or whose mothers live outside of the research hamlet of Tanjung Batang.

9. Terms that carry somewhat the same idea in Minangkabau (*kapalo warih, kapalo kaum*) refer to heads of lineage segments.

10. I was unable to determine how much either husbands or wives contributed to their households in earned income since people were reluctant to give me exact amounts.

5

Senior Women
and Ceremonial Strategies

Moving beyond households, I turn now to a location that raises considerably greater difficulties in terms of evaluating gender and power. While I began this book by situating rural Minangkabau women within households, I did so to locate a broader domain of kinship within distinctly household affairs. In this chapter I want to expand the view beyond the household by situating women within village lineage structures.

If in earlier writings Minangkabau women had some authority within a domestic sphere loosely defined as household and sublineage, village life was considered the domain of men par excellence. In a village governed by *adat*, the *adat* functionaries such as titled men, security officers (*dubalang*), clerks (*manti*) and religious officers (*malim*) were considered the "the guardians of social norms" who regulated social reality (Abdullah 1972:197). Men who held these positions were said to make the decisions about lineage problems and ceremonial events. Pak challenged this view, arguing that "women, not men, are the principal agents managing, animating, and organizing village life" through their control of ritual activities (1986:169).[1]

Because Minangkabau village life is embedded in the idiom of kinship, lineage activities constitute the core of social life in the village. The whole range of activities involved in carrying out ceremonies as well as the interactions among elites and between elites and their subordinate kin are political events. The point I take up here is not just that women, as elders, are key actors in these events. In this chapter and the next I explore how elite women define and reconstitute the larger community as they manage and carry out lineage activities.

In this chapter I look at elite women's relations to those who are kinfolk beyond the household but within lineage and clan, while in the next chapter I examine hierarchical relations between elite women and their subordinate client and servant kin. I explore how *adat* ideology validates elite women's authority over others in their lineage (both extended kin and client kin) and show how *adat* ideology is used and manipulated in negotiations of status and rank.

SENIOR WOMEN AND "SISTER'S CHILDREN"

As noted in chapter 1, the kinship system provides the basis for ranking within the village. Elite lineages hold the highest rank within the community; client and servant families occupy the middle and low rank, respectively. Among elites there are also gradations in ranking. Each clan and lineage has its highest-ranking sublineage (*pucuk*) with its associated titled man and senior woman. Senior women are also referred to by the name *Bundo Kanduang* (literally, womb mother or one's own mother), which means in a deeper and more respectful sense ancestress, mother of the kin group, or senior woman (see also Reenen 1996).[2] Villagers in Taram used the term to identify the woman who has responsibility for overseeing the clan, lineage, or sublineage (see photo 5.1).

When I asked Yetri, Hartati's daughter, about the rights and duties of senior women (*Bundo Kanduang*), she said, "to give advice to the children and guide them in the proper way." This image resonates with the state and Islamic ideals

Photo 5.1 Two senior women and a daughter-in-law
(*pasumandan,* on left) at a ceremonial gathering

of woman as the mother who is educator and guide to her children. Yet it disguises a much broader relationship. Senior women's responsibilities extend well beyond that of mother.

One day while I was talking to Dt. Rajo at his sister Hartati's house, a woman came to the house asking for Hartati. The two women talked for ten minutes about the arrangements for the wedding of the woman's son. I asked Dt. Rajo why this woman sought out his sister. He explained that the woman was a member of Hartati's lineage. Then he said, "She [Hartati] is the commander" (*komandan*, a term derived from English). His use of the term *komandan* surprised me, as I had never heard it used before nor seen it mentioned in the literature. By using it, he was emphasizing the senior woman's authority over others below her in the lineage. Later he elaborated:

> The senior woman controls and gives direction to those in the sublineage, lineage, and clan [*kaum, payung, dan suku*]. The role of *Bundo Kanduang* is broader than that of just taking care of children. Yetri (Hartati's daughter) only takes care of her children, but *Bundo Kanduang* can have two or three households that she manages. That is in matters of *adat*, not in everyday life. [*Bundo Kanduang*] manages lots of people, including client kin [*orang bamamak*].

I asked Hartati about her responsibilities as senior woman. She mentioned a number of things that she was involved in:

> Bundo Kanduang leads [*membimbing*] her children [*anak*] and relatives [*kamanakan*]. A mother takes care of her family; *Bundo Kanduang* takes care of her *kamanakan*. If she doesn't take care of her *kamanakan*, then people will talk about her and say she isn't resolute. She must be able to resolve the problems of her *kamanakan*. If a relative comes to *Bundo Kanduang* and complains about another relative or sibling, then *Bundo Kanduang* must settle the problem. For example, she will call the other person and talk to her/him, "Don't be like that, etc.," and they will accept her advice.
>
> When my children were small, I needed to be there to take care of them. But at the same time, I still had responsibilities as *Bundo Kanduang*. I can't refuse that. Our responsibilities as elders [*mamak*] are heavy. For instance, a relative will come and say, "Well, my daughter has a prospective groom [*jodoh*], what about it?" We go to the *mamak* [of the candidate's lineage] and propose the marriage to them. *Bundo Kanduang* is the one that carries it out [*menjalankan*].

In her description, Hartati makes an important distinction between mothers in the sense of those who raise their children and mothers (*Bundo Kanduang*) who are responsible for all the kin within their sublineage.[3] Like other women I talked to, she had no difficulty explaining the difference between the two categories. The responsibilities of a senior woman as *Bundo Kanduang* encompass all her "children" (*anak dan kamanakan*). The term *kamanakan* is usually defined narrowly as "sister's son" or "nieces and nephews" because it is thought to be the term men use for their matrilineal kin. But as used by Hartati and other people in

Taram, it has a more general meaning of "relative". For instance, when I was talking to Dt. Rajo about the lineage elders' responsibilities to their "sister's children," he said, "There are lots of titled men in the village without *kamanakan*, including Dt. X." The titled man he referred to had several sisters and many, many nieces and nephews. What Dt. Rajo meant was that this man had no client kin. Hartati referred to *Bundo Kanduang's kamanakan* several times in the above quote, by which she meant both her blood kin and adopted kin. Thus, *kamanakan* refers not just to sister's children but to "classificatory" sister's children, that is, all the "relatives" in a woman's lineage, whether elite, commoners, or servant kin.

A senior woman's responsibilities over her "children" extend beyond her immediate household to those in her lineage. It involves the guidance and supervision of the members of her sublineage throughout their lives. In terms of actual numbers of families, senior women in Tanjung Batang have anywhere from two to fifteen elite families under their responsibility and usually supervised a number of client families as well. Only a few have servant families belonging to their sublineage. Since many of these families are scattered throughout the village of Taram, the senior woman's influence extends throughout the village.

Among elite women, the highest-ranking woman at the lineage and clan levels has more prestige and influence than those below her. Fitriani and her nephew, Dt. Sango, are the highest-ranking members of their clan, which has four lineages and fifteen sublineages. Fitriani's position is highly respected by members of her clan. Another senior woman in Fitriani's lineage, who is approximately the same age as Fitriani, said that if she does not help out at a ceremony within the lineage, Fitriani will ask her why she did not attend. According to this woman, Fitriani makes the decisions and the others just go along with whatever she wants. Although this woman was probably underplaying her own authority to give the impression of harmony so important in village life, it suggests that, in like manner with titled men, rank bestows greatest authority to those at the top.

Within the lineage the most senior woman has to be notified about the affairs of sublineages under her supervision. If there are problems in the sublineage, then the senior woman is called in. Fitriani said, "If there is something that can't be resolved, *Bundo Kanduang* will check into it." As noted in the last chapter, the senior woman handles marital problems not only of the daughters of her lineage, but of out-married sons as well. As far as Hartati's daughter Yetri is concerned, she is glad she is not *Bundo Kanduang* yet. "As *Bundo Kanduang*, it's difficult. You're busy all the time. My mother has client kin in the farthest hamlets in this village." When these kin need the advice of the senior woman, she takes care of them, which in many cases means going to their houses to supervise day-long ritual gatherings as well as spending many long hours in careful deliberations concerning the proper *adat* to follow.

CEREMONIES AS DAILY POLITICS

The implications of women's authority and control within the lineage and community can be seen within the domain of ceremonial *adat*. The ceremonial context comprises a critical domain for the analysis of women's power in the village because social relations appear in high relief during ceremonies. The enactment of ceremonies is an enactment of social networks, obligations, duties, and rights. According to Prindiville (1981), the exchange of labor and food at ritual gatherings solidifies kin ties centered on the matrilineage. Ng calls these Minangkabau rituals rites of transition in which "the principles of their social universe are inculcated, re-affirmed and transmitted" (1987:121). Ng goes on to say that ceremonies are more than just expressions of solidarity. Ceremonies are "also occasions when villagers compete for social prestige" (Ng 1987:76). Ritual activities as a way to accumulate prestige are a common practice throughout Indonesia (Kipp and Rodgers 1987:11). On these occasions lineages demonstrate economic and social dominance through conspicuous display and consumption of food and knowledge of correct ritual dress and behavior (Ng 1987).

Following Ng, I see ceremonies as more than the expression of social values and meanings displayed in ritual tableau. Ceremonies are important in terms of constructing and redefining social ties as well as in confirming or enhancing the prestige or influence of one's lineage. Ceremonial events provide one of the stages on which to express and contest prestige and power in the village. They constitute the site of daily politics enacted in many small ways. In the following I show that through their position as lineage elders and *adat* experts, senior elite women and men control ceremonial practice.

Although the "formal" speeches of ceremonies are often the only part recognized as the official ceremony, an approach Geertz (1960) took in analyzing Javanese ceremonial feasts (*slametan*), ceremonies are complex activities. Stoler (1977) provided important insights into the *slametan* ritual and women's role in mediating inter-household relations by taking into account women's collective social labor preparing and distributing food for the feast.[4] Following Stoler's lead, I discuss below the myriad deliberations, preparations, and activities that occur in the course of a ceremonial event to provide insight into elite women's control over ceremonial activities and their meanings.

Ceremonial *Adat*

Hardly a month goes by in which villagers are not caught up in the planning and preparation for a ritual gathering. During my stay in Taram a ritual gathering took place in Tanjung Batang at least every month. I attended twenty-five ceremonies (and missed several others). Such ceremonies are referred to as *kenduri*, an Islamic term, or *baralek*, a Minangkabau term. Each one typically involves butchering an animal for meat and preparing large amounts of food for a ritual feast. In addition each ceremony is preceded by deliberations among the lineage elders, for whom food must be prepared and served. Ceremonies are held for engagements, weddings, *penghulu* installations, male circumcisions, births, and deaths. Following a death, additional ceremonies to commemorate the deceased are usually held on the third, seventh, fortieth, and hundredth day. During Ramadan small feasts are an on-going part of ritual observances. Each household usually holds a *buka bersama*, breaking the fast together, by inviting friends and kin to share an evening meal. Although Ng (1987) distinguishes between major and minor ceremonies, in Taram any ceremonial occasion can be turned into a major event, depending on the wealth of the family. Most families make the greatest expenditure for weddings, but even a birth celebration can become a lavish event.

A myriad of events throughout the ceremonial process provides ample means for elites to assert and negotiate lineage standing and power. These events include the deliberations, preparations, the invitation giving, the ceremony itself, and the thank-you gathering afterwards. *Adat* provides the guidelines for proper execution of all these events. Ceremonial *adat* in Taram has three levels, referred to as high, middle, and low *adat*. A high *adat* ceremony must include butchering a water buffalo for the feast, as well as other elements of ceremonial dress that are excluded from lower-level *adat* ceremonies. For mid-level ceremonies a cow is butchered for meat and for low-level ceremonies one or more goats are butchered. A water buffalo is the most expensive to purchase and slaughter, and the most prestigious. Cattle (*sapi*) are less expensive, but still constitute a significant outlay for a ceremony. A single goat costs only $25–27 (45,000–50,000 rupiah).

High adat ceremonies are infrequent because of the cost involved of slaughtering a water buffalo for meat and providing food for the large numbers of guests that attend. Arguably the most recent high *adat* ceremony took place in the mid-1990s for the wedding of Yonalis's granddaughter, although there is some debate about whether it was actually a high or mid-level *adat* ceremony. The previous one was in 1982. Even mid-level ceremonies are held infrequently. Most elite families opt for what I call a high-end low-level ceremony, that is, they hold a low *adat* ceremony in which the bride dresses elaborately but the family butchers goats for meat instead of a cow or water buffalo.

The inclusion of some elements of high *adat*, or even national culture, in a small ceremony reinforces elites' standing in the community. For instance, at the wedding of the daughter of an elite but poor family, only two goats were slaughtered and a small bridal dais rented. The bride, however, proudly wore a large headpiece (*sunting*) and large gold bracelets, the tokens of her elite rank that are forbidden to non-elites (see photo 5.2). In another elite wedding that was equally small, the groom's side, from Payakumbuh, rented a large dais and large *sunting* for the bride. Some of their young kinswomen arrived at the ceremony wearing the horn-shaped headcloth that only elites are allowed to wear (and Taram elites wear for high *adat* events only). Some elites hire local entertainers to play Minangkabau folk music, while others hire bands that play Indonesian pop

Photo 5.2 Bride wearing a large headpiece

music. Both types of entertainment serve in small ways to underscore the status of the family in the village. Client and servant families are usually only allowed to hold small feasts for which one or a few goats are butchered. These small ceremonies are not considered *adat* ceremonies and are simply referred to as *mendoa*, or ceremonial prayers (saying prayers for the celebrants/deceased). Such ceremonies garner little attention or prestige for their hosts.

Ritual gatherings incorporate Islamic practice in a number of ways in the village. As I discussed in chapter 2, Minangkabau social life interweaves Islamic and Minangkabau practice (see also Whalley 1993). According to my consultant Dt. Rajo, *adat* ceremonies adhere to Islamic tenets. Villagers feel that they are expressing their Islamic faith in the ritual style of these ceremonies, despite the fact that in many ways ceremonies follow *adat* prescriptions.[5] Each *adat* ceremony minimally includes an Islamic prayer offered by the religious functionary (*khadi*) of the lineage.[6] Minangkabau perform the major Islamic rituals (according to Martin's [1982] inventory of Islamic rites): a ceremonial feast following birth, male circumcision, marriage, and death. At the death ritual, the body of the deceased is washed and wrapped by an *imam*, or religious specialist, if available, and buried before the third call to prayer after death. The marriage rites (*nikah*) are performed before the religious specialist. The marriage ceremony also follows the Islamic style of an all-day celebration, but following matrilineal practice, the groom is brought to the bride's house and retires to her bedroom following the ceremony. Thus, Islamic and Minangkabau practices are incorporated into every ceremony.

Ceremonies and their preparation involve an enormous amount of cooperation with a wide range of kin and affines. Depending on their relation to the host family (the family holding the ceremony), different groups of kin form either the pool of labor or the respected guests (see also Ng 1987). There are five groups of kin involved in ceremonies. From the senior woman's point of view, the first group is her own kinfolk, both women and men of her matrilineage as well as client and servant lineages, who help with preparations, cooking, serving, and speech-making. Kinswomen cook and decorate the house and bridal room, while kinsmen build cooking sheds and platforms, and butcher and cook the meat. The host family works for several days before a ceremony to prepare enough food for all the guests. The second group is her *bako*, members of her father's matrilineage, who attend the event as respected guests. The third group are the *pasumandan*, the women (including their matrikin) married to men of her matrilineage (making her their *bako*), who help with preparations and also attend as guests. When not helping at their mother-in-law's house, the *pasumandan* and their kinswomen work at home baking cakes or preparing sticky rice rolls for the trays that they will carry on their heads to the ceremony. The fourth group constitutes the women who are grandchildren of men of the matrilineage (*anak orang tua*, *anak buah*). This group also provides food for the ceremony. The fifth group is composed of *urang sumando*, the men married to her kinswomen, who provide cash for some of the expenses, particularly to purchase the animal to be butchered. They also attend the deliberations and the event as guests.

Lineage elders spend considerable time, particularly for marriages, working out the details of ceremonial events so that all obligations and duties are understood by all groups involved. Negotiations may commence months before the actual ceremony. It often takes several meetings (*musyawarah*, deliberations) to settle questions of *adat* and draw up lists of invitees. For each meeting, kinswomen work together that day to prepare food to serve to the attendees. Lineage members, both women and men, attend these meetings and discuss the arrangements for the ceremony until they reach consensus. An early question that must be resolved is what level of *adat* to use for the ceremony (this question was the sticking point in the deliberation discussed in chapter 2). Other matters are either men's or women's concerns. According to Dt. Rajo, "the senior woman has more responsibilities than the senior man in matters of ceremonies and their negotiations. She is responsible for certain decisions made concerning ceremonies, such as for marriages or deaths." The senior women discuss what food to prepare, what women need to be invited, what women can be asked to help, and how many items should be included in food trays brought by *pasumandan*. The senior men decide on what men to invite or ask for help, whether or not to build a shelter to cook the meat in, whether to build a platform for the trays, and who will make speeches. These decisions are then discussed and agreed on with all members at the deliberation.

At the early stages of deliberation only members from the sublineage confer, but as planning progresses, members from the lineage and clan are invited to join in the planning as well. For large ceremonial events hosted by an elite lineage, a final meeting is held to inform the village—either the hamlet or, in a high *adat* ceremony, the whole village—which means that other families without kin ties to the families involved are invited or asked for assistance. State-sponsored organizations, such as PKK and *Karang Taruna*, the neighborhood youth association, are asked to help out.

RITUAL PRACTICES

The ceremony itself is a many-faceted event composed of several interlinked elements. Of particular importance for this discussion are the social and ritual aspects involved in the preparation and presentation of food trays, ceremonial dress, guest seating and treatment, and speeches. Each of these elements can be reworked in seemingly endless variation that provide host and participants with a number of ways to highlight or downplay their relationships.[7]

Tray Service

Part of the spectacle of a wedding ceremony is the arrival of *pasumandan* (women married to men of the host lineage). These women bear elaborate trays of food on their heads and wear their smartest clothes to show their respect to their husband's matrilineage (see photo 5.3). A number of other women also

Photo 5.3 Daughter-in-law arriving at a
ceremony bearing an elaborate tray

bring trays, all of which are used to help feed the guests. As guests arrive at a ceremonial gathering and sit in the main hall, trays are brought in and placed before them; particular categories of trays go to particular guests. The *pasumandan* trays contain a set number of cooked food items; the number of items on these trays is decided at the lineage deliberations, and no one is allowed to bring more or less items than specified. As Hartati stated, "You can't just have people bringing anything." Trays are displayed prominently either in a large room of the house or on a platform specially built for that purpose until they are needed for the guests. Guests who bring trays of cooked food return home with small packages of raw food, usually rice and bananas, given to them by the hosts.

The following story illustrates the use of trays during a ceremonial gathering hosted by Hartati at her big house. The event was a low-level *adat* ritual (called an *akikah* or *turun mandi*) for Hartati's infant grandson, Yetri's second son.

Nurani and I arrived at the big house for the ceremony at 10:45 a.m. It was a busy scene with women entering and leaving the house, both guests and those there to help serve them. We were greeted by Dt. Rajo, who was standing with two other men in the yard. There were several women working in the kitchen downstairs. Leli and Yeni, Hartati's client kinswomen, were busily helping out, running upstairs and down, getting things when asked, and helping serve food. Siti, Hartati's sister, greeted us as we climbed the steps and ushered us to a place to sit near the head of the main hall. The front area of the main hall had been cleared of furniture, covered with mats, and set out with dishes and food. Yetri was sitting in her room [*anjuang*] at the head of the main hall with her infant son wrapped in a small sarong, waiting for guests. She was dressed in a very fine pink overblouse [*baju kurung*] and cloth sarong. Hartati had a headache and was lying down for the moment in the bedroom next to her daughter's.

We sat down in the main hall with our backs to the outer wall. Lining the middle of the floor was a row of trays bearing *agar-agar*, a sweet dessert made with gelatin, cake, and bananas. After we sat down, Siti and then Hartati brought over plates of food to set in front of us, and told us to eat. Hartati then brought over a plate with a large baked *gurami* [a type of fish] on it, as yet untouched, and insisted we eat it, too. As soon as we finished eating, Nurani got up and we made our way to the line of women going into the end bedroom where Yetri sat with her baby. We each shook hands with Yetri and gave her an envelope of money for the baby. Then we slowly made our way out of the big house.

The women who arrived in the morning came with trays of food, the most important being those from the wives of Hartati's brothers. Nurma arrived with Noni, a young client kinswoman, who was carrying a tray for her mother, the wife of one of Hartati's brothers. Both Noni and her four-year-old daughter were dressed very nicely in respect to the father's lineage [*bako*]. The second sister-in-law arrived early with her granddaughter and brought a tray. Dt. Rajo's wife is deceased. Her tray, a very elaborate one containing a layered cake with five or six plates of food, was brought by her daughter, who arrived with a large contingent of her kinswomen. Each of these women were received in the main hall. Hartati made sure they were served food before they left.

About 1:00 p.m., a number of elite and titled men, including Dt. Rajo, arrived from their Friday prayers. They came in and sat in the main hall, which had been reset with fresh plates and food. Several client men set out rice and tea for the guests, who then engaged in a short exchange of speeches lasting about five minutes. Yetri's baby boy was brought in and held by the wife of Hartati's youngest brother, while the *wali hakim* [man who acts on behalf of the father of the boy's mother] fed the baby. Then the men ate. When they were finished, client men cleared their plates away and handed them to client women who took them downstairs to be washed. At that point the trays were carried in and set in front of the men. It took two men to carry each tray. A close kinswoman of Hartati supervised this and told the carriers what trays to take and exactly where to place them. The most important trays went to the elite men sitting at the head of the main hall away from the kitchen end of the big house. When the trays were in place, there was another short speech [*pidato*], lasting about two minutes, then they ate the food on the trays. After the men finished, there was about fifteen more minutes of speeches, spoken very softly.

In this event the most elaborate trays were those brought by the women who had married Hartati's brothers. Each of the sisters-in-law who attended was well-dressed as a sign of respect to her husbands' kin. The daughter of the deceased sister-in-law brought many kin with her in honor of her father's family. One sister-in-law was absent from the event, the client women of Nurma's family. She was represented by her daughter, granddaughter, and her elite kinswoman, Nurma, who brought the tray herself rather than the client woman to show greater honor to the host family. By their attendance and presentation of elaborate food trays, these kinswomen each in different ways reaffirmed their connection with Hartati's matrilineage and their continued interest in maintaining family ties.

The senior woman hosting the event pays close attention to tray placement because a misplaced tray can cause serious problems. The most important trays are those of the wives of the titled men of the lineage and clan. Hartati described the process: "Trays can't be placed just anywhere. In this house, the tray for Dt. Rajo has to be placed at the head. Trays from the relatives [*kamanakan*] would go to one side. The senior woman has to know this and make sure things are arranged right." Misplaced trays can cause serious insult to kinsmen who are not given the appropriate tray; it is an equal affront to the women who bring them. If the important trays are placed near the kitchen, Hartati said, the women who made the trays would be offended (*hati sakit*) and would go home. Just such an event did happen at another wedding in the village. At this wedding one of the sister-in-law's trays had not been placed "high" (in front of the titled men) but was placed lower (*di bawa*). The woman who brought the tray became very upset (*sakit hati*) and felt humiliated by the error. Such misplacement suggested to her that her in-laws thought little of her. Given the usual careful placement of the trays, it would be easy to conclude that the misplacement was purposeful. In all likelihood, the woman was client kin; her tray was not considered as respectable as the others brought by elite sisters-in-law.

The contents of the trays are another of the key culinary elements in a ceremony. Trays for simple ceremonies usually contain only three items, usually bananas, cake, and *agar-agar*, while for larger ceremonies five items might be allowed. Ng (1987) suggests that the restriction on number of food items may be the result of sumptuary regulations put in place to prevent the escalation of ostentation. Her argument fits quite well with Minangkabau efforts to prevent boastful or excessive behavior, but in Taram the regulations still allow quite a bit of room to express difference. Although the number of items on a tray is decided beforehand, women use the lavishness of the tray's contents to convey certain meanings about their relationship with the host family. Because the trays are displayed for all to see before they are served, women spend time looking over the trays and can readily judge how lavish or cheap the different trays are. (see photo 5.4)

Photo 5.4 Kinswomen inspect the trays for a wedding

Tray contents express the relationship between the bearer and the receiver of the trays. The following story indicates the significance of tray contents from the point of view of those attending a wedding. In this case Dela asked her sister Nurani to represent her at two weddings being held by client kin of her husband Dt. Sati. As the wife of a titled man, Dela has a responsibility to attend and bring a tray to ceremonies held by members of her husband's lineage, but she asked her sister not only to make the cakes for the tray but to attend in her stead as well.

Nurani was busy mixing batter for cakes on August 30. The preceding two days she had supervised the harvest in her large rice field across the river and had shuttled back and forth between her house, the rice mill, and the field. Today was a home day to make cakes for her sister. Nurani was not in a good mood as she worked on the cakes. (Usually she is pleased when others need her services, but today she seemed only irritated.) "Dela is lucky to have an older sister," she said. She complained that Dela asks her to do everything she doesn't want to do herself, but if asked, Nurani has to go to. She sighed and said, "The oldest has the most responsibilities."

Nurani had three cakes to make that day. She called her mother Yenita over and made her help, saying she couldn't do it all alone. The cakes were single-layer cakes; each layer had to be cooked separately in the tiny gas stove that Nurani uses for such occasions. Dela was actually busy selling food in her small shop that she set up outside the nearby elementary school. When Dela showed up at Nurani's house around 12:00 p.m., Yenita quickly got out of her duties and made Dela help Nurani.

The next day, August 31, Nurani had to go to the two weddings [*baralek*]. In the late morning she changed from her house dress into a *baju kurung* [overblouse]—an ordinary one, she said—and went to her mother's house to pick up the tray for the first wedding. Her mother had put several other items on the tray after the cakes were finished. This tray was just a flat silver tray with a plain single-layer cake, *agar-agar*, and bananas. Nurani took two young girls with her, Santi's granddaughter and a neighbor girl, and made the long walk across the bridge to the other side of the village with the tray on her head. She returned to her house in the early afternoon, changed her overblouse, picked up the second tray from her mother, and this time went with two elite women to the second wedding. The tray Nurani took this time was much nicer. It had three small raised silver platters on it, one with agar-agar and the others with her cakes. One of the cakes was covered in white icing and had several plastic flowers in the center that she had bought at the market. *Pulut* [a sticky rice dish] and bananas covered the bottom of the tray.

I asked Nurani why the two trays were so different. She said the people hosting the first wedding are not client kin of Dt. Sati but of another family in that lineage. Besides, the ceremony was only a small one, she said. Since they are more distant kin, she only needs to bring a small tray. The other family are client kin of her sister's husband. So they get a nicer tray. She said, "Everything has to fit the occasion. Besides, the [second] ceremony was much bigger. They butchered four goats and had a band playing."

According to Nurani, though both families were client families, she prepared the contents of the trays to correspond to the perceived closeness of each family to her sister's husband. What she did not state explicitly but hinted at was the difference in the relative status of the two families. The second ceremony she attended was hosted by a well-to-do client woman who was a rice merchant associated with one of the mills in the village. Her economic standing was attested to by the size of the ceremony, the number of goats, and the fact that she could afford a band. Though the ceremony was hosted by a client woman, Nurani's efforts in dressing up, bringing a very nice tray, and attending with other elite women rather than the young girls she took to the earlier ceremony accentuated her relationship with this woman's family, signifying that she considered her an important woman closer to her own rank.

As can be seen from the foregoing trays, their content, and their placement constitute an integral and important part of the ritual. Trays are not just simply markers of status or static reflections of relationships among people and kin in the community. Elite women can affirm, accentuate, or minimize their relationship to the host family by bringing more or less lavish trays. Host families choose which of their guests to honor by serving them the best trays. They speak back to the tray-bringers by placing their trays in more or less auspicious locations. Trays thus constitute a conversation among kin, affines, and neighbors that underscore established kin ties or create new alignments.

Photo 5.5 Women in ceremonial dress attending an engagement ceremony

Ceremonial Dress

The ceremonial dress worn by guests depends on the *adat* level of the ceremony and the guest's relationship to the host family. At low *adat* events, women guests typically wear *baju kurung* (a tight-fitting overblouse with long sleeves), a cotton print or woven sarong, *selendang* (a wide scarf draped over one shoulder), and gold jewelry. Women always wear their gold jewelry at ceremonial events; it signifies the wealth of their family. For mid-level *adat*, they wear one or two woven sarongs covered with a simple sarong draped so that only the gold-embroidered bands at the bottom of the woven sarongs show beneath the simple one. Depending on the event, women wear either a white or print headcloth wrapped in such a way as to resemble water buffalo horns (see photo 5.5). In Taram, women only wear the traditional horned headdress (*takuluak tanduk*) and red velvet tunic for high *adat* events, so these outfits are rarely seen. (See Ng 1987 for further details on women's costumes and their meaning.)

What women choose to wear takes a certain amount of deliberation as they work out their relationship to the host family and their own investment in that relationship. As noted in the story above, Nurani took great pains to make the right appearance when attending ceremonies. Clothing says a number of things about one's status and the status of the family hosting an event. Dressing too elaborately for a small ceremony is inappropriate, giving it more respect than it deserves, just as dressing too simply conveys a lack of respect.

Host kinsmen usually wear a simple sarong and shirt. At low *adat* events kins-men's dress is even less elaborate. They wear plain white shirts over cotton print trousers with a rimless black cap (*peci*) on their heads and small woven cloth wrapped at the waist. Only at high *adat* events do elite men put on special cloth-ing, including a black velvet tunic and trousers, an elaborate headcloth, and cane. Young men without ceremonial responsibilities usually wear jeans and shirts.

Guest Seating and Treatment

Elite ceremonies are held in the big house, if the family has one. Women dominate the space inside the big house while men cluster outside the house in small groups and are occasionally called into service to help the women. As Ng, among several others, have noted, "women are the principal figures in adat ceremonies either as organizers or as participants" (1987:78). Kin, guests, and neighbors, predominantly women, come and go all day during a ritual gathering. At such times the atmosphere in the main hall is dignified and restrained. Women engage in polite conversation but refrain from loud noise or laughter. Only in the side rooms and kitchen, where other women are busily cooking or serving up the food, is there much talking.

Fitriani, the highest-ranking (*pucuk*) woman in her clan, explained with pride how she handles the women guests at a ritual gathering when she is the host. She explained as follows:

"I greet [each guest] and tell her where to sit. I know exactly where they should sit, and I'll tell them, "no, no, not there, come over here and sit down" [seating them nearer or farther from the head of the main hall]. Then I sit with them and make sure that they have enough to eat and drink. [Guests are always encour-aged to '*tambah, tambah*' (take more) and '*jaan baso basi*' (don't be so polite)]. If they run out, I call one of the women helping to get more water or food for them and talk to them, make them feel welcome. All of that, including the chat-ting, is important so that they feel honored. I won't let them sit just anywhere. I keep an eye on everything. I know exactly how it should be done."

Irwati, who had been listening to this recitation of proper procedure, looked a bit worried. Although Irwati is about the same age as Fitriani, she has lived in Padang for most of her adult life and has not had the benefit of on-going training from her own mother. Consequently, she is a little unsure about all the ins and outs of running a proper ritual gathering.

At a ritual gathering for a deceased person (*mendoa*), women are ushered into the main hall to sit with other women, while men hang about outside waiting to assist with the burial. At one gathering I attended, I noticed how the senior woman went to great efforts to have some of her women guests sit more centrally, even to the point of having everyone else move around. No one but me seemed flustered by all the maneuvering for space. I also noticed that a number of women brought small bags of *sirih* (a quid of betel leaf, areca nut, and lime) that they offered to the sen-ior woman. When a woman could not get close enough to hand it to her, she would toss her bag to the senior woman, who took a quid for herself. Then the woman who brought the bag would point out who else should get the bag, resulting in more tossing of the bag around the room. Fitriani explained what was happening:

"Wives of the men of the lineage [*pasumandan*] and kinswomen of in-married men [*bako*] bring bags of sirih and offer them to the Bundo Kanduang of the deceased. That's so the family knows who has come to mourn with them. Otherwise there are so many women coming and going that you might miss someone and not remember whether or not they had come. This way, you give the bag to the woman, who recognizes you and takes the sirih." Then she said proudly with a smile, "Sometimes my mouth has been all red from getting and chewing so much sirih."

Sirih bags are a way to ensure that the host knows that her affinal kinswomen have come and honored her family in their time of mourning. Not coming to such an event could be interpreted as a slight to the family and might lead to strains between the two groups. By telling me how much *sirih* she had chewed, Fitriani was relating that many, many people had come to honor her family, an indicator of their high status and respect in the community.

Ritual Speeches

Critical to a proper ceremony is the exchange of speeches made by titled men representing the host lineage and affinal lineage. Around mid- to late afternoon of a wedding ceremony, these kinsmen enter the main hall to carry out their portion of the event. Women promptly vacate that space for other parts of the house, and those who sit on the edges of the main hall remain relatively quiet and attentive during the men's speeches. I say "relatively quiet" because after the first half-hour or so they begin talking among themselves, moving around, even laughing quietly with each other, until the men are finished.

The length of ceremonial speeches varies depending on the importance of the families and the event. Ritual speeches are different from everyday language; they are usually punctuated with Minangkabau proverbs and aphorisms, some in archaic phrases whose meaning is obscure to the listeners, particularly the younger ones. Most titled men learn the art of ritual speech-making, but if none of the lineage men are adept, a specialist may be used for the occasion. Several titled men speak during the exchange of speeches at wedding ceremonies. The other men sit quietly by, smoking and occasionally seconding the comments being made. At intervals during the speeches, the assembled men are served a main course and dessert. Once the speeches are completed and a prayer said, most of the men retire immediately from the house. Women then take over the main hall again and continue receiving and serving women guests until late in the evening.

Men elders use ritual speeches to underscore the importance of elite events. At one low *adat* ceremony I attended for the daughter of an elite woman, the men

Photo 5.6 Titled man (*second from right*)
giving a speech at a wedding ceremony

exchanged speeches for several hours, ignoring the fact that the wedding was low
adat. In this way they signified the importance of the wedding of an elite couple,
despite the fact that it was not a lavish ceremony. Men also use these speeches to
extol the glories and achievements of their lineage and poke fun at the other lineage, and so help to maintain or heighten the prestige of their kin group.

Speech-making is not the domain solely of men, however. Ritual gatherings
for elite engagements (*tunangan*) are conducted solely by women, who make the
speeches. In the following event, the engagement ceremony for a young couple,
who were both from well-respected elite families in the village, included
speeches by the senior woman of both lineages.

Well over sixty women attended the engagement ceremony, filling the cav-
ernous main hall of the big house. The big house belonged to the grandmother of the woman getting married. She and her own mother lived in
another house. All the women present wore expensive overblouses, shawls,
and several layers of expensive woven sarongs underneath their cotton
sarongs, and to the last woman wore white headscarves. As they sipped on
their tea and ate the rice cakes and bananas offered, there was only low talking in hushed voices. The senior woman of the young woman's lineage
(*sapayuang, M.*) presented a ritual offering of *sirih* to the women of the young
man's lineage. Then everyone got up, filed out, and walked en masse to the
big house of the young man's side (*fihak laki-laki*).

Once there all the women sat down as before, but the seating was reversed. The kinswomen and affines (*bako*) of the young man's side (the host family) were on the upper level of the main hall, and the kinswomen of the young woman's side were seated on the lower level of the main hall. The *Bundo Kanduang* of the young woman's lineage, Fitriani, brought out a gold box containing *sirih* [betel]. From a kneeling position she offered it to each group of women in turn, starting from the most rear with the kinswomen of the young man's side. After everyone chewed sirih, food and tea were brought out, the same as before. Following a second offering of *sirih*, the formal speeches began, lasting for about ten minutes. Several senior women took turns speaking, one asking the other side if they accepted the marriage. Once it was established that both sides agreed to the marriage, all the women immediately got up, filed out, and went home. The ritual had ended.

In this case the senior women of the two lineages involved, not the sublineages, were the ones making the formal presentations of *sirih*. The women who attended were representatives from all the different sublineages within the two lineages, as well as members of affinal lineages, making it a large event. Compared to the speeches that men make, the women's speeches were shorter and more to the point, but the women speakers relied on the use of well-known Minangkabau aphorisms in their speeches, as do the men. As ceremonies go, the engagement ceremony is fairly short; this one lasted about two hours. Despite its brevity, it begins the formal relationship between the two sides, bringing all the women together in a first test of relations between them. In their dress, demeanor, and conduct of the ritual, both sides show how well respected they are and how properly trained in the conduct of *adat*.

CEREMONIAL MEANINGS

Ceremonial events represent in myriad ways the matrix of social life, its fine-tuning, reworking, and reconstitution. Women are the primary organizers, managers, and actors during these events but ceremonies are not complete without the men's attendance and speeches. The lavishness of a ceremony speaks to the standing of a host family in the community. Host families are under pressure to sponsor ceremonies whose sumptuousness corresponds to their means and rank. According to Ng (1987), the wealth of the host family displayed through the ceremony is a frequent subject of discussion. Villagers deride ceremonies that are "stingy on *adat*." Ceremonies in which inadequate amounts of expensive and complex dishes of food, cakes, and rice are served reflect poorly on the hosts (Ng 1987:82). Hartati's efforts to produce a lavish ceremony (described earlier) served to underscore the high status of her family as an elite family.

Kin and relatives respond to such efforts by turning up in large numbers to show respect to the family. They also ensure that the host has ample assistance so that the senior woman herself has only to supervise her guests during the ceremony itself. Kin of affines take great care to make sure that their trays are well prepared and presented so that their kinswomen will feel honored.

Attendance itself, as well as which member of a kin group attends, is an important statement regarding relations among elites. Nurani told me that for events within her own lineage, she would not think of sending someone younger in her place; it would be impolite, even disrespectful. The level of participation in any particular event can be used to gauge the standing of the host family and its connections to other lineages and neighbors. The absence of expected individuals or a lack of generosity in helping out sends a clear message regarding a relationship between the two families. Ng notes, "[T]o refrain from participating in the ceremony of either a matrilineal or an affinal relative shows one's disapproval of, or hostility towards, the sponsoring lineage" (1987:80). In Tanjung Batang, senior women from most of the lineages in the hamlet make an appearance at major ceremonies hosted by other elites, even those not related.

People who give generously of their time to help with the preparation for a ceremony, even distant kin, are held in high regard. Most kin do actively help with preparations, although some high-ranking women come and sit and chat but do not help materially with the cooking or other preparations, or they consistently send a younger sister or daughter instead of coming themselves. Such behavior is acceptable for elderly women, but for younger elite women, it creates bad feelings toward that family. A woman who does not help with ceremonies implies that the host family does not deserve the respect which her help confers. Some of the strongest complaints I heard from women in Tanjung Batang was that certain people did not attend ceremonial events hosted by relatives or neighbors. Such people were considered arrogant and their lack of participation just cause for others to reciprocate in like manner.

Ceremonial gatherings are a dialogue between host and participants. A woman's decision in helping, attending, and bringing trays carries significant meaning concerning the relations between the two families. By the lavishness of the ceremony, the senior woman and her family assert or reinforce their own standing in the community. For their part the participants through their actions facilitate, undermine, or counter the importance and social standing of the host family.

NEIGHBORHOOD NETWORKS

Despite the hegemony of kinship in the village, social relations are not all based on kinship. Ceremonial events reach beyond kinship networks to incorporate neighbors, co-workers, and social organizations within and beyond the community. Stivens (1996) makes this point for the villagers of matrilineal Negeri Sembilan, although in her case, kin ties are not as extensive as those in Taram. Women in the village rely on several social and civic groups in addition to their kin to help with the labor and expense of ceremonies. Women in Tanjung Batang have organized a Village Committee (*Panitia Desa*) headed by three elite women that provides help with the food for ritual gatherings within the hamlet. In addition to that group, the members of PKK, the state-sponsored Family Welfare Organization, volunteer their services for ritual gatherings, providing additional plates, glasses, cooking utensils, and chairs for a small fee. When elite families host a major ceremony, they arrange with these groups for the needed assistance.

Women also provide assistance to their neighbors in the village, whether or not they are related. This relationship, called *julo-julo* (exchange partners), is an ongoing exchange relationship. *Julo-julo* partners are families that agree to help each other out with ceremonial preparations, usually by bringing a tray of food. This relationship is not based on kinship but on the principle of exchange. If a woman provides a tray for another family's ceremony, later that family will reciprocate and bring a tray when she has a ceremony. If she does not help out, then they do not feel obligated either. Neighbor trays are a way to have enough food available for all the guests, which at large celebrations would be beyond the ability of the host family. These trays are served to guests and neighbors who have no kinship relation to the host family. These exchange relationships provide another source of labor outside of kin networks. From the point of view of a senior woman, bringing in additional help from non-kin extends her influence and connections throughout the village. These neighbors and friends help to maintain, solidify, and increase the reputation and respect of her family.

CONCLUSION

Ritual events are more than oratory and eating of food. Though ritual oratory is often considered the primary element of such events, for rural Minangkabau the trays brought to the ceremony and prominently displayed on special platforms are equally significant to the conduct of a successful event. In defining the relative roles of women and men in ceremonies, Prindiville states that "men exchange words while women exchange food" (1981:29). Trays, like speeches, cement or barter relations between two groups. As men exchange artful speeches punctuated with proverbs and maxims, women contest and assert allegiances and identities through their food presentations.

But women's contributions to ceremonial events involve more than just food exchange. As I noted throughout this chapter, not only trays but ceremonial preparations, dress, and guest seating and treatment convey important meanings in these events. Each aspect of an event makes a statement about the status and reputation of the senior woman and her family. The amount of money spent, the number of guests in attendance, and the number of kin mobilized to help are all indicators of the status and popularity of the host lineage (Ng 1987:81–82). For elite wedding ceremonies, the swirl of guests and large numbers of kinfolk assisting in the event serve to underscore the rank of the family, even if it is a small ceremony. The significance of these events ripple throughout the community as kin from different hamlets arrive and depart.

I view these events as key sites in the creation and negotiation of social identities. Each event is a reprocessing and legitimating of the social order, reconfirming and reasserting the place of elites in the village and the position of each lineage in relation to others. Through these events elite women maintain and strengthen family status and reputation and also build networks of exchange and cooperation that serve as the foundation of the community.

Ceremonial practice maintains solidarity, but it also underscores difference. Elite women's use of and control of ceremonial elements such as dress sets boundaries between groups. More elaborate dress marks elite ceremonies as higher status than those of non-elites. By determining tray placement and proper seating, elite women confirm their own rank and consign client kin to lower rank. Even in their low *adat* ceremonies, elites reinstantiate their privilege and difference from others in the village.

I interpret ceremonial events as strategic sites of power. This interpretation, however, is not the only one that can be derived from ritual practices. Although I have steadfastly positioned people as strategists, there is another side to ceremonial gatherings. These ceremonies represent people's caring for family, hope for the future, joy in well-being, and grief at death. My intent in focusing on the negotiated quality of ritual is, on the one hand, to avoid representing people as simply reproducing "custom" and, on the other, to show how people create meaning through ritual practice.

NOTES

1. Prindiville (1981) makes a similar point in her suggestive article, but does not provide ethnographic data to support it.

2. In the following I use the terms *Bundo Kanduang* and "senior woman" interchangeably.

3. Interestingly, Hartati also calls herself *mamak*, taking on the term usually associated with men lineage elders. Her usage seems to substantiate Abdullah's (1972) statement that *mamak* refers to the elders of the family in general. See also discussion in chapter 2 on the process of adoption (*bamamak*).

4. Other anthropologists whose attention to women in ceremonial activities revealed important insights into women's power include Gailey 1987, Linnekin 1990, Weiner 1976.

5. Later I discuss how Islam is used to make certain statements in ceremonies but I leave questions concerning the interpolation of Islam and *adat* to other writers.

6. At weddings, this prayer is delivered at the end of sometimes long-winded ceremonial speeches. Women who have not been following the oration too closely have to resort to whatever is handy to cover their heads as the prayer starts. A doily, small tablecloth, or even a paper napkin will do.

7. See Pak 1986 and Ng 1987 for further descriptions of ritual elements in Minangkabau ceremonies.

6

Ceremonial Practice
and the Ideology of Rank

In this chapter my focus shifts to relations across the kinship hierarchy between elite elders and their client and servant kin, a relationship that falls within the category of "patron-client." As noted in the previous chapter, a senior woman is responsible for all her relatives (*kamanakan*), not just her children and her sister's children but also those who are adopted into or brought into her lineage. These subordinate kin are expected to follow the advice and guidance of their senior kin, a relationship that is justified through *adat*. As heads of elite lineages, senior women are empowered to make decisions about the social and ceremonial practices of their subordinate kin—a position that gives them control over the social identities and statuses of those below them.

The ideology of rank, however, is malleable. Kinship rank is constantly challenged, reshaped, and circumvented by subordinate kin through marrying up (hypergamy), throwing lavish ceremonies, gaining higher education, and adopting symbols of modernity and national culture that reflect well on a family's worth. This view of kinship as a negotiable commodity has been a somewhat neglected topic in studies of the Minangkabau. Interest in the effects of modernization and the global economy has meant greater attention to Minangkabau as a cohesive entity contra the world and less attention to questions of social identity within rural Minangkabau villages. Here I examine social conflicts between elites and subordinate kin and the strategies that they use to construct or reshape identity in the effort to achieve higher standing.

ELITE-CLIENT RELATIONS

As adopted kin, client families come under the control of the senior woman and the titled man of their elite sublineage, and by extension all elders within the lineage and clan. The material differences between elites and their subordinate kin are not extreme, although wealth tends to correspond with rank. As noted in chapter 2, kinship rank cross-cuts class status, yet more poor families belong to the client and servant ranks (60 percent). The differences between the groups are signified through certain rights and privileges. Only elite families have the right to bear titles and conduct lineage meetings, to build big houses (*rumah gadang*) and rice granaries, to wear certain ceremonial clothing, and to attend certain ceremonies from which all others are barred.

The relationship between elites and clients falls under the category of "patron-client," a term used in the literature to refer to many different types of relations between superiors and subordinates (e.g., Lehmann 1986, Littlewood 1980). Some restrict it to agrarian relations between a landlord and tenant, in which case it often has the negative connotation of exploitation. Others use it to refer to a broader relationship that includes kinship, friendship, or exchange (e.g., Hefner 1990, Jay 1969, among others). I prefer to use it in the broader sense because it best reflects the complexity of the relationship for rural Minangkabau (see Blackwood 1997).

Using the term "patron-client" as a category for the elite-client relationship is somewhat misleading, however, for a couple reasons. First, it tends to reify a relationship between two individuals, "the patron" and "the client," who are usually perceived as the respective "heads" of their families. For rural Minangkabau "patron-client" relations are established between two kin groups or families, the elite elders and the women and men of the client family, not just the "heads" of families. All of these individuals have specific obligations and duties to each other. Second, the term "patron" evokes the image of a male superior, which creates further conceptual problems in this case, since both elite Minangkabau men and women have positions of superiority over their client kin. Consequently, I choose not to use the term "patron" but substitute it with the term "elite."

Elites portray the elite-client relationship as one of benevolence and assistance to those who are new to the village. Hartati, who has several families of client kin, described the situation of newcomers as follows: "Newcomers have just come here. They have to depend on those that are already here. They of course don't know what things are like here yet; they have no experience. They look to the elites and are adopted by us. They are helped in matters of daily subsistence. So that they can become one of us, we protect them and guarantee their livelihood." Her statement reflects the advantages a family gains by becoming client to an elite family. Besides gaining access to elite rice land through sharecropping, adoption into an elite sublineage situates a family in the community. It gives them an identity—they are so-and-so's kin—and hence an entrée into the social life of the community. As new members of an established lineage, client kin broaden their own social connections, which increases the number of people they can work for or ask for help with family ceremonies. Through adoption, client kin become part of the round of ceremonial festivities and exchange labor that makes up the core of social life in the village.

Although elites represent their relation to clients as mutually beneficial, client status is a subordinate status. Client kin "on the whole [enjoy] fewer rights and less power" than elite kin (Bachtiar 1967:378). The democratic structure within elite families (i.e., that all have equal voice and all have the same status) does not apply between elites and their client and servant families.[1] Client and servant families come under the authority of senior women and men, which means that they have little voice in deliberations for ceremonies hosted by their elite kin and must be represented by elite kin in matters of intra- and interlineage or village disputes. Because only elites can decide on proper *adat*, client and servant kin have to abide by the decisions of the elites. In addition, client kin's status as newcomers and commoners means that they are less respected and less influential in the community. Junus noted in his study of the village of Silungkang in Tanah Datar that elites "regarded the newcomers as less respectable than themselves" (1964:308). Although differences among the kinship ranks fall short of class distinctions, they do represent "unequal opportunities in the realm of political power and social prestige" (Bachtiar 1967:378).

Although the elite-client relationship is a hierarchical relationship, it is firmly grounded in the idiom of matrilineal kinship. Adopted families are incorporated into elite lineages as "kin." As I discussed in chapter 2, although they are not "blood" kin, they are considered relatives (*kamanakan*), people who are bound by the same expectations of mutual assistance, respect for elders, generosity, and loyalty that pertain to "blood" kin. I refer to the expectations of kinship that are contained in the words *kamanakan* and *famili* as the ideology of relatedness.

The ideology of relatedness gives client kin a greater degree of flexibility and maneuverability than their subordinate position might otherwise allow. The differences between a client relationship and a contractual relationship, such as those sometimes invoked for land tenancy, make this point clearly. Whereas contractual relations specify labor obligations, costs, and reimbursements, a client relation embedded in kinship follows codes of exchange and assistance that have no specific timeframes for reimbursement nor expectations about amounts of labor contributed. Where family crises or bad harvests due to environmental problems might result in the severing of a contractual bond, the ideology of relatedness allows client kin greater leeway to produce results or make up for weak contributions in ceremonies. Although clientage is based on unequal relations of power, for rural Minangkabau the client relationship provides a stable, on-going relationship that downplays class distinctions and creates a strong security net against misfortune.

Elite Responsibility

The authority of elite kin over their clients applies to all contexts that fall under the sphere of *adat*, including, for example, plans to lease-in rice fields or plans for marriages or other ceremonial events. If a client family is involved in a marital dispute or accused of some wrongdoing, such problems are addressed to the elders of the elite lineage, who bring moral and economic weight to bear on their client kin to keep them in line.

As elder to all her relatives, the senior woman has power over those who are client and servant kin to her sublineage. Most senior women have a number of client kin that they are responsible for. In addition to resolving disputes, they are called on whenever there are births, marriages, or deaths in the families of their client kin. Each of these occasions requires their supervision and advice regarding the proper *adat* to be followed.

The authority of senior women to resolve disputes and reprimand client kin is evidenced in the following stories that Nurma told me. Nurma's mother Yonalis is no longer involved in arbitrating the disputes of her client kin but leaves it to her daughter. Although quite proud of her rank, Nurma is regarded as a fair-minded, intelligent woman and has considerable clout in the village.

> Noni, Nurma's client kin, has been married only a few years and has one daughter. She is an energetic and vivacious woman who has her own food stall and also manages her mother's rice fields for her. Noni was having problems with her husband, resulting in his moving back to his mother's house and refusing to return to Noni's house. She told Nurma what was going on and asked her to try to resolve the conflict. Nurma asked her nephew, who held the title in her family, to talk to the husband's family to attempt a reconciliation. Noni's own uncle and older brother were not involved in these discussions. Despite the efforts at reconciliation, no one was able to resolve the problems, resulting in a permanent separation between Noni and her husband.

In this case a marital dispute resulted in the intercession of both the senior woman and the titled man of the elite sublineage. In another instance, Nurma's intercession resulted in disciplinary action for a client woman. This woman was married with two children and lived in the dilapidated big house that belonged to Nurma's family. The family lived on the income her migrant husband sent home as well as the profits from rice fields that her brother sharecropped for her.

> It was rumored about the village that Nurma's client kinswoman was sleeping with another man while her husband was away working [*merantau*]. No one had any evidence of adultery but the rumors had to be cleared up. As the senior woman, Nurma had a talk with her client kin about the situation. She reprimanded her wayward kin, advising her not to associate with other men anymore. Rather than risk greater problems in the future with her elite

kin, the client woman had to respect Nurma's authority over her and avoid any questionable behavior.[2]

As attested to in this situation, the senior woman of the kin group has the authority not only to arbitrate disputes but to advise and reprimand client kin.

If a wedding for a client family needs to be arranged, senior elite men and women act as advisors; their approval should be obtained before a marriage ceremony can take place. Dt. Rajo said, "If their child wants to marry, they must report first to *Bundo Kanduang*; it must be given consideration first by *Bundo Kanduang*. She will decide whether the candidate is a good person or not. If *Bundo Kanduang* gives permission, then they can go ahead and marry." In some cases a client family may even ask for help in finding suitable marriage partners for the family's children.

Senior women have a broad range of responsibilities for their client kin. As experts in ceremonial *adat*, they must be consulted about proper procedures. Fitriani explained her responsibilities to her client families as follows:

> When a person dies, the family will come and ask when I will attend, when should the person be buried, what should relatives take to the family, and I will tell them. For marriages, [I tell them] when it will be, what type of clothes they should wear, and what should be slaughtered. For circumcision ceremonies, [I tell them] what to provide, what extent of ceremony can be carried out. I decide what is appropriate [for ceremonies] and then let the male lineage elders [*ninik-mamak*] know at the deliberations [*mufakat*].

Her recitation of responsibilities puts the decision-making squarely in the lap of the senior woman, who then informs the titled men in the lineage. Nurani was equally explicit in her description of her responsibilities to oversee and manage events: "At a ceremony [of client kin], I am the one to tell everyone to eat, or give the sirih, because I'm the *tuan rumah* [head of the house or host]." As the senior woman of the client's lineage, the senior woman is considered the head of the house and host for any ceremonial events in her client kin's house. Without her presence, the ceremony could not take place.

The senior woman's responsibility to her client kin involves frequent visits and consultations with them concerning proper ritual proceedings. The amount of time involved in such duties is evident in the following description of events surrounding the death of the grandmother of one of Nurani's client families:

> About 5 p.m. on June 12, Sahril, a member of Nurani's client family, came to her house to inform her that his grandmother had died. The family, whom Nurani described as *famili kita* (our kin), live in a small, neat wood-frame house with sparse furnishings. They were adopted into Nurani's sublineage over thirty years ago when the grandmother and her husband moved to this village. Although they are poor, the family is well liked in the village. They regularly help out at ceremonial events, whether those of their neighbors or elite

kin. The family lives in another hamlet about a half-hour's walk distant. Nurani left right away and didn't get back until 8:00 p.m., returning on the back of a borrowed motorbike. She left again the next morning at 7:30 a.m. to attend the burial. Nurani asked Reni to stay home from work that day and take care of the baby so Nurani would be free to attend to matters.

On the 14th Nurani returned to the client family's house in the morning. Reni had gone to work but Nurani left as soon as the baby fell asleep in his bed. Shortly after she left, her mother Yenita came by to check on the two children. She told the kids to quiet down a couple times but didn't pay much attention to them. She commented to me that her back hurt all the time and kept her from doing much anymore. Yenita left after only fifteen minutes and then Dela, Nurani's sister, came over just as the baby was waking up. She stayed and took care of the children until Nurani came back.

I asked Nurani what she was doing at her client kin's house and she said they were discussing (*berbincang-bincang*) when to hold the seven-day ritual prayer (*mendoa*) for the deceased. She went to participate in the decision-making. The next night Nurani again went to the client kin's house to visit with guests at the three-day ceremony following the death. Another elite woman who attended helped serve food. Nurani returned home about 10:30.

As this story suggests, any events that take place among client kin have to be attended to by their elite elders. Certain decisions have to be made or agreed on by the elite senior woman. Her attendance and participation convey both her respect and concern for her client kin, maintaining the bond between them, while at the same time ensuring that her wishes are followed properly.

Client Obligations

A client relationship obligates client kin to help at any ceremonies hosted by their elite kin. Client men and women provide labor for ceremonial preparations and are present during ceremonial festivities to dish out and serve food. Their help is expected not only for events hosted by their elite kin but for any events that their elite kin are involved in, including those for their *bako* (the matrilineage of the father), those hosted by the elite's *pasumandan* (women married to men of the lineage), or even those hosted by client kin within the same lineage. The nature of client kin's assistance depends on their relationship to the host. While all women work together preparing food, client family members tend to work more in the kitchen during ceremonies. At ceremonies held in the big houses, client women normally work downstairs in the kitchen and client men run errands; if they do participate upstairs, it is usually as servers.

As noted earlier, the client relationship is built around certain expectations contained in the terms *famili* and *kamanakan*. Client kin are judged for their generosity and willingness to help their elite kin and are treated according to how well they fulfill their obligations. When client kin maintain good ties with their neighbors and kin, elite kin reciprocate by helping with ritual occasions. Smaller numbers of elite kin turn out to help in these ceremonial feasts, but without the client tie, they could expect the help of only a few neighbors. In contrast, client kin who fall short of their obligations to elite kin can expect less in assistance and help from them. Over time a client kin's relation to her elite kin can either solidify or weaken her own standing in the community.

The events surrounding Henita's death illustrate the results of failing to maintain a client relationship adequately:

> Henita's family is a client family to Fitriani. They have lived in Taram for four generations but are one of the poorest families in the village. Henita married a man from outside Taram and they had two sons. When Henita died, women from the neighborhood came to her house to pay their respects but only stayed for a few minutes and then left. A few neighbors stood around outside Henita's house as the funeral preparations were carried out. Dt. Sango, Fitriani's nephew, was called but never came. A lower-ranking elite woman of Fitriani's lineage took charge of the arrangements. Henita had worked in this woman's rice fields in the past as a day laborer. Later two other elite kinswomen brought the necessary cloth to cover the body, but the cloth was not the expensive kind normally used. Fitriani later told me about her client kin, "Henita wasn't well liked. She never went to other people's ceremonial feasts. She didn't fit into the social life of the community and was not really involved with her lineage, so we only used regular cloth [*kain*]. That's why only neighbors came to her house when she died."

Henita's failure to maintain her part of the client relationship resulted in only minimal assistance and help from her elite kin and even from her neighbors. Only client kin who hold up their end of the bargain can expect good relations with their elite kin throughout their lives.

Client kin are not bound to follow the advice of their senior kin but if they disagree, they risk the disfavor and loss of goodwill of elite kin and of other elites in the village as well. If client kin are unwilling to accept the decisions of elite kin, elites have the power to impose sanctions against them. The most serious sanction forbids a family to socialize with other members of the community or participate in any ceremonial events. Restitution is made when the family apologizes and pays a monetary fine decided on by the *adat* council of titled men. Some client kin have been known to sever their relationship with their senior kin when they felt they were not being treated fairly. In one case a family then established a client relationship with another elite family in the village. Such behavior, however, marks them as problematic and tends to marginalize them in the community.

CONTESTING IDENTITIES

Though the client relationship is built on notions of *famili*, the disparities in prestige and power accorded to each rank make the social identity of rank one of the primary contested domains in the village. The conflict over rank is not new to this era; it has been a significant feature of village life for generations. The tensions between wealthy or educated client kin and their poorer or less educated elite kin has been noted at least since the early part of this century. Minangkabau novels of that period poked fun at the arrogance of the "nouveau riches" (Kato 1982:189). Observers reported meeting wealthy Minangkabau whose resentment at their inferior client status led them to "gleefully describ[e] the stupid ignorance of chiefly families" (Swift 1971:258).

Client kin have not been powerless to improve their standing and rank in the community. Families of client rank are eligible to move into elite rank when their elite sublineage dies out with no female heirs. If their elite elders agree to it, they can then inherit elite property and title. In their efforts to move into the elite rank, earlier arrivals to Taram sought to marry men of elite rank. Through the practice of hypergamy, marrying a man of higher rank, a women could raise the rank of her descendants. This is possible because the rank of the father is taken into consideration in the rank of the children (see also Reenen 1996). If a husband comes from a wealthy lineage, a good marriage means access to rice land that can then serve as the material basis for increasing the woman's family wealth. Wealthy families can afford lavish ceremonies, which have long been used throughout Indonesia as a means to accumulate prestige (Kipp and Rodgers 1987:11). The first European observers who arrived in West Sumatra in the early 1800s noted that "upwardly mobile" families would give feasts and expensive gifts to win a following and improve their chances of claiming a title (Dobbin 1983:17). Marriage to titled men has enabled several women within recent memory to claim rights to higher status for their children. By changing their fortune and improving their "blood line," a few client families over time have been able to make claims to elite title if the elite lineage failed to produce a female heir.

The decision concerning which client family makes the best candidate for elite rank is made by the elites. Their decision is based on a number of factors, including any marriages client women have made to men of elite rank, as well as the status and wealth of the family. In the contemporary period the transformation in the process of improving rank reflects changes at both the local and national level. Avenues similar to those used by client kin in the past are apparent today, but new practices and discourses have become available to substantiate claims to high rank. The best option is to maintain loyalty to elite kin while at the same time taking advantage of new avenues to improve one's wealth, although some elites complain that clients with sufficient money or influence can simply buy off their elite kin by paying them money to gain the right to a title.

CONTROL OF CEREMONIAL ADAT

Elite control over *adat* and the lives of client kin is realized in practice at each ceremony. As noted in the last chapter, ceremonies provide the grounds for elite kin to reinstantiate their privilege. It is also an opportunity for client kin to contest and alter the balance of power within the kinship hierarchy. The gains a client family has made over time in wealth, education, and good jobs can be tested against community reaction each time it hosts a ceremony. Ceremonies thus become sites of contestation between elites and their subordinates.

Client families have to negotiate with lineage elders who make the final decisions about the proper procedures for any ritual gathering. Several senior women told me that there are some things in ceremonies that are just not permissible for families who are not elites. If there are disagreements between clients and elites over the procedure to follow, the event may be postponed. According to Fitriani, "If the senior woman doesn't give her permission, then nothing happens. If the client kin agrees to the restrictions, then okay. If not, then it doesn't happen." In asserting their right to govern ritual gatherings, elites argue that only they know proper *adat* and so they must make the decisions concerning any matters involving *adat*. What that means, in effect, is that the symbols of elite status are preserved for the elites.

Although most marriage celebrations that took place during my stay in the village were small ceremonies, the restrictions imposed by elites mark client ceremonies as less important than those hosted by elite families. Client families are not allowed to hold high or even mid-level *adat* ceremonies. At one client wedding I attended between the daughter of a client family and the son of an elite family, only one goat was slaughtered. Although the groom's side received the kinswomen of the bride's side in their big house, the bride's family had to host the event in their small house. There was no bridal dais for the couple, who had to sit on the floor. The men elders exchanged speeches that lasted for only one-half hour. Only a few elite kin of the sublineage were present and there was none of the coming and going of guests usually seen at elite ceremonies. Although lack of resources affects both client's and elite's ability to host large ceremonies, the restrictions placed on client ceremonies make clear the differences in status. In effect, by insisting that client kin hold low-level ceremonies, elites ensure that their client kin do not overstep their rank.

Taking Attendance

Despite the restrictions on client ceremonies, there are myriad ways for client kin to manipulate ceremonial events to make claims about their worth and importance in the community. One strategy invoked to contest status revolves around one's presence or absence at a ceremonial event. By not helping their wealthy client kin as much as elite kin, elite kinswomen can use such actions to manage relationships with their successful client or servant kin. It serves to keep these kin in their place. Elite generosity in terms of time and labor or the lack of it reinscribes elite control and dominance within the ceremonial context.

Wealthy client women can engage in similar tactics, but they risk censure if they act too arrogantly toward their elite kin. Rather than taking the time from their own work to help out, some wealthy client women have been known to simply give money to their elite kin to help with ceremonial events. In discussing one instance in which this happened, Dt. Rajo made the following comment:

> Actually, she should be present to help out, not just help out by sending money. Her whole family should come to help [with preparations] but they are rich now and less inclined to help. Her *mamak* [elite kin] will understand if she is busy. But if she is always like that, then eventually, if she needs her elite kin for something, like a ceremonial event [*baralek*], they may refuse to help out, or refuse to handle it as they should.

Elites resent this type of arrogant behavior. Dt. Rajo's attitude toward this woman, however, reflects the flexibility of the ideology of relatedness. It is understood if she is busy and cannot help out now and again, but continued behavior of the sort that seems to flaunt her wealth may cause elites to be less generous in their attitude toward her. Perceived arrogance on her part will cause elites to refuse their help in return. She may be wealthy but she is still obliged to help out as others do.

With the increase in profits realized since the New Order push for agricultural development, an increased number of client families have become as prosperous or more prosperous than their elite kin. The ability of these families to attain middle-class status has heightened the tensions over the inequalities of rank and the desire for higher status. These changes put pressure on elites, who are often hesitant to embarrass their wealthy client kin by insisting on certain protocols in ceremonies. It is harder for elites to refuse the requests of wealthy client kin when they know their subordinate kin can afford a lavish ceremony. For their part, clients may be less willing to abide by the prohibitions enforced by elites who are less well off.

Lacking access to elite kinship rank and power, those with money try to negotiate a better standing in the community based on their wealth. The attempt to redefine mutual assistance in terms of money suggests that ideas of commodity-based relationship are replacing those defined by the ideology of relatedness. For wealthy client women like Anna, whose story I will present shortly, such tactics provide an avenue past the restrictions of the *adat*-based hierarchy.

ADAT AND NATIONAL CULTURE

As I mentioned in the opening to the chapter, challenges to the kinship hierarchy are made in part by adopting the symbols of modernity and national culture. In the same way that daughters' desires reflect in part the discourses of modernity and individualism, client kin draw on national culture to contest their position in the community. The "metropolitan superculture," as Hildred Geertz called it

(1963:35–36), has provided new elements for ceremonial practice. Although little unanimity exists among scholars as to what constitutes national culture, or how much of national culture is Javanese culture (Kipp 1993), as I use it here "national culture" refers to the symbols and acquisitions of modernity represented in media and reflected in urban middle-class lifestyles (Dick 1985).[3] The inclusion of urban elements in village ceremonies is a common practice throughout Indonesia. In West Sumatra Minangkabau call this practice *diadatkan*, or *adat* that has been made *adat* (Abdullah 1966, Johns 1958). Although the Minangkabau maintain the centrality of adat to ceremonial practice, its boundaries have always been exceedingly permeable. The ideas and symbols that constantly flow through West Sumatra appear readily in ceremonial practice.

As noted in chapter 2, the practice of migration (*merantau*) is a direct venue for the transmission of state and global discourses. Of individuals born in Tanjung Batang, currently 19 percent migrate to other cities but maintain on-going ties with their families. This figure means that most families have at least one individual temporarily living elsewhere.[4] When migrants return home at Ramadan, they bring with them physical evidence of urban lifestyles in their city clothes, their cars, and their gifts. Family members who visit their kin in the cities are prompted by their experiences to question the relevance of *adat* to their lives. A young woman told me that when she visits her kin in Jakarta, the rules about sex segregation in the village do not apply in the city. She feels freer to ignore village custom and behave as she thinks a young urban woman would.

The great increase in literacy in Indonesia since the 1950s has brought urban and foreign culture more readily into rural homes through newspapers and magazines. Stores in Payakumbuh sell all the popular, glossy, teen and women's magazines. Young women's magazines in particular emphasize a middle-class urban image in their advertisements and articles (Lutz 1992). A typical Indonesian magazine for youth, such as *Cemerlang* (meaning brilliant, dazzling, or radiant), resembles *Glamour* magazine in the United States with its numerous articles full of fashion advice and beauty tips. One of the articles in a 1988 issue was entitled, "Beauty Secrets of a Top American Model." The consumerism of these magazines translates quite literally into the desire to imitate the styles they represent; young women pay village seamstresses to make fashions copied directly from magazine ads. Not surprisingly, young brides now don white wedding gowns in the later hours of wedding ceremonies in imitation of Western-style weddings.

State television made its entry into the homes of many villagers after the introduction of electricity to Taram in 1976, bringing with it further reinforcement of the status and desirability of urban lifestyles. State television became available to rural Indonesia in August 1976 (Chu et al. 1991). Up until the early 1990s only one channel was available: TVRI (*Televisi Republik Indonesia*), which was controlled by the Indonesian state. Through its programming, the state furthered its "specific mission of promoting national unity and integration, national development, and political stability" (Chu et al. 1991:15). Since the early 1990s Indonesian television has expanded to include a number of private television stations, increasing viewers' access to a wide range of cultural representations. By 1996 satellite dishes were common throughout Taram, bringing in stations from Singapore and more movies from Hong Kong. Many television programs made in urban settings, such as popular serial dramas like "Sartika," about a wealthy Javanese woman doctor, portray an affluent urban culture, where cars, large houses, multiple servants, and lavish furniture are the norm. These programs have considerable impact on viewers, encouraging acquisition of luxuries as indicators of class status.

Although national culture and ideology are increasingly hegemonic in Indonesia, the creation of a pan-Indonesian citizen holds sway primarily in urban areas. Rural villagers are well aware of national culture and ideology, but rather than simply subscribing or succumbing to it, or contesting it, they use it to supplement or challenge *adat*-based claims of social identity. Urban culture provides an alternative discourse of legitimization that people can lay claim to in their bids for higher status.

It is predominantly wealthy elite and client families in the village who can afford to incorporate elements of urban culture and lifestyle into their ceremonies. The incorporation of a white wedding gown or Indonesian pop singers in an elite wedding serves to underscore high status. For client kin the use of non-*adat* elements, which are outside the control of lineage elites, can become an avenue for circumventing elite control. The following case illuminates the various strategies a client family used in the context of a ceremony to negotiate their standing in the community.

THE MARRIAGE OF THE RICE MILLER'S DAUGHTER

A complex reading of a ceremony reveals the opportunities it presents a client family for improving its status in the community and making claims to higher rank. A clear example of the conflict between client and elite kin over claims to elite rank occurred at the wedding of the rice miller's daughter. In this particular ceremony the negotiation of identities took place between a wealthy client woman, Anna, and her poorer elite kinswoman, Fitriani. The wedding provided the grounds for contesting identity and making claims to higher rank through the manipulation of cultural symbols.

> The rice miller, Anna, threw a big wedding for her daughter, Esi. It was the most festive, well-attended wedding I observed while I lived in the village. All day long, well-dressed guests, bringing expensive gifts, came to Anna's house to eat some food and congratulate the bride and groom. Some of the trays that women guests brought contained fancy layer cakes. One even had blinking lights and a little Western-style bride and groom figure on the top. By the end of day I counted at least twenty lavish trays of cakes set in the front room, plus a large number of plain trays of food. These trays filled one whole

room in Anna's house plus her rice shed. The gift tally was running at 170 by early evening. The amount and quality of food spoke to the wealth and generosity of the family. The usual joke about ceremonial feasts—that meat cannot be found in the meat dishes (because the family is trying to make it stretch too far)—did not hold for Anna's food. The bridal room was lavishly decorated in pink satin drapes and filled with beautiful, expensive furniture. A rock band serenaded the wedding party with very loud pop music amplified by huge speakers. The bride herself was enthroned on an elaborately decorated dais, waiting for the groom, who was brought later in the afternoon by his kinsmen. The groom arrived at the house in a dark suit and white shirt, but later put on the wedding finery of an elite man. He sat quietly on the lavish dais next to Esi, while Esi sat slumped to one side of the dais in a rather undignified manner, complaining to her attendants that the *sunting* (ornamental headpiece) hurt her head. That evening Esi changed to a white wedding gown.

Given the lavishness of the wedding, the bride's family appeared to be members of the elite rank. Anna, a stocky, pleasant and shrewd business woman in her early fifties, is one of the wealthier women in Taram. Her house is a small big house with a sizable two-story attachment made of brick and plaster. Next to her house is the rice milling shed that she owns. Her venture in rice milling capitalized on the Green Revolution's transformation in local agriculture. Anna bought her first gas-driven rice huller in 1974, taking early advantage of the rapidly expanding rice market. At that time there were only two other gas-driven mills in Taram. Not only has rice production continued to increase since that time, but government regulations compel farmers to have their rice milled in order to meet the standards for marketability. Over the course of a year Anna employs anywhere from five to thirteen workers to keep her mill running. She also owns her own rice fields, most of which are sharecropped for her.

Due to the continued expansion of the rice market, Anna's business has been so profitable that she went to Mecca with her husband on the *haj.* They are two of the few people in Taram who have been able to afford to do so. Anna commands respect as a wealthy business woman. By achieving the *haj,* one of the primary duties of all Muslims, she has also achieved another level of respect from the solidly Islamic community of Taram.

Because of Anna's wealth and position in the village, I assumed at first that she was elite, but later found out that her family is client kin to an elite lineage. Consequently, despite her stature in the community as a businesswoman and *haji,* Anna must follow the advice and recommendations of her elite kin in matters of *adat* and kinship. In the social network of the community, which is defined by kinship, she is simply a commoner.

Fitriani, Anna's senior kinswoman, is by contrast the highest-ranking member of Anna's clan. Though elite, Fitriani is no longer well off. Having pawned a large part of her ancestral property, Fitriani is chronically in debt to one of the local rice merchants. She only has one plot of rice land remaining, which her daughter Lina works. Despite her poor economic situation, she commands considerable respect and influence in the village.

Because Anna's decisions in areas governed by *adat* have to be approved by her senior kin, she had to notify Fitriani of her daughter Esi's marriage. Esi's marriage to an elite man was a testimony to the respect her family commands. Her fiancé's grandmother and family own a magnificent big house built in 1978, one of only three built since 1970. Esi's marriage to a man of higher rank invoked the long-standing strategy for client women to improve their kinship rank through marriage, giving Anna a better chance of getting a title from her senior kin in the future.

Manipulating Adat

Fitriani and other elite elders had no problem agreeing to Esi's marriage because it was within *adat* prescriptions. The wedding itself, however, raised a number of questions regarding proper *adat*, the most important being the level of *adat* to use. Problems with the wedding occurred when Anna decided that she wanted her daughter to wear a large *sunting* and gold bracelets. The bracelets alone cost upwards of 1 million rupiah ($550) each, but it was an expense Anna could afford. According to Fitriani, Anna's request was not permissible: "In wedding ceremonies, if [client kin] want to wear *adat* clothes, they can. But they can't leave the house in it. They can only wear the large headpiece [*sunting*] in the house. If they are not descendants of a *datuk*, they are not allowed. They are also not allowed to wear large gold bracelets." The bride from a client family is not allowed to wear a large headpiece or large gold bracelets in public processions because both are insignias of elite status.

Despite these restrictions, Fitriani made an astute compromise, refusing to allow the bride to wear the symbols of elite status in the public processional, but in other ways accommodating the desires of her client kin. The bride wore a traditional red velvet overblouse with a large gold necklace and a small headpiece (*sunting*) for the public procession to the groom's house and back (see photo 6.1). The small headpiece and the lack of elaborate gold bracelets marked the bride as a commoner. Fitriani's compromise consisted of allowing a large headpiece to be worn by the bride during the ceremony in her mother's house and allowing to a cow (*sapi*) to be slaughtered. Although Anna had wanted to slaughter a water buffalo, the compromise gave the wedding ceremony the status of a mid-level *adat* ceremony, a significant accomplishment for a client family.

Nevertheless, the limitations on *adat* for the wedding were upsetting to Anna. According to another client woman, Anna was upset (*sakit hati*) because certain restrictions were imposed. In defense of her position, Fitriani said to me, "We have to make sure *adat* is followed properly, because if something is done wrong, the [council of] titled men may later call us to account for giving wrong advice, or for allowing the misuse of *adat*." Fitriani invoked *adat* as the foundation and validation of her decision. In her interpretation of her responsibilities, *adat* sets the guidelines that she and the men elders carry out. Her statement suggests that

Photo 6.1 Bride with small headpiece in
wedding procession with her kinswomen

adat is unchangeable and therefore non-negotiable, although as the final compromise suggested, if there is consensus among the elite elders, it is possible to
make changes. In fact, as in all community affairs, the final decisions made by

elites were both strict and flexible, since Anna was allowed some mid-level *adat* practices but denied high-*adat* status markers.

To create a lavish ceremony in ways not circumscribed by adat, Anna invoked elements of national culture. Anna, her head covered in a manner befitting a *haji*, chose to wear an expensive peach colored dress instead of the typical Minangkabau dress for ceremonies, the overblouse and sarong, thus accentuating both her identification with national culture and Islam. Anna's daughters wore elegant outfits which emulated the Javanese national style of dress for ceremonies rather than the Minangkabau style. Set up on a stage with huge amplifiers, the rock band that she hired could be heard for miles around, adding to the festive air and excitement of the celebration. The female lead singer's outfit of jeans and a satin shirt contrasted glaringly with the dignified clothes of the wedding participants. Because of the cost, bands are rarely hired for weddings in the village. Their presence at this wedding served to accentuate the lavishness of the ceremony.

Elite individuals disparaged the ceremony because its ritual elements were not "pure" *adat*. The combination of high and low *adat* with elements of national culture was somewhat derisively said to mix things that do not belong together, like apples and oranges. Yet the elites could not ignore the fact that large numbers of people came to a wedding that was not supposed to be too terribly important by *adat* standards. In fact, the lengthy two-and-a-half-hour exchange of speeches by the titled men was a good indication of the respect and importance of this family.

The strongest impression the ceremony created, and the one to cause elite families to take the most notice, was the amount of labor Anna mobilized for the preparation and management of the celebration. On the day the bridal room was decorated, a few of Anna's senior kin were present, including Fitriani, but none of them were helping out. The one exception was Lina, Fitriani's daughter. Fitriani and one or two other senior kin were present throughout most of the day of the ceremony but did not assist with cooking, serving, or other tasks. Fitriani's youngest daughters, however, sat at the guest reception table and signed in guests. A large majority of those present and helping were from client and servant families. Even with only minimal assistance from her senior kin, Anna had plenty of people to handle the minute-by-minute problems of managing such a large celebration. The amount of labor available showed that Anna commanded the allegiance and support of a large number of people.

Her authority was all the more clearly shown by her casual manner at the celebration. She moved through the crowds all day long to welcome people, appearing content and unharried by the problems of handling such a large celebration. Her husband's demeanor was equally unperturbed as he wandered among the guests all day, welcoming male guests and taking pictures. Anna's conduct contrasted sharply with the weary aspect of certain poorer elite women at another ceremony I attended, who, because of lack of money or insufficient help (suggesting insufficient influence over their kin), were overcome by the magnitude of the labor involved.

Remaking Social Hierarchy

Anna's efforts for her daughter's wedding constituted a political act to reinforce and resignify the importance of her family. It drew on her importance as a wealthy *haji* and businesswoman. As a wealthy client woman with a number of sharecroppers and other laborers under her influence and providing a strong network of support, Anna contested the power of her elite elders and won several concessions from them. The elite remained secure in their control of *adat* by insisting that Anna use a mixture of mid- and low *adat* elements, preserving high *adat* for themselves. As this story shows, in ceremonial practice, elite women and men have ultimate control over status markers; they set limits to what is permissible and what can be contested. But the lavish nature of a ceremony incorporating national culture accentuated the notion that importance does not attach to rank alone. Even though Anna lacks elite rank, her ability to mobilize labor and throw a lavish ceremony marks her as a person to be reckoned with—and one less likely to be cowed by the dictates of *adat* in the future.

Thus, the rice miller turned her daughter's wedding ceremony into an occasion for contesting her family's place in the social hierarchy. Anna's claims to higher rank made use of the conflict between national and local culture. She used elements from national culture to support claims of equality and the importance of wealth for community standing. At the same time the marriage actually reinforced the Minangkabau concept of rank. After all, her daughter did not just marry anybody; she married a high-ranking elite man. But by incorporating national culture through the use of non-Minangkabau elements in the ceremony, Anna took advantage of alternative discourses to negotiate social identity in the village. Anna's manipulation of multiple claims to assert her identity as an important person, and the response of the elites, constituted a slight shift in accepted practice (*habitus*). This shift both reinforces and alters local social relations. It revalidates the social hierarchy at the same time that it creates new possibilities for social identity.

SERVANT KIN AND STRATEGIES FOR CHANGE

As descendants of slaves, servant families hold the lowest rank in the kinship hierarchy. People generally are reticent to talk about rank, particularly in light of the state's principle of equality as expressed in the *Pancasila*. According to state ideology, all citizens are equal and have an equal opportunity for advancement and success. Villagers acknowledge that the Indonesian state does not recognize a servant class any longer. Nevertheless, the low rank of servant kin continues to inform people's understanding of social relations in the village. During an interview with Yonalis, Nurma's mother, I asked her the rank of a particular family in the village. She was hesitant at first to say anything, but when I persisted, she exclaimed, "They were bought!"

Servant kin are firmly under the authority of elite men and women. Mariam, a grandmother and member of one of Santi's servant families, told me, "If one of us wants to get married, we ask Santi first. If she doesn't like the prospective spouse, she can refuse to agree to the marriage and then it won't happen. We can't go against her because we can't do anything alone as one family. We need her help and support." Like client kin, servant kin must have the permission of the senior woman and titled man in any activities that involve *adat*. They too must be loyal and ready to assist their elite kin whenever asked. Servant kin, however, are seen as more closely bound to their superiors than client kin and have greater restrictions imposed on them than do client kin.

The control of elite women over their servant kin was illustrated in an incident I witnessed between Yenita and Tisra. Tisra, whose own family lives in another village, is a woman in her early thirties. She married and lives with Jasir, a man from another of Santi's servant families. The couple has very limited income, most of it coming from the food stall that Tisra set up in the front of her house and from Jasir's work on road construction projects.

When Jasir married Tisra, Santi did not approve of the marriage. With no help forthcoming from Santi, the couple turned to Yenita, who lives next door to Santi and is in the same clan. She let them build a small house on the edge of her garden. For several years they maintained a good relationship. Tisra helped her in-laws whenever she could, including babysitting for Dela and Reni and helping with preparations for ritual gatherings. But there were murmurings about Tisra. People said she was arrogant (*tinggi hati*) and didn't help out like she should (*tolong menolong*). She only wants to work for money (*upah*), they said, but that's not the way mutual help (*tolong-menolong*) works. It means you just help someone, and later it will be returned in some way. But Tisra, it was said, doesn't like to help.

When Yenita's eldest son fell ill, Yenita left with her eldest daughter Nurani to visit him in Jakarta, leaving other younger family members in charge of the household. Yenita expected Tisra to help out those at home. Instead, Tisra went to her home village to attend a wedding and was gone overnight. When Yenita returned from Jakarta and found out that Tisra had been gone, she confronted Tisra in a rage and told her to get off her land. Within two weeks, not only had Tisra left, taking her young daughter with her back to her mother's village, but even her house disappeared. Tisra took most of the furniture from the house and Jasir tore down what was left for firewood. No one intervened on Tisra's behalf. Because she was an outsider in her husband's family, community sentiment held that she was in the wrong for attending the wedding. Even if some people thought Yenita was especially hard on Tisra, no one intervened. Her responsibility was to help her husband's kin, sharing their pain as well as their prosperity, they said. Therefore, as senior woman, Yenita's decision was final.

Although Tisra felt she was acting as a responsible member of her own matrilineage by going home to attend a ceremony, her elite kin felt that she failed in her responsibilities as their relative (*kamanakan*). This incident proved to be the final straw for her elite kin. Servant kin can choose to go against the will of elite kin, as Jasir did in the first place by marrying someone that Santi did not approve of. But that meant that Tisra, who was already in a vulnerable situation as an outsider, had to rely solely on Yenita's goodwill, which was never excessive. She had no one else to go to since Santi, who could have influenced Yenita, had never been fondly disposed toward her. Community sentiment also turned against her for breaches of the ideology of relatedness.

The severity of restrictions on servant kin are especially apparent at ceremonies. Although servant kin provide assistance, they are forbidden from attending mid- or high-level *adat* ceremonies. According to Nurma, "Those of low caste [servant families] are not allowed to attend ceremonies because they are lowly [*hina*]. If a servant should appear at a high *adat* ceremony, such as a ceremony to pass on a title to a new titled man, then that ceremony would fail, or have to be aborted." Because most ceremonies in the village are not high *adat*, the difference between servants' role and that of client kin is not often obvious. But at any mid or high *adat* ceremony, servant kin are not allowed except downstairs as help.

Servant families, like client kin, make efforts to renegotiate their identity. If their elite sublineage should become extinct, servant kin may be able to live in the big house. But, unlike client kin, they cannot gain possession of the rice lands or the title. Title and land go to the closest elite sublineage. It is possible, however, for a woman of a servant family to move up given the right conditions, as with client kin, although her origins will not be forgotten for a long time. Although marriage between an elite man and a servant woman is disapproved, the practice of polygyny in the past made it possible for an elite man to have a wife from the servant rank. The daughters or descendants of such a marriage might later be raised to middle rank (if they also marry well). One woman in the village who married a titled man is said to be in line for client rank because the number of elite sublineages in her lineage is shrinking. Generally, however, the strategy of hypergamy, which is part of the older pattern of rank negotiation, is not very successful for servant families.

Servant kin who are able to accumulate some wealth turn that into education and civil service jobs as a way to circumvent *adat* and their low status in the community. As I noted in chapter 4, servant families have a higher level of education than those of client rank. Although approximately the same number in both groups have received advanced degrees, 16 percent more individuals from servant families have completed a high school education than client families. A small number (3 percent) have joined the civil service (the village average is 8 percent), working for the state or teaching at local schools. The obstacles to

Table 6.1 Percentage of Migrants by Rank out of the Adult Population of Tanjung Batang (N=449)			
	Women	*Men*	*Average*
Elite	18	20	19
Client	15	22	18.5
Servant	20	39	29.5

achieving equal citizenship are greater for servant than client families, however. This fact is attested to by the higher percentage of individuals from servant families who migrate to other areas (29.5 percent versus the village average of 20 percent; see table 6.1). By migrating to another area, migrants can lose the stigma of their rank because no one will question them about their family origins

CONTENTIOUS EVENTS

Servant kin who have been able to achieve some degree of success as defined by the modern Indonesian state have more ability to contest *adat* and the kinship hierarchy. One servant woman, who has had experience living in other parts of West Sumatra, participates in the state-sponsored village women's organization, headed and run by elite women, and serves as an elected officer. Participation in this organization is outside of the controls of *adat*, so no on can restrict her attendance there. As an officer in a state organization, she gains visibility and respect for her performance of her duties as treasurer. This position provides another avenue for gaining status in the village, one that does not ignore *adat* but one that draws on an ideology of modernity to circumvent an ascribed identity. Although servant kin do not repudiate the kinship hierarchy that places them at the bottom, they take advantage of the state ideology of equal citizenship to assert their equality with all other individuals.

As servant kin quietly push for greater equality, elites are forced to reconsider what is appropriate treatment of subordinate kin. Elites hold diverse and sometimes contradictory opinions about servant rank. Some point out that servant rank does not really matter anymore in day-to-day life. According to this view, it is only in *adat* ceremonies that people still have to abide by the rules of *adat* for proper behavior. As long as people remember their place in ceremonies, they can live as they want. Since ceremonies constitute a significant portion of village social interaction, however, the fact that servant rank is only pertinent to ceremonies means that servant families continue to feel the restrictions of their rank, though to a lesser degree than in the past.

Other elites insist that rank can never be changed, no matter how economics or education may alter family status. Nurma, true to her feelings about her rank, said, "Even if [servant families] become very wealthy and are doctors and professors and civil servants, they would still be low. Even if I become very, very poor, my rank would still be high." As a wealthy elite woman, Nurma does not feel that economic distinctions make any difference to kinship rank.

A series of events in the village that created considerable consternation and debate about the status of servant kin illustrates the contentious and shifting nature of the category and of elites' efforts to find some middle ground.

Mariam's family is a good example of strategies by servant families to improve social standing. Mariam and her sister Rahmah [met in chapter 2] are members of Santi's lineage. Both are haji and are respected for their devotion to Islam. Of Mariam's six children, the four youngest have all completed high school. Two of her daughters married husbands from outside the village (one a career military man) and moved away with their husbands; one son is attending a college in Padang. The youngest daughter, Aziana, a sweet and pleasant-looking young woman, lives at home and runs a small shop nearby. Despite their low rank, Mariam's family is moderately successful in the eyes of the state and better off than many families of client rank.

Living near Mariam's house was Yonalis's nephew Dt. Kuning, a young and newly titled man who had been hanging about the village without a job. Dt. Kuning held the highest-ranking title in his clan, which had been passed on to him when his mother's brother, Hartati's husband, passed away. He and Aziana wanted to marry. Normally men who bear the family title are discouraged from marrying someone of servant rank. Neither the senior women of his lineage nor the *Bundo Kanduang* of Mariam's lineage, Santi, approved of the marriage, but they did not stop it.

Not surprisingly, there were difficulties with the wedding. Aziana wanted to wear a large headpiece at the wedding, but needed Santi's permission. Santi was well-known for being very strict about *adat*, a fact that her servant kin knew only too well since it was Aziana's aunt Rahmah who had been denied the use the big house for her daughter's wedding. Even though Aziana only wanted to wear the headpiece in her mother's house, Santi, unlike Fitriani, would not allow it. At deliberations, when the issue was raised, Santi got angry and said, "That's mine [*itu punya saya*]," meaning that the right to wear a headpiece belongs to elites and she was not about to give up that right.

The situation after the wedding only got worse. The wives of titled men play important roles at ceremonies (as noted in chapter 5), both by their presence and by bringing the most elaborate trays to be served to titled men. Despite now being wife to a titled man, Aziana was not supposed to even attend mid- or high-level ceremonies held by elites except to assist in the kitchen.

When Nurma's daughter got married a year or so later, the elites decided to hold a high-level *adat* ceremony. Dt. Kuning, Nurma's cousin, was of course centrally involved as the titled man. Unbeknownst to Santi, the titled man of Aziana's elite sublineage, who ranked lower than Santi and her nephew Dt. Mangkuto, gave permission to Aziana to participate in the wedding. When Santi saw Aziana walking in the bridal procession to the groom's

house, she yanked her out of the procession and told her she could not go.
Aziana and her whole family were greatly embarrassed by this turn of events.

Santi's actions toward her servant kin evoked strong responses from others about
adat and the kinship hierarchy. Elites that I talked to thought that Santi's action
was mean-spirited but mainly because it was done in public. Most believed she
had the right to forbid Aziana from participating, agreeing that as a servant
woman, Aziana had no right to be in the procession.

Santi's behavior caused some titled men to grumble that she was out of line
for going against the decision of the titled man. Once a decision has been made
by the men elders, Dt. Rajo argued, *Bundo Kanduang* should not stray from that
decision. The problem from his point of view was not whether her action was
right or wrong, but that it was a public embarassment to the titled man, whose
decision she overruled. But apparently Santi was not consulted about Aziana's
participation in the ceremony. According to Nurma, the first mistake was made
by the titled man. "The [titled man] didn't have the right to approve her attendance without agreement and shouldn't have anyway. The problem was that the
issue should have been settled beforehand in a deliberation and not in public like
that." No action was taken against Santi for her behavior.

Some elites felt sympathy for Aziana, but felt that *adat* had to be maintained.
Hartati stated, "[Ceremonial] *adat* is difficult because some people are not
allowed to attend. People are having a ceremony and they're not allowed, we feel
sorry for them. They feel sad, lots of people attending and they can't. That's a
pity. But if a goat isn't slaughtered for the ceremony, then they can attend." Hartati put the problem in terms of what *adat* allowed. She found a solution to the
difficulties by suggesting people not hold high *adat* events.

Other elites were more willing to compromise with subordinate kin. Fitriani,
who had been faced with a similar situation with her client kinswoman Anna,
told me that she did not like to forbid her client or servant kin from doing certain things in ceremonies. "Some people would ... but I don't like to do that. I
don't like to oppress people. Their blood is the same red as ours. Just our fates
are different. Really, it's too bad! If they are able to buy things, then why
should we forbid it? That's evil. Personally, I think it's not right. You know,
wearing the bridal headpiece [*sunting*] is only for half a day. We [elites] are not
lessened by that."

Fitriani saw no problem with letting the bride in a wedding of subordinate kin
wear what she wanted in her own house. She drew the line, however, at her subordinate kin wearing elite status symbols in the wedding procession. She
explained that it was fine if a bride wore the headpiece in her own house but then
added, "Of course they can't go around the village in it. That would be acting
haughty, they'd get a big head." She said, "There are lots of people now who
have money; they can afford things and they want everything. What is not
allowed is for them to take what we have. That's not right. There is still a dis-

tinction." To Fitriani some changes are acceptable. She feels bad when others are humiliated. But like Santi, she believes the status markers that distinguish her and other elites from subordinate kin need to be preserved. The reason for maintaining these distinctions, according to Fitriani, was that, "If it isn't followed, then there is no difference between us and them."

According to Dt. Rajo, if subordinate kin are not restricted to low *adat*, "then their *mamak* will be encroached upon. They'll be higher than the *mamak*." Elites claim certain rights in ceremonies should not be given away. Their statements suggest that these status markers are one of the few things that serve to distinguish them from their subordinate kin. Without these markers, their subordinate kin might surpass them in status.

Part of the conflict over Santi's actions comes from the importance of the ideology of relatedness and mutual aid in the village. People value generosity and loyalty, both of which come into question when elites act in domineering and arrogant ways. Several people questioned the propriety of Santi's actions as a senior woman. Hartati commented about Santi that "when she gives advice or guidance, she doesn't do it gently, she is heavy-handed. She treats people harshly. That's not good, you have to treat everyone the same. We all have the same red blood, after all. We can't be haughty [*sombong*], we will not be esteemed by others if we act that way." Such behavior threatens the bonds of relatedness that hold families together in the village. People expect to be treated with respect even if they are not all the same status. These differences of opinion suggest that elites are concerned about maintaining *adat* principles as well as preserving harmonious relations. To do both they must maneuver between acting generously toward their subordinate kin and maintaining the distinctions between them.

Ironically, it was Santi's daughter Irwati, university-educated and a civil servant in Padang, who raised questions about the necessity of maintaining rank distinctions. She suggested avoiding high adat ceremonies in the future. Her beliefs reflect village sentiment about relatedness as well as her experience living outside the village.

> Too many people who can't attend ceremonies get offended. It's too exclusive and why should we want to exclude people? That's like the caste system in India where some aren't allowed to be near high-ranking people. It's the same with high *adat*, servant and even client kin can't go in the procession or sit in the big house because it's not proper and doesn't show respect. I wouldn't do that anymore. Mid-level ceremonies are okay, though, because not everyone is excluded.

In her opinion, rather than continue to offend people, elites should refrain from having prestigious ceremonies. Distinctions between the ranks appear to her to be unfair and exclusive. Taking this argument further, Irwati stated that economic considerations should be more important these days than considerations of rank. "Economic well-being is more important than having 'blue blood' [high rank].

Younger women do not pay much attention to rank anymore when they marry. They are more interested that the husband will make a good income. But for those whose whole world is the village, yes, rank is still important." As an elite woman who has appropriated some of the class values of the Indonesian state, Irwati argues for a more modern attitude, one that recognizes the importance of maintaining an adequate income over that of rank. From her perspective, the valuation of rank above all else does not reflect the realities of the world anymore. When Irwati returns to the village at retirement to take her mother's place, her views of *adat*, shaped by her years in the port town of Padang as a civil servant, will undoubtedly have an impact on her relations with those of lower rank, reconstituting yet again elite relations to subordinate kin.

Every time there is a ceremony, the points of contention between elites and subordinate kin are revisited. By making claims that elite views are old-fashioned, outdated, or arrogant, villagers make use of the discourse of modernity to revise the codes of *adat* and limit the power of elites to define others as subordinate. Dt. Rajo remarked that "things are different now and *adat* is changed to fit the times. We have progressed and some things about *adat* have to change as well, like the clothes worn at wedding ceremonies or who is able to slaughter a cow or even water buffalo." By being sensitive to changing attitudes, elite women and men adjust *adat* to fit new circumstances while preserving the power of *adat* to define the community.

CONCLUSION

The kinship hierarchy and the inequalities it fosters in access to power and privilege lead to conflicts over rank. Deliberations and ceremonial events highlight the differences in kinship rank, making these events one of the primary arenas for contesting rank. As people attend to and discuss the meanings of ceremonial activities, they daily register slightly different meanings and statuses for the families and lineages that make up their community. Through ceremonial practices that draw on a range of symbols and ideologies, rural villagers rework, reassert, and redefine people's identity. Ritual in this view is more than a display or reflection of social status; it is the stage on which new meanings are introduced, weighed, incorporated, or rejected. Ceremonial practices are one of the more visible ways in which culture—*habitus* in Bourdieu's (1977) term—is created, reproduced and reconstituted in understandable form.

Through their control of *adat*, senior women shape social identities and political alliances within the village. Lineage elders' claims to *adat* knowledge allows them to regulate ceremonial events. Although they participate in all decisions, senior women in particular set the standards of ceremonial dress and food presentation for their subordinate kin. By limiting the style of dress and adornment worn in ceremonies and preventing subordinate kin from attending important elite ceremonies or using the big house, senior women redefine their own privilege and set limits to the status subordinate kin can achieve. In their role as guardians of ceremonial procedures, senior elite women and men define and reinforce client and servant rank as positions of lesser prestige and power at the same time maintaining their own greater privilege.

Although I have emphasized the inequalities of the kinship hierarchy in this chapter, the relationship between elite and subordinate kin is not exploitative. Elites' power is held in check by the idiom of kinship itself. A senior woman gains benefits from maintaining positive relations with her subordinate kin. If she is not too heavy-handed or arrogant, she can build a network of kin who will support her and her family in lineage affairs and help to build her influence with other elites.

In the politics of ceremony, is *adat* being circumvented? Is the kinship hierarchy changing shape as new avenues are found to breach the ideology of rank? Women of client and servant families both use similar strategies to change their situation in the village. These women work hard to be loyal members of elite lineages and to increase the wealth of their families through farming. In their efforts to achieve higher status and greater respect in the village, they encourage their children to attain higher education, particularly in servant families, and are more likely to allow their daughters to go to the *rantau*. They make use of national and religious status markers to aid in their efforts, including participation in state-sponsored organizations in which rank does not matter. They invoke the symbols of national culture, the state ideologies of equality and class distinction based on education and employment in salaried jobs, and Islamic expressions of faith, represented by attaining the *haj*. But they also maintain the idiom of *adat* expressed in the ideology of relatedness.

Elites face pressure both from above, at the state level, and from below, in the kinship hierarchy, to change the shape of *adat* and thus the structure of social identity in the village. Although elite practices tend to reinforce the boundaries between ranks, elites have broadened the definition of social worth. In the conflict over the status implications of increasing wealth, higher education, and prestigious jobs, elite women and men find ways to negotiate changes without undermining the vital foundation of community life vested in kinship relations. The proverb that is often quoted by Minangkabau concerning *adat* continues to ring true. Minangkabau say, "It doesn't dissolve in the rain; it doesn't shatter in the heat," which means that even though conditions change, *adat* stays the same; it will not disappear.[5]

NOTES

1. Regarding status, the Minangkabau quote the aphorism, "[We] stand equally high and sit equally low [*tagak samo tinggi, duduk samo randah*]" (Bachtiar 1967:378).

2. If evidence is found of wrongdoing, the matter has to be taken up with the titled man of the sublineage.

3. For work on Indonesian national culture and its production, see, for example, Heider 1991, Hooker 1993, and Schiller and Martin-Schiller 1997. My intent here is only to give a brief overview of some sources of national culture.

4. Of the ninety-two individuals who have migrated temporarily, 84 percent are living outside of the West Sumatran highlands. Two-thirds migrate to cities in Sumatra, while others have migrated as far as Sabah and Kuala Lumpur, Malaysia. The most popular destinations are Pekan Baru (Riau), 27 percent; Padang (West Sumatra), 23 percent; and Jakarta (Java), 17 percent.

5. The Minangkabau saying goes as follows: "*Indak lapuk karena hujan; indak lekang karena panas.*"

7

Controlling Labor, Controlling Kin: Village Farm Relations

In this chapter I extend the analysis of elite women's control of subordinate kin to the rice field, that is, the domain of agricultural production. In the Minangkabau literature many scholars agree that women control economic production in West Sumatra, by which they usually mean that women manage their rice fields on a day-to-day basis and use the produce for household needs. In contrast to this somewhat limited view of women's control of the "economic sphere," the actual picture that emerges is far more complex. As feminist scholars have pointed out, the "economic sphere" is not separate from other social relations; among other things, production processes are informed by gender relations in households.[1] In the case of the Minangkabau, production relations are not just family and household relations; they are deeply embedded in a complex web of kinship, rank, and clientage. As shown in chapter 3, elite women control ancestral land and the labor needed to work the fields. Two things happen as a result. One, it creates a network of kin who are dependent on elite women landowners for access to land and labor. And two, these kin help to maintain the power and influence of elite women within lineage and village affairs. Consequently, women landowners' control in the "economic sphere" is inextricably related to their control over social and political relations within the village.

I highlight in this chapter the embeddedness of the economy in the cultural system, or the cultural economy, to use Halperin's term (1994). But where Halperin emphasizes cultural institutions over agency in the construction of the economy, deemphasizing individual actors, I see actors as consciously negotiating and manipulating larger processes as they rework local relations. I argue that agricultural production and its transformations cannot be understood adequately without interrogating the interplay of kinship, clientage, and state-supported agricultural policies with production relations in the village.

In the following I explore the interrelation of economic practices and kinship practices in village social life. I first sketch a brief history of agricultural production in wet-rice farming in Taram and the transformations resulting from agricultural development policies promoted by the Indonesian state since the late 1960s. Then I investigate the relation between elite women and those dependent on them for access to land and work. For rural Minangkabau this dependence is subsumed within the kinship bond of clientage. Although sharecropping remains one of the primary arrangements for working the land, increases in wage labor threaten the practice of clientage. I examine the tensions between elites and clients created by this movement toward wage labor. I also explore collective labor groups and how they act as a wedge both against the control of wealthy landowners and against individualized wage labor. The differences in access to land among women underscores the point that class interests cut across gender, as Stoler (1977) first suggested in her article on Javanese women rice farmers.

AGRICULTURAL PRODUCTION AND ITS TRANSFORMATIONS

Before the push for agricultural development in the late 1960s and early 1970s, wet rice was grown on an annual cycle in Taram. This cycle has been adequately described elsewhere (Ambler 1989), but I will briefly sketch the division of labor and labor process of the annual rice cycle. Because some of these practices remain in place in the 1990s, I provide detail from the experiences of farmers that I interviewed. Due to the efforts of the Dutch who built a dam in the 1920s on a river on Taram's eastern border, the village has long had the advantage of an irrigation system that ensures adequate water for the growing season. As the rainy season approached, men plowed the field, using water buffalo, cattle, or hoe, and cleared or repaired the water canals. After harvest they burned the stubble in the fields, the ash providing fertilizer for the next crop. Women transplanted, weeded, and harvested the rice using small hand-size sickles called *tuai*. The landholder set aside a portion of the rice harvest as seed for the next year and deposited the remainder in her granaries. The whole cycle lasted approximately eight months; after harvest, the field was left fallow for three to four months until the beginning of the next rainy season. During the off-season women farmers grew dry field crops or tended gardens. During that time and between plowing and harvesting, men also worked on dry field crops, usually cash crops such as tobacco or coffee, which were located on land at the edges of the rice fields or in the nearby hills.

Since 1965, agricultural development has transformed the way the land is worked. By the late 1970s almost all farmers in Taram had switched to high-yielding varieties of rice, which they sold as a cash crop. Because of the shorter maturation period for these varieties, farmers were able to raise two crops per year where they had previously only grown one. Farmers now work year-round with much less concern for seasonal rainfall. Little time is allowed for fields to lie fallow; if water is plentiful, a field just harvested is plowed as soon as possible and the cycle started again. Only a severe dry season prevents farmers from turning their fields over quickly. Given adequate rainfall and use of the fastest-maturing rice varieties (which take only four months), some farmers push their fields to produce almost three crops a year. Further, because the agricultural cycle no longer follows the seasons, fields in Taram are nonsynchronous; different areas are planted and mature at different times throughout the year.

Technological changes include a switch from the small knife (*tuai*) used at harvest to the sickle. Some farmers rent hand blowers, a simple hand-operated machine that cleans the *padi* more quickly than hand winnowing, but this equipment is not used uniformly by all farmers. In the early 1980s motor-driven hand tractors became available in Taram. The use of tractors shortens the time needed to prepare the rice field for planting. If it took one man four days to plow the soil of an average field, now it takes one man one-half day with a hand tractor. Most landowners have switched to tractors because the cost of hiring a tractor and driver is less than that for hoe plowing. Larger equipment such as combine harvesters have not been adopted in Taram because rice plots are small and divided by bunds, making access to the fields nearly impossible for large machinery.

The changes in technology have meant that more men are involved at harvest time cutting and threshing than in the past, a trend common throughout Southeast Asia. But in Taram by far the great majority of cutters and threshers are women. Since tractors do the same task as plowing, only men drive the new motorized hand tractors. None of the landowners have purchased tractors, however. Instead, a local farmer-businessman rents tractors and drivers to farmers. The change in plowing has had the greatest impact on the availability of agricultural labor for men. Many of the earlier exchange groups of men plowers are no longer in existence because of the replacement of hoe plowing with tractor plowing. Only the fields that are unsuitable for tractors are worked by men plowers.

Rice was originally hulled by water-driven machines owned by the wealthier families in Taram. These machines have been replaced by gasoline-driven hullers and polishers, which are also locally owned and operated. The first one in Taram started operation in 1963 and produced 300 kilograms of hulled rice in one hour. Currently there are seven mills in Taram, the majority having started up in the 1970s; the largest machine now mills 1,000 kilograms of rice an hour. These mills usually employ three to ten men or women to spread the *padi* on concrete to dry, and two to five men inside to process the *padi* through the huller. Each mill has arrangements with certain rice merchants in the village to bring their *padi* to that mill. Rice merchants (called *tokéh* locally) lend money to farmers and then buy the crop from the farmer in payment of the loan. Mill owners charge their merchants a smaller fee for milling rice than they charge individual owners for milling.

The technological requirements of the new strains of rice make access to cash essential to farming. Although farmers produce two crops per year with a resulting increase in income, cash requirements have increased the difficulties of farming for smallholders. Several women complained to me that now they have to pay for everything—the seed, the fertilizer, and all the labor—whereas under the old system, they did not need cash for farming. Cash requirements mean that many more farmers operate on a credit basis than in the past, borrowing cash from rice merchants at the beginning of the growing season to pay for seed and fertilizer, as well as labor, and repaying the loan at harvest by selling the *padi* directly to the lender.

CHANGING LABOR PRACTICES

In addition to changing technology, agricultural development has transformed the types of relationships between owners and laborers. Prior to the adoption of the new high-yielding varieties of rice, the most common labor practices were for owners to work their own land as owner-operators or to lease their land to tenants in a sharecropping arrangement. To supplement labor during peak labor periods, most farmers also engaged in exchange labor practices with other farmers. Following the switch to high-yielding varieties of rice, these labor practices remain in use, although the conditions have changed. Some practices, such as exchange labor, are employed much less than before.

Owner-operators, like Fitriani, are generally smallholders who carry out most of the agricultural tasks with the assistance of family members or close kin. Fitriani has retired from farming, but her daughter Lina works their one plot of rice land for her now with the assistance of one or two other close kinswomen. Wira, Lina's elder sister, provided some labor when she first moved back home. To help with planting and weeding, Lina works on an exchange labor basis with a few other smallholders.

Larger landowners such as Hartati, Nurma, and Nurani generally lease their land to tenants for sharecropping. Older women who no longer have daughters at home to help, like Santi, are more likely to have their land sharecropped for them. In Santi's case, her eldest son and his wife are among her sharecroppers. In the typical sharecropping arrangement, the landowner supplies the seed and pays for half the fertilizer, while the sharecropper handles all other inputs, keeping the owner informed of the progress of the crop. The sharecropper splits the produce with the owner fifty-fifty (*paduoan*, M., to split in half).[2] Sharecroppers are usually husband-and-wife teams like Nurani's client kin Intan and Sahril. They split the labor along customary gender lines. Sharecroppers use the same labor strategies as owner-operators, either relying on the assistance of kin, exchanging labor, or paying for help. On the final day of the harvest, the owner goes to the field to supervise as the sharecropper measures the *padi*, pays off the laborers, and bags the *padi* for transport to the mill.

There are several reasons farmers lease their land to sharecroppers. Share-cropping provides a high degree of flexibility in production by reallocating land and labor among households over time (Robertson 1980). It is mutually benefi-cial to landowners and land-poor families because both are able to derive income from the land. Some landowners have surplus rice land they cannot work them-selves; others have nonagricultural occupations that do not allow enough time for farming, and some are elderly and unable to work (Syahrizal 1989:106).

> Nurani, who manages her mother Yenita's and her own rice fields, has most of her rice land worked for her. "It's expensive to have land sharecropped, but I have to," she said. "I don't have a husband or a son-in-law to help with my fields." (Her son-in-law Ahmad is not a farmer.) She commented that the men in her family, in particular Dela's husband Dt. Sati, do not have the stamina for that kind of work. In fact, neither he nor her son was ever very interested in farm work. Dt. Sati has always had other means of income and other responsibilities as a titled man that prevent him from helping out. Nurani's son sought a college education and has plans for a salaried job. Conse-quently, rather than paying a worker to do what a kinsman or in-law would do for free, Nurani prefers to have most of her land sharecropped for her.

Exchange labor continues to fill an important need for smallholders and share-croppers in Taram. Although exchange labor predominates in Minangkabau vil-lages where there is little economic differentiation among households (Syahrizal 1989), in Tanjung Batang in 1989–90 there were several active exchange groups with five to seven members each. Women exchange labor for transplanting or weeding their rice fields, while men exchange labor for plowing. This type of labor is used so that tasks can be finished more quickly. If one woman takes a week to plant her field, the plants will not ripen all at the same time. With sev-eral women working together, the field can be planted in a day and the plants will mature at the same time (Syahrizal 1989). Most of this labor is performed through small exchange groups (*lambik ari*, M.) that work together from year to year. Exchange labor is based on the principle of reciprocity or mutual assistance (*tolong-menolong*). Exchange groups of women alternate working in each other's rice fields during the growing season; no one gets paid. According to Lina, Fitri-ani's daughter, "We pay with our bodies." Lina gets very busy because of these exchange arrangements; sometimes her own rice field has to wait while she goes off to help another woman with her planting or weeding. She said they just ask each other, can you do such-and-such tomorrow at my rice field, and if they can (*boleh*), then the next day they go there. Relations in these exchange groups are not strictly regulated; members do not always have to work together all the time.

Harvest time requires a large number of workers to bring in the harvest within a day. It used to be customary for owner-operators to ask kin first to help bring in the harvest. Exchange groups typically work for each other at this time, but they also work together for other landowners, especially those with large landholdings, in

Photo 7.1 A woman cutting *padi* at harvest time

which case they are paid for their labor. Each exchange group cuts and threshes the *padi*, putting the cut stalks into their own pile (*ungguk*) and threshing from that pile. They are paid twelve *gantang* of padi for each one hundred *gantang* that they harvest; the padi is then divided among them.[3] The groups earn different amounts depending on their speed and skill. Lina said her exchange group always makes about a *gantang* more per person than the other groups, signifying their greater speed and efficiency.[4]

With the intensification of rice agriculture, most farmers sell their crops on the market. Cash has increasingly become the preferred medium of exchange for agricultural labor as well. For smallholders the need for cash has increased the desire and need for wage labor. Consequently where most of the agricultural labor was done on a household and exchange basis, with only harvesters being paid in kind, much more of the agricultural labor process, particularly plowing, planting, and weeding, is currently paid in cash. In fact, the need for immediate cash prevents some smallholders from working in exchange groups at all.

Several different types of paid labor are now available. Individually hired laborers (*buruh*) are paid for that day's labor. For transplanting and weeding, women earned 1,250 *rupiah* a day in 1990 for six hours of work. Men were paid 2,500 *rupiah* a day for plowing with an animal they provided (see *rupiah* in glossary for exchange rate). Contract labor groups (*borongan*) work for a specified number of days doing transplanting or weeding for a set wage. Contract work is arranged between a landowner and a woman who has several other workers that she can call on to work with her; in some cases they are members of her exchange group. Contract laborers usually receive a slightly higher wage for their labor than day laborers.

Another type of work group has developed out of the exchange labor groups: the collective farming group (*kelompok tani*). Owners who need laborers for planting or weeding contact the group head, who then contacts group members to work the next day. The collective in Tanjung Batang works twice a week planting or weeding and is paid at harvest for the days worked. Most of the women in the collective are small landholders or sharecroppers. If not all members are needed for one day's work, then on the next work day, the members who did not work are called.[5] Large landowners, owner-operators, and other group members hire the group to work for them.

The collective charges a slightly higher rate than that paid to individual day laborers (1,500 rupiah per day in 1990). Because the collective is not paid until harvest, however, farmers who use the collective avoid heavy expenditures of cash for labor during the growing season. For smallholders who might otherwise have to borrow money from rice merchants to pay the cost of labor, this delayed payment is an incentive to use the collective despite the higher rate. By avoiding borrowing money from a rice merchant, farmers are able to sell their rice directly to the mill at market prices and make more money for their harvest.

For the workers, many of whom have their own fields and labor costs, the collective provides a means to make extra income. Collective members regard the collective system as a way to save money. Each day worked is like money in the bank, I was told. They use the lump sum at harvest for things other than daily expenses, such as purchasing livestock or paying for house repairs, renovations, or additions.

FARM HOUSEHOLDS

As discussed in chapter 2, Tanjung Batang has a total of 106 farm households out of 125 total households. Of these 106 farm households, 94 percent have access to some land they work themselves and only 6 percent have no land and no access to land through sharecropping or other arrangements. Those without access to land survive on agricultural wage labor plus other sources of income. According to my survey, there are several different strategies used by farm households to work or gain access to land, from overseer, owner-operator, sharecropper, to laborer (see table 7.1). Even farm households who own land (owner-overseers and owner-operators in table 7.1) employ a number of strategies to earn income through farming in addition to working their own land, including sharecropping and various forms of agricultural wage labor, such as collective labor and contract labor. Agricultural wage labor is now common throughout the village for both women and men, although renting land through sharecropping has continued to be a predominant form of land tenure. Households that rely solely on sharecropping and/or agricultural labor comprise only 17 percent of the total, although 44 percent of all farm households do some sharecropping and 40 percent of all farm households engage in some agricultural wage labor (these are overlapping percentages). The mix of

Table 7.1 Control and Access to Land of Farm Households by Rank (N=106)

	Owner-Overseer	Owner-Operator	Operator/ Sharecrop/ Laborer	Overseer/ Sharecrop	Sharecrop/ Laborer	Laborer	Total
Elite	28	7	14	1	1	0	51
Client	7	3	15	2	10	5	42
Servant	7	1	2	1	1	1	13
Total	42	11	31	4	12	6	106

Table 7.2 Rice Production of Farm Households by Rank (N=106)

	None	Poor <400 gt.	Average <1000 gt.	Well-off >1000 gt.	Total
Elite	0	17	17	17	51
Client	4	18	12	8	42
Servant	1	5	5	2	13
Total	5	40	34	27	106

strategies reflects the fact that smallholders continue to dominate the land-scape of rice production in Taram. Seventy percent of farm households have small to medium-size landholdings producing under 1,000 *gantang* of rice per harvest (see table 7.2).

An important factor governing access to and control of land in the village is the intersection of kinship rank with class in farm households. Although many families in Tanjung Batang own or have access to land, wealth tends to correspond with kinship rank since it is predominantly elite households, and particularly elite women, that control land and labor. As Table 7.2 indicates, a greater percentage of well-off households come from elite lineages (63 percent), although some client families rival elites in wealth. While poor families are found in every kinship rank, over 60 percent of the poor come from client and servant families. In terms of rice production, elites produce 72 percent of the total rice harvest. Elite women constitute two-thirds of all women overseers, meaning that they supervise the labor but do not work the fields themselves (see table 7.1). Further, of all the women landholders who use sharecroppers to work their land, almost 80 percent are elite women. This group of women holds the land that sharecroppers need access to; they also hire much of the agricultural labor in the village. Both the sharecroppers and those hired to work the fields depend on these women landowners to gain access to fields or earn an income.

OVERSEERS AND THEIR CONTROL OF LABOR

As noted in chapter 3, women who control the land control its use. Women overseers supervise the work on their fields but do not get involved in the day-to-day operation. To better illustrate the meaning of women landowners' control over their workers and over the production process, I followed Nurani as she managed her several rice fields through one agricultural cyle. Nurani owns and manages several rice fields for herself, her mother Yenita, and her sisters. Some of the land she manages herself, other pieces are taken care of by sharecroppers. Nurani is a smart, hard-working farmer who prefers to keep close tabs on the work in her fields. Eschewing the aloof attitude of some of her peers toward farm labor, Nurani is not above helping with some of the (lighter) work herself at harvest time. She works closely with Intan and her husband Sahril, two of the share-croppers who work for her family, a young couple who have built up a good reputation as farmers. They not only sharecrop for Nurani, they also help her with the work on the field she manages. Sahril's family is client kin to Nurani.

Sept. 9, 1989. Sahril came to the house in the morning to tell Nurani that her field was ready to be fertilized. They talked about it briefly and then she wrote down for him what to get and how much. Later I went with Nurani to oversee the plowing of her large rice field across the river. She had hired a tractor and driver to do the job. We sat and watched from her small shelter (*dongau*, M.) built on the edge of the rice field. Intan and Sahril joined us and then the farmer-businessman who rented the tractor to Nurani stopped by and sat with us as well. Nurani had invited Intan to come along as we walked by her house on the way to the rice field. Before the plowing was finished, we left for home; the others stayed and ate lunch. Nurani said of the sharecroppers, "They provide the labor (*tenaga*), we have the rice field."

Sept. 19, 1989. Nurani said her rice field that was just plowed would be planted on the 21st. On the 20th she had Sahril prepare the seedlings for the planting. Intan and Sahril both were at Nurani's house last evening after dinner. Nurani asked Intan to find workers for the planting tomorrow.

Sept. 22, 1989. Nurani was busy in the early morning preparing food to take to the rice field. She made lots of rice, eggplant, and *rendang* (a meat dish), put each dish in a separate container and placed all of them in one large metal bowl, with plates and cloths. Then she put the very heavy bowl on top of her head, with my help, balancing it with one hand and holding a tea kettle in the other. She carried it all to her rice field, about a twenty-minute walk across the bridge to the fields on the other side of the river. We arrived at her field about 10:00 a.m. and put the bowl of food in the small shelter.

The women, including Intan, had already finished planting Nurani's field and had moved on to plant two small fields next to Nurani's. They moved slowly across the flooded field, their feet deep in the mud, planting long, neat rows of seedlings about a foot apart (see photo 7.2). They had started about 8:30 a.m., and finished all three by 11:30 a.m. (some planting had been done the day

Photo 7.2 Women planting a rice field

before). There were fifteen women in all, working as day laborers. Intan had gotten them together the day before. They all belonged to one labor group (*rombongan*). The women ranged in age from late twenties to early fifties. Sahril stopped by the field for a while before the planting was finished to watch.

Nurani only supervised that day. Planting is not something she likes to do. She says she gets sick if she works in the mud of the field. She walked around the edge of the field, checking the seedlings that had just been planted. Then she walked along the edge of the field where the women were planting and watched, saying a few things to some of the women, mostly Intan. The women worked steadily, bent over, rarely pausing to straighten up except when they needed more seedlings. Later Nurani went over to her mother's field nearby, which was being harvested, to check on that also. When she came back to her small shelter, she got the food ready for the workers. The women continued planting on their own, taking the seedlings out of the trays, pushing them into the mud, and moving on to the next row. No one told them what to do; no one needed to.

When the women finished around 11:30, they came over to Nurani's shelter where the food was waiting for them. Nurani seemed to know all the women. There was a lot of bantering and conversation among the women as they dished up their plates. Not all of them fit in the small shelter, so some ate as they squatted next to the shelter. Nurani ate at the same time, but she sat off to one side of the shelter slightly away from the rest of the women. Intan joined her there and ate with her, both of them squatting on the ground. When the women were finished, they rinsed off their plates in the irrigation ditch and put

Photo 7.3 Landowner paying her workers after planting

Photo 7.4 Measuring the harvest

them back with the leftover food. As they got ready to leave, Nurani took out a roll of rupiahs that she had been carrying and paid the women for their labor (see photo 7.3). As the women left, Intan helped Nurani collect the dirty plates and left overs, and then the two walked back to Intan's house.

Nov. 14, 1989. Nurani was harvesting her sister's and her mother's rice fields. Intan sharecrops these fields and had brought seventeen workers to the harvest, including her sister-in-law (Sahril's sister). When I arrived around 1:00, the rice stalks were all cut off and threshed, and only a few workers were still winnowing (*diangin*) the *padi*. Intan was busy measuring one pile of *padi*. Sahril and another man worked with her, holding the sacks as she poured in the *padi* and then tying up full sacks and carrying them to the edge of the field. Nurani had already been at the field earlier, left to go to the miller's, and then returned again. She talked to Intan and watched for a little while until Intan finished measuring the pile. When Intan moved off to another part of the field to measure another pile, Nurani went over to two different groups of harvesters who were still winnowing and talked to them. Then she walked to the far end of the field where one woman was working alone winnowing. Nurani had a winnow basket with her and started helping this woman winnow her pile of *padi*, while Intan continued measuring *padi*. It was 4:30 p.m. before Nurani got home.

As these journal entries suggest, even though landowners such as Nurani have farmers that work for them, they oversee and keep track of the work on their fields. Intan was asked to get the workers for the planting, whom Nurani paid directly, in addition to providing a meal for them. Nurani likes to go to the field whenever work is being done. She also consults frequently with the sharecroppers, who come to her house to talk about what is going on and what they need. Although she does not give orders while work is being done, by visiting the fields she can tell how well the work is going and whether the workers are skillful and efficient enough.

Although Nurani has contracted with both Intan and her husband, Intan is the primary person responsible for the work on the field; most of the labor is done by women that she calls and it is she who takes charge of measuring the *padi*, while her husband stands by to help carry off the sacks of rice. Intan is considered a good sharecropper because she is reliable, has access to a number of women that are also reliable, skilled workers, and has a husband who is a skilled farmer. Nurani treats her sharecroppers with respect, but as the ones in her employ, they are the ones who need to come to Nurani's house to consult with her in the evening.

Even though owners have higher status than their workers, status differences are muted. When an owner like Nurani works in her own fields (winnowing), status differences between sharecroppers, workers, and owners are apparent only by the difference in clothes: the owner's clothes are nice and clean, while the workers are in torn and faded work clothes. Terms of address remain the same, dependent on age differences. Owners are not addressed as *tuan* (boss), although sometimes workers joke about the owner being the boss. I heard sharecroppers address a slightly older owner as *kak* (older sister) and a younger one by her first name. Muted public acknowledgement does not obviate the fact, however, that sharecropper and workers depend on the owner for their income.

Over the course of the agricultural cycle, large landowners employ a considerable number of workers. At one harvest Hartati had more than thirty people working one of her fields. They were organized into nine groups, each group containing anywhere from one to eight people. The workers were primarily women, but there were also four or five men and older boys who were cutting and threshing, and several teenaged girls threshing and winnowing. In addition to those working the harvest, during the agricultural cycle Hartati might hire twenty women for planting, ten women to weed twice, plus two or three men (including the male sharecropper) to plow, fertilize, and fix the canal, and several men to help haul the sacks to the miller—more than seventy-five workers in all. Because the same workers are usually called by the sharecropper for the different tasks, the total number of individual workers may be thirty-five to forty. Hartati also has another large field on the other side of Taram that is worked by a sharecropper who employs a completely different set of workers. Thus, with just those two fields alone she has seventy to eighty workers in her employ either directly or indirectly, resulting in many households that are dependent on her for their income.

SHARECROPPING AND CLIENT KIN

Sharecropping as a major form of land tenure in Taram is not just an agrarian relationship but a relationship embedded in kin ties. For landless or near landless farmers, access to land comes through elite members of lineages to which they belong. The sharecropping relationship, often based on kinship ties or residential propinquity, has been described in Southeast Asia in general and Java more particularly as a benevolent or moral relation that advantages small landholding peasants who can claim such ties (Hefner 1990, Hüsken 1989). Jay noted that the Javanese landholder becomes a patron to the sharecropper, giving material aid in emergencies, as well as advice and gifts, in return for labor and social gestures that acknowledge his "quasi-paternal role and superior rank" (1969:230). Although there is disagreement over the direction of change in the patron-client tie (see Hart 1986, Pincus 1990), and an assumption that agrarian change erodes these ties, patron-client ties seem to persist despite the transformations caused by agricultural development. Even poor landless farmers in Malaysia were unwilling to give up their patron-client ties, although such ties, according to Hart (1991), work to co-opt and mute men's resistance to increasingly unfair labor practices by large landowners.

Patron-client ties in Java are similar to those in West Sumatra in terms of the perceived advantage and moral obligations of the relationship. The broader social and economic conditions in West Sumatra, however, differ from Java. As discussed in the last chapter, the client relationship involves landowners and tenants in a wide range of social and ceremonial obligations and duties, situating the client within an idiom of kin relations that surpass the economic relationship. Hartati explained the importance of client kin as tenants on her rice fields as follows: "[Client kin] can get rice land if there is an agreement between us. They work our rice land, but they divide the produce in half with us. It's better if it's our *kamanakan* [relatives] who work our rice land than other people, if they're good workers. We're already related [*famili*] and we help each other. Client kin help the elite family and it's returned, it's an exchange of help [*tolong-menolong*]." For Hartati and other wealthy landowners, it is better if the person working the land is a client because they have a permanent bond (*hubungan famili*) with their client kin. Of client families in Tanjung Batang who sharecrop (and who identified the landowner), 90 percent of the landowners are their elite kin. Some client families have sharecropped the same land for their elite kin for more than a generation.

Not all sharecroppers fall into the client category; many of them are close relatives, in some cases daughters, but more likely sons, as well as other kin within the same clan (*sasuku*) or relatives of the husband's or father's lineage. As noted in chapter 3, a daughter is given land to use outright, but a son who gains access to land through his mother is obliged to return half of the harvest to his mother in the same way a sharecropper would. Those landowners who rent land to close kin for sharecropping tend to be small landowners or elderly women who no longer work their own fields. In some cases, landowners find a sharecropper from close neighbors or people who live near the field. Over time, however, even non-kin sharecroppers come to be seen as related (*famili*) to the landowner.

As Hartati's comment above suggests, sharecropping is more than an agrarian relationship in this village. Because it is framed in terms of the larger client relationship, the same expectations as those discussed in the last chapter apply to sharecroppers. It is in the sharecropper's best interests to maintain the goodwill of their landowner by providing assistance at ceremonial events or being helpful in other ways. If a client family does not adequately maintain its client relation, it is much easier for an owner to end a sharecropping relationship. In contrast, hardworking, loyal, and respectable client kin cannot be so easily dismissed as tenants. The relation of clientage embedded in the idiom of kinship makes elite landowners more hesitant to withdraw land from their client kin, if they are loyal clients, giving these kin greater security in access to land and making their relationship less likely to be an exploitative one (see also Robertson 1980).

Sharecropping as an alternative (or addition) to land ownership provides the security of an on-going land tenure relationship despite the fact that sharecroppers only receive half the income for their labor. Permanent access to the land, however, is not guaranteed (except in the case of immediate kin). Access is affected by the changing circumstances of the landowner's household as well as that of the sharecropper. For instance, leased land may be taken back at the marriage of a daughter, given to other kinfolk who request it, or pawned to pay for a large wedding, a serious illness, a funeral ceremony, or a new house. For the sharecropper's part, serious illness or the death of a spouse may lead to the loss of land to another family with adequate laborers. Failure to bring in a good crop may also result in the termination of a sharecropping agreement. Thus, although the sharecropper's access to land is more secure when based on a client relationship, many other factors enter into their ability to maintain long-term, stable access to land.

The ability to provide access to land to subordinate kin secures the bond between these kin and elite women landowners. Many elite women have one or two client or servant kin who are sharecroppers. A few wealthy landowning women, like Hartati, have several sharecroppers, both client and non-kin, as well as large numbers of agricultural laborers who work for them. Their control over others' livelihood is a great incentive for loyalty. Not only does elite women's ability to hire workers or sharecroppers give them higher status than those who work for them, it also strengthens their authority and influence over large numbers of families in the village. Such kin will fall in line with the opinions of their superiors and generally support their decisions, a situation that assures the political power of senior women and their families within the village.

THE THREAT OF WAGE LABOR

Before agricultural development, much of the field labor of plowing, transplanting, and weeding was done through exchange. Following the commodification of rice agriculture in the 1970s, wage labor has become a regular aspect of wet-rice farming. The increased use of wage labor, however, has ramifications that affect the relationship between client kin sharecroppers and their elite kin. In the following I examine some of the problems created by the increase in wage labor and then in the next section explore the way elites and clients are renegotiating their ties of kinship (*famili*).

Some of the largest landowners, primarily from elite families, have replaced their sharecroppers with wage laborers, either on an individual or contract basis. This practice removes surplus land from sharecropping. In 1990 a third of landholders who produce more than 400 *gantang* per harvest used a wage system for some or all of their labor needs, while 42 percent of the largest landholders (producing over 1,000 *gantang* per harvest) did so. The reason for using wage labor, according to one landowner, is that although she has to pay for the labor, the harvest is not divided with a sharecropper, so on balance, she makes a greater profit than if the land was sharecropped. While some of these landowners hire kin or clients as wage laborers, the long-term relationship they had with tenants is replaced by a temporary wage relationship that ends as soon as the wage is paid.

Many client kin do work as day laborers during planting and weeding seasons, but they prefer to take on this type of work as an addition to a primary source of income. The difference between wage and sharecropping relationships is significant. Where sharecropping is the basis for a long-term stable relationship between the landowner and the sharecropper, wage labor cannot guarantee anything past one day's pay. The daily wage for transplanting or weeding amounts to 1,000 to 1,250 rupiah a day, less than a subsistence wage—too low to do more than meet the basic daily food requirements of the worker and her family. One farmer showed me just how far a day's wages go. This woman has no land of her own but holds some in pawn, has access to another piece through her husband, and works a third piece as a sharecropper. She also works as a day laborer. She and her husband, who is also a farmer, have been hoping to make some improvements to their house, but have not yet had the money to do so.

> She brought out a small liter can filled with husked rice (*beras*) to show me how much they eat each day. She said she cooks four liters of rice a day to feed her family of five, which amounts to 800 rupiah per day just for rice. That doesn't figure in anything else, such as condiments (*sambal*), shopping, or cooking oil (*minyak*). She said it's hard, if you only earn 1,000 rupiah a day— there just isn't enough for anything, and she has two children already in school with their school fees to pay.

Daily wage work does not cover subsistence for most families. It is a less reliable source of income than sharecropping due to widely fluctuating seasonal demand, loss of wages due to illness on a scheduled work day, ceremonial obligations that take time away from work, and other problems. The vagaries of agricultural wage work are evidenced in landless households that depend solely on wage labor. These households are all poor primarily because wages are simply too low to support a family. For client kin the prospect of depending solely on wage labor is not a happy one. Losing a sharecropping relationship that provides the main source of income is devastating to client kin. Not only does it decrease their income, it disrupts the elite-client relationship.

While there are some benefits to be gained from wage labor for landless farmers in the village community, it tends to weaken the position of the worker in relation to the landowner. "Free" wage labor allows workers to choose whether and where to work. It also frees workers from social responsibilities to landowners. Under wage labor, an individual can work for any landowner who needs labor and receive a wage that is fairly standard throughout the village for each task performed. A laborer with a good reputation usually can find as much work as she or he wants. However, because agricultural wages are so low, a laborer is hard put to earn a subsistence wage. Consequently, for client kin, wage labor alone is not an adequate replacement for sharecropping rights or smallholding. The benefits of clientage for smallholders and landless farmers outweigh any small advantage gained through wage labor.

The increased use of day laborers poses a threat to client kin who depend on the client relationship to give them an advantage in gaining access to elite lands through sharecropping. Intan and her husband Sahril were faced with this problem when Nurani shifted some of her family's land from a sharecropping arrangement to wage labor.

Intan had been sharecropping for Nurani's family for several years. When Nurani's son started college, she asked her mother Yenita to help pay for her son's college education. So Yenita gave her control of some ancestral rice land that Nurani had only managed according to her mother's wishes up until then. Despite the fact that Intan worked as a sharecropper on that land and was a reliable worker, Nurani decided to take over complete management of the field and pay day laborers to work the field for her. She didn't completely leave Intan out, however; she asked Intan to help find workers for her, and hired Intan to work on the land at a daily rate. So now, instead of receiving half of the harvest, Intan only earned a daily wage and perhaps an extra *gantang* of *padi* at harvest for her help hiring workers. With the loss of sharecropping rights, Intan's income decreased, which meant that she and her husband would have to find other land to sharecrop to make up the lost income.

Overall, the advantages of using wage labor fall somewhat more strongly on the landowner's side. Landowners do not contract the same relationship with laborers as they do with their client kin. They can hire anyone to work as laborer for a minimal wage and do not accrue further obligations to their laborers beyond that day's wage.

For Intan, the loss of sharecropping rights changed her relation to Nurani from one of land manager (as sharecropper) to merely wage laborer, a significant demotion that affected their relationship. Because Intan no longer had the privileged position of sharecropper with its higher status than that of laborer, it created ill will for her toward Nurani. Over time she was less and less apparent at ceremonial events hosted by Nurani's family. The change in land tenure weakened the bond between the two women and lessened Nurani's ability to count on this woman, which affected her ties with Sahril's family as well.

Changes in the land tenure relationship threaten social bonds between owners and their tenants. Production through wage labor loosens social relations and loyalties on both sides. Laborers lose the guarantee of continuing income and access to land, while elites lose assistance at ceremonies and the increased status of having numerous kin. For workers as well as elites, wage labor has the potential to break down vertical alliances between clients and elites. Consequently it has created tension between clients and elites who are forced to renegotiate the meaning of mutual assistance and relatedness, the values that form the bedrock of kin ties. While some resist the changes in meaning, others are trying to shift the terms of the elite-client relationship.

NEGOTIATING KIN TIES

The tension over the shift to wage labor is evident in the contestations over land rights and kinship obligations. The loss of sharecropping rights leads client women to ask why they should heed the dictates of elites if the terms of their relationship have changed. Elite women who are divesting themselves of tenants are forced to justify their actions or face community disapproval. Underlying this jockeying for position is the very real threat to client kin and their concerns not only about economic conditions but the nature of social relations within the community.

The following case describes the relationship between Hartati and her client kin, Leli and her daughter Yeni. Hartati's rice fields amount to almost two hectares. Like Nurani, she decided to hire day laborers to work the large fields closest to her home and left the farther fields with a sharecropper. Leli and Yeni are both farmers who rely in part on Hartati for access to land.

Leli, an aging, rotund woman in her fifties, is the senior woman of a client family that has been part of Hartati's lineage for at least three generations. After Leli's first husband died, leaving her with four children, Hartati let Leli build a small one-room house on Hartati's land just a few yards away from the big house. Leli, who remarried and is now divorced, has been a farmer all her life, but age and failing knees have limited the amount of farm work she can do anymore. With one child still at home and in school, she works as a day laborer (primarily for Hartati) to make ends meet.

Leli's eldest daughter Yeni is also a farmer. Like Leli's other children, Yeni only finished elementary school (SD). She married a man from another client family and together they built their own one-room house across the path from Leli's house. Yeni has not had any children yet. In the past Yeni had a share-cropping arrangement with Hartati, but when that piece of land was given to Hartati's daughter Yetri at her marriage, Yetri leased it to a different share-cropper. Economically both Leli's and Yeni's small households fall into the category of poor households because they do not produce enough rice on which to subsist (less than 400 *gantang* per harvest).

Although Leli and Yeni no longer have access to Hartati's land, their obligations to their elite kin remain the same. They are expected to help at ceremonies and assist Hartati when she needs help. Leli and two of her daughters assisted at every ritual gathering at Hartati's house that I attended. At the ritual for Hartati's grandson (described in chapter 5), they were busily helping out, running upstairs and down, getting things when asked, and in general doing whatever was needed.

One of the things Hartati occasionally asks Yeni to do is to catch fish from her pond. In return for her help, Yeni is allowed to keep a few of the fish she catches. Yeni said to me, "It's only enough for one meal, not anything I could profit from," implying a lack of generosity on her kin's part. But if Yeni feels any resentment, she does not mention it to her elite kin nor does she stint in her help. Any resistance to Hartati's requests could jeopardize her relationship with her elite kin. She and her husband might not be asked to work on Hartati's land again or they might be told to move off the land where their tiny house is built. Despite her apparent loyalty, it is clear she has some questions regarding the level of reciprocity from her elite kin.

Though Yeni and her mother Leli both seem to be having difficulties due to their inability to get steady work from their elite kin, elites suggest that the problems of Leli and her family stem from their lack of productivity as workers. As one elite woman explained:

Yeni is lazy [*pemalas*]. She only thinks about today; if she has enough for today, that's it. She doesn't worry about tomorrow. If she has money, she spends it—she goes right to the store and spends all her money. She and her husband could be rich by now if they both worked all the time—they have no children. If someone doesn't call her to work, she doesn't look for work anywhere else. She just waits to be called. If you want to work as a farmer, there is enough work.

According to this account, Yeni could be doing well for herself but she is too lazy to work hard. Other elites suggest that in Leli's case her difficulties getting work come from having bad knees. Further, without a husband, it is too hard to manage all the work involved in sharecropping, so no one will give her land to sharecrop anymore.

From Yeni's perspective these arguments overlook the fact that her family is landless. They only have access to low-paying wage work and no land of their own from which to build up some income. When I asked Yeni if she had any land, she held out her hand palm up and said, "This, this is my rice field." Although Yeni has no children, some of her income goes to help her mother and sisters, so there is never extra money even in her own small household.

The statements by elites support the current relationship between Hartati and her client kin. By not arguing for Yeni's right to sharecrop, they also signify their acceptance of wage labor as a way for elite women to manage their land. From Yeni's perspective as client kin, she does not have access to rice land that a client relationship is expected to provide, a fact that creates hardship for her family.

Client families can and do resist the change in elite-client relations brought by wage labor by questioning the generosity of elite kin. Although in this case client kin are careful not to accuse their elite kin directly, wealthy elites are criticized when they fail to uphold their responsibilities to client kin, particularly hardworking, loyal clients. They may be talked about behind their backs and accused of being stingy, not only by client kin but by other elites. Over time such criticism and loss of community support act as a brake on elites' actions toward their client kin; it also serves as a wedge against the loss of access to elite lands. Despite the shifting terrain of land tenure and the move by some elites to replace sharecropping with wage labor, the expectations about mutual assistance founded in the ideology of relatedness continue to hold the elite-client relation together.

STRATEGIES OF THE COMMON FARMER

Moving beyond the owner-sharecropper relationship, I focus on a group of women smallholders in the village to show how their participation in a collective labor group serves as a wedge against the control of wealthy landowners on the one hand and individualized wage labor on the other. Although this group of farmers cuts across all kinship ranks and class divisions, they are alike in that most own very little of their own land. Most of them, however, have access to some land, through husbands, fathers, or sharecropping arrangements. Only two or three members of the collective are landless.

During the 1970s the state instituted a development program that promoted the creation of farm groups (*kelompok tani*). Through extension services, these groups were given direct access to new technologies, information, and credit as well as improved processing and marketing (Directorate General 1977). In Tanjung Batang the first state-sponsored women's farm cooperative, Sinar Jelita, grew to approximately one hundred women members. In addition to attending meetings and other activities sponsored by the state farm program (*Koperasi Unit Desa*, KUD), this group worked as a collective labor group planting and weeding for pay. After the head of the group died, the group split into two. One group of about forty members still claims the original name. The second group, which is no longer directly involved with KUD, is informally known by the name of its current head and only man in the group, Husein.

Husein is the only man who does planting and weeding in the village, a fact that causes some amusement among the members of the collective. He and his wife are both farmers and joint heads of a client household. Although their family looks quite poor with their shabby clothes and small, unkempt house, they have a decent income from sharecropping that has allowed them to pawn-in some land from several struggling elite landowners, including Fitriani. Husein is client kin in Fitriani's clan.

The success of Husein's collective comes not from the support of the state program but from its ties to several women's exchange groups. In Taram a number of exchange groups transformed themselves into collective labor groups as wage labor became more available. Hart (1991) notes this same phenomenon occurring among women in the northern Malaysian district of Kedah. Several mother-daughter units and kin-based exchange groups form the nucleus of this large collective. Because of their long-standing kin ties, these exchange groups play a key role in the collective in terms of holding the group together. Lina, who has worked with the collective for several years, expressed the importance of the kinship tie to exchange groups in the following way: "I can depend on family to help me. They won't go off and work for someone else." Kin ties are privileged over other ties and ensure that a group member will give priority to other members when they need help. Exchange labor groups stay together for years because the women have developed good working relations with each other. Long-term exchange groups become well-known in the village and often work together at harvest for other landowners. With the increase in availability of paid labor, those exchange groups with a good reputation find themselves in demand for wage work in both planting and weeding. Exchange groups thus moved easily into paid work as a group, and then became part of the collective labor group as well.[6]

Husein's group numbers about thirty women and is composed almost equally of elite and client women, plus two women from servant families. Most of these women live in one part of Tanjung Batang, forming a fairly close-knit group of kin and neighbors who help each other in ceremonial activities as well. The collective works every Wednesday and Sunday during planting and weeding season, but group participation is flexible; members work as much or as little as they want, or when they are not working on their own fields. Some members tend to work more while others only occasionally join in. Most jobs are not large enough for everyone to work, so very few members work every day the collective works. One mother-daughter pair alternates working for the group and is treated as one unit.

Collective group members are only paid at harvest. For each time they work with the group, they accumulate 1,500 rupiah, a wage that is slightly higher than the average rate of 1,250 rupiah a day for planting or weeding. I asked who decided the rate of pay and was told simply that the group did. The head of the group keeps track of how many days each woman worked. At harvest, the owners for whom the collective worked pay Husein, who then divides the money among the members. Some women work as many as thirty days in a season, earning 45,000 rupiah at harvest. In addition the head gets one day's wage from each woman in the group as payment for coordinating the group.

Managing the Collective

The collective was headed by Lina, Fitriani's daughter, for the first two seasons, but she did not like the problems associated with managing the group. She told me that she quit because she could not always get the number of workers that she promised the landowner. It made her look bad when not enough women showed up to work. I also heard similar complaints from the woman who heads the other collective in Tanjung Batang. Husein then became head of the group, a somewhat unusual move for a man to take responsibility in an area in which women normally are in control, made the more so because Husein is client kin and of lower rank than many of the women in the collective. Despite the apparent success of this group, the switch from a woman leader to a man points to certain tensions in the village about women's leadership.

Women's exchange relationships entail responsibility and expectations of reliability and hard work, the same expectations that apply to the collective. Lina herself has been part of a six-woman exchange group for several years. Exchange groups, however, are based on kin ties with their long-established expectations about loyalty to kin and mutual assistance, whereas collectives have a number of women of different rank, not all of whom have kin or even neighbor ties to each other. Another contrast between the two is that the collective works for wages whereas exchange groups have no financial accounting. Since Minangkabau women are well-known as entrepreneurs and managers of money, the reluctance Lina felt in managing the collective was not about handling money. I locate the problem in the shift from a labor relationship based on exchange (mutual assistance) to one based on a wage. The commodification of the exchange relationship calls into question the ideology of relatedness within which kin usually operate. Without kin-based ties to rely on, management of a collective becomes more difficult as expectations become more ambiguous and negotiable.

Lina's reluctance may also be suggestive of women's unease in taking charge in an organization that falls within the domain of state-sponsored projects. As I mentioned in previous chapters, the state validates men as leaders while representing women as domestic caretakers. Although the collective no longer attends state (KUD) functions, men's control of state programs serves as the prevailing model for modern state-sanctioned groups. According to one member of the group, Lina was too easygoing (*lunak*). "If a person promised to work and then didn't want to go that day, Lina wouldn't say anything, just keep quiet. So after her, Husein became head. He's a man, and if a person doesn't go when they're supposed to, he gets mad. He tells them, 'Quit the group then if you don't want to work.' He'll tear up their worksheet [a sheet that lists the number of days they worked]." Lina was reluctant to confront group members who were irresponsible. In contrast, these women expected a man to be able to enforce the rules of a wage-based collective, reflecting the persuasiveness of the state's validation of men as leaders in a modern world. This case is unusual for collectives, however, since the sexual division of labor usually keeps men's and women's groups separate. Most collectives are managed by women leaders. In a neighboring hamlet, a large collective farming and milling group called Shinta is headed by a woman, who has become well known in women's and development circles in Indonesia as a result of her leadership of the group. Such contradictory practices suggest that the persuasiveness of the state's hegemonic model of men's leadership for large wage-labor projects is unevenly expressed.

Collective Advantage

The advantages of working for the collective are several. First, the collective provides security for its workers. They can be assured of work and a small supplemental income. Second, because they belong to a group, these women have an edge in getting wage labor. Group members are known as reliable and hard workers and so are more likely to be hired. Third, this group has been able to demand a slightly higher rate of pay than that earned by individual laborers. The amount is figured by estimating how many average workers it would take to do the work. The group contracts to do the job with less workers than the average but is paid the same amount of money—thus each individual earns more per person.[7] Further, the group has been able to shorten the hours of work per day without losing any income. Where the workday for hired labor used to start around 7:00 a.m. and end at 4:00 p.m., now women work only until 1:00 or 2:00 p.m. for the same wages.

By organizing collective groups, these women have improved the terms of their labor. With access to land through sharecropping dependent on the owner, and the possibility of losing that land ever present, their participation in the collective helps them survive the uncertainties of sharecropping and wage labor. It has created a hedge against complete dependence on landowners and their interests, and an alternative to individualized wage labor. These advantages work for both client women and poorer elite women. For client women, who make up the largest proportion of sharecroppers, their participation suggests that they are particularly interested in finding other means to secure a stable income. It also represents an attempt to assert their class interests against those of wealthy elite women. In moving away from dependence on their elite kin, they are redefining their own identity as clients.

For both client and poorer elite women, working in the collective maintains the spirit of kin ties by incorporating, if uneasily, the ideology of relatedness into a wage system. Collective labor integrates the tradition of mutual aid into the contractual relations of the market. It preserves kin ties yet also lays the groundwork for greater reliance on the market as a means to achieve prosperity and social identity. The development of the collective is an eloquent statement about both the demands of modernity and the importance of solidarity.

CONCLUSION

In the last chapter I showed how women's control of "sister's children" extends to client and servant kin in social and ceremonial relations. Through land ownership, elite women's control over subordinate kin extends to agricultural production as well. The ability to provide access to land to subordinate kin helps to secure the bond between these kin and elite women landowners. It also assures the political power of senior women and their families within the village. A few wealthy landowning women have a number of sharecroppers, both client and non-kin, scattered throughout the village, as well as many agricultural laborers who work for them. With a large number of sharecroppers and workers under their control, these women are more visible and well-known in the community; such visibility does several things for them politically. It increases their control over clients because these families depend on them for access to land and income; it increases the standing of their families because more individuals will feel obliged to attend their ceremonies; and it increases their influence in lineage decision-making because of the status and respect of their family. In the final chapter I show how this political power has carried some elite women into the domain of state-controlled, male-headed, village government.

Agrarian transformations have resulted in an increasing complexity of peasant relations—without, however, undermining women's control of land. Earlier assumptions that the penetration of capitalism in Southeast Asia would result in the development of a peasant proletariat dispossessed from their land and living off wage labor have proved inaccurate as numerous case studies revealed the continued presence of smallholder farming and sharecropping in peasant communities (Bray 1983, Hart 1989, White 1989). In Taram, despite the transition to double-cropping and the use of new technologies, smallholders and sharecroppers continue to dominate the landscape. The more problematic change confronting farm laborers is the increase in wage labor. Although it provides supplemental income for many families, it has the potential to undermine the vertical alliance between elites and client families.

As rural farmers, women act as manipulators as well as resistors of changing production relations. Some wealthy elite women have taken advantage of wage labor to increase their profits, while poorer client and elite women have used collective labor as a tool to assure reliable work and income and increase wages. In resistance to increased wage labor, subordinate kin uphold the ideology of mutual help embedded in the client relationship as a way to prevent elites from severing the client tie and, with it, clients' access to land.

The tying of elite-client relations to the idiom of kinship has created bonds of loyalty and community solidarity that make it difficult to disentangle any one part of the relationship without damaging the whole. The ideology of relatedness prevents elites from acting too freely to disengage from client relations, thus minimizing loss of land access for client kin. By articulating social and economic relations through the elite-client tie, client kin continue to have value as dependable sharecroppers and additional labor for ceremonies and other occasions.

Labor relations in this village are hedged about with kin and client ties that act as a brake against individualized wage labor, increased class stratification, and poverty. Other studies have noted the importance of kin or personal ties in maintaining the sharecropper relationship and abating proletarianization or the development of a privileged class.[8] The continued viability of sharecropping as a strategy for land tenure in Taram, even with the availability of wage labor, is consistent with other areas of Southeast Asia where sharecropping has persisted despite agricultural development. In Taram many landless or near-landless farmers remain tenants despite agrarian change because of the benefits of a relationship that gives most households some access to land and provides elites with a source of steady, loyal labor. Its persistence can be credited to the value of the sharecropping relationship, both socially and politically, as well as the value to both elites and clients of maintaining a kinship relationship within the context of a kinship hierarchy. Completely free wage laborers in this community would be worse off than those who participate in the client system. Although as members of subordinate families, client kin have less rights and lower status than their elite elders, they can rely on the client tie to build security and social standing in the village.

Landlord/tenant relationships in Taram go beyond relations of owner/laborer to incorporate other social and ceremonial ties. In this village the transformations of agricultural development are bound by the terms of local culture. There is no simple movement from peasant to proletarian; each change is directed in this instance by kinship, clientage, and rank. Women figure prominently in this process, as both manipulators and resistors of agrarian change. Elite women's continued dominance in agricultural production assures the operation of land and labor within the terms of kinship and rank. Elite women and their client kin are both bound to and invested in a complex relation of land, labor, and obligations that supports the continued interdependence and solidarity of households and maintains a viable peasant community.

NOTES

1. See, for example, Guyer and Peters 1987, Hart 1991, and Moore 1992.
2. During the 1950s, the Indonesian Communist Party (PKI) attempted to change the split to sixty-forty in favor of the sharecropper. This proposal met with considerable resistance by owners and was never successfully implemented in West Sumatra.

3. A gantang is a dry measure that equals approximately three liters of unhusked rice (*padi*).

4. For example, Lina's group has five members, and the other group has six members. Each group harvests 300 *gantang* of rice, but each woman in Lina's group gets a little over seven *gantang* (12 gt. paid per 100 gt. harvested = 36 gt. divided by the number of workers in the group), while the other group earns only 6 *gantang* per person.

5. In practice, things do not always work so smoothly. Enough people are not always available, while sometimes a person is available to work but does not get called.

6. Probably because these groups overlapped, people in the village used a confusing variety of terms to refer to the collective, which in Indonesian is called *kelompok tani*. Sometimes it was called *gotong royong* (community self-help), which was also used to refer to community cleanup days; *julo-julo sawah* (literally, rice field lottery), which is probably derived from the fact that they work many days but get paid only once at harvest; or *kongsi*, a term taken from Chinese that means partnership or association. Kongsi, however, was usually used for the smaller exchange groups, as was the term *lambik ari* (M.)

7. For example, if it usually takes ten women to plant a field in one day, each of whom would make 1,200 rp., the ten women would be paid a total of 12,000 rp. (wages are paid by the day not the hour). The labor group may bring in only six women, who can plant the field in one day. They divide the 12,000 rp. among themselves to earn 2,000 rp. each for their day's labor, 800 rp. more than they would earn working individually as day laborers.

8. See, for example, Coughenour 1992, Gastellu 1987, Robertson 1980, and White 1989.

8

✛

The Politics of Power

In this book I have circled through many facets of a rural Minangkabau village to draw out the different contexts in which power operates, moving from households, to lineage affairs, to ceremonial events and agricultural practices. Despite the fact that historically elite men's power has been defined as official, public power, I view village politics as a multiplicity of nodes of power that incorporates titled men and other functionaries of the *adat* hierarchy within a more complex system. In the previous chapters, I showed that lineage affairs and ceremonial events constitute the core of social life in the village, thus extending elite women's power throughout the village. Here I take a final look at power at the "village level." I turn first to the state-mandated political structure in the village, the village (*desa*) government, in order to explore one final time what constitutes power.

LOCAL POLITICS

As I discussed in chapter 2, titled men have greater access to "public," state-validated venues of power at the village level. During the period of Dutch occupation, men elders were elevated to positions of power beyond that which women held. Under Indonesian state rule, men have again been privileged as heads of households and village leaders. Men use their titles and status as elite lineage elders to gain positions within the state system of administration at the village level and beyond. Few rural women seek to turn their power into political venues outside the community, but some have become powerful in state-sanctioned political offices within the community. Elite women organized a successful local chapter of the Family Welfare Organization (*Pembinaan Kesejahteraan Kelu-*

arga, PKK) in Tanjung Batang. With its orientation to "domestic" issues of family and child welfare, it is somewhat limited in scope. In contrast, village government has broader functions that integrate several categories of people from the village into its offices, primarily titled men, but also influential members of the community. This system has opened the way for a few wealthy elite women to take leadership positions.

A new village administrative system established in 1979 created more opportunities for participation in government as well as opportunities for new status positions. Village administration was reorganized into the village council (*Lembaga Musyawarah Desa*, LMD) and the village security council (*Lembaga Ketahanan Masyarakat Desa*, LKMD). LMD is the smaller and more prestigious council, composed of seven members and neighborhood (*dusun*) heads. In Tanjung Batang all nine members of LMD are from elite lineages. Out of the seven members, six are titled men and one is a woman, a leading member of an elite family. LKMD consists of officers and general members representing various sectional interests within the village: *adat*, religion, youth, and women. It advises the village head on development activities and helps to coordinate all organizational activities at the village level. The members of LKMD pass their plans and recommendations to LMD, whose members then make revisions and send them to the subdistrict head for approval (MacAndrews 1986, Sinaga 1985, Watson 1987).

Members of both councils come from among the leading influential and educated village members. Although most are men *adat* leaders, some council members come from the ranks of wealthy farmers and business people, usually those who are well educated or hold civil service jobs. Villagers make the distinction between *adat* leaders (*pemuka adat*), those whose leadership is based on *adat* principles, and community leaders (*pemuka desa*), prominent and respected, usually well-off members of the village without high rank in the kinship hierarchy (also referred to as *cerdik pandai*, those considered intelligent or brainy). Though these categories are predominantly made up of individuals who are members of elite families, the presence of community leaders, who are called "big people" (*orang besar*), suggests that status categories distinct from kinship rank have become salient in the village.

LKMD consists of twenty-eight members: eight of the nine members of LMD (seven men, one woman), the village officers (all men), the two neighborhood (*dusun*) heads, the leaders of the youth organization *Karang Taruna* (both young men), ten women from PKK, and one woman designated as *Bundo Kanduang* according to state-defined rules (not necessarily the head of a lineage, see Blackwood 1995). Ninety percent of LKMD members are elites; only two come from client families and one woman from a servant family. Women make up 40 percent of LKMD and 11 percent of LMD (one of nine). LKMD women come from the ranks of younger, educated women (mostly in their thirties and forties), who are either *adat* leaders or *orang besar*, and who are also members of PKK (at an

LKMD meeting, eleven out of the twelve women attending were PKK). As PKK representatives, these women are directed to handle issues of family welfare. Thus, women's authority as members of LKMD ostensibly derives from their involvement in the state-sponsored women's program rather than their position as representatives or leaders of their lineages. PKK leaders, however, come from the ranks of up-and-coming elite women, thereby complicating the state's efforts to slot women as domestic authorities and men as public leaders (see Blackwood 1995).

NURANI'S STORY

A closer look at the one woman appointed to the village council (LMD) brings together in one person the multiple and contradictory sites of power in the village. Other stories throughout this book have revealed many aspects of Nurani's life.

As a member of an elite family, Nurani takes her social responsibilities seriously. She is constantly involved in the rounds of ceremonies in the village, always ready to give of her time, whether with the ceremonial preparations or during the ceremony itself. Her knowledge of *adat* is already quite extensive, as evidenced both in her management of ceremonies for her family and her client kin, and her participation in a wide range of ceremonies hosted by other lineages in the hamlet and village. She is a very devout woman, who prays faithfully, fasts, and tithes. As noted in the last chapter, Nurani manages her family's many rice fields and has numerous sharecroppers and laborers under her supervision. Her success in making use of the new farming technologies prompted others to call her a modern farmer (*tani moderen*). Her rice is considered to be high quality and earns a higher price on the market than that of others in the village. Due to her business acumen, she became a rice merchant when her children were in their teens. Consequently, in addition to the numerous people who work for her, many of the village's elite are her clients, including the village head. Not only is Nurani a senior woman in a well-to-do family, she is considered a big person (*orang besar*) in the eyes of village folk. Her visibility and reputation in the community led to her position as the only woman member of the village council.

Much of Nurani's political work as a council member follows the pattern used in family deliberations. Council issues are discussed in private discussions with other women or with the head of LKMD. Women from PKK, including Nurma and Fitriani, come to Nurani before council meetings to discuss the matter at hand and reach some consensus with her. The head of LKMD comes to Nurani's house to discuss both business and village council matters with her. Council meetings maintain the sex-segregated fashion typical of all Minangkabau gatherings as well as the gendered style of discussions. Men sit on one side of the village hall and women sit on the other nearer the

door. The men, many of whom are members of the *adat* council, carry the
discussion, while women interject their opinions only when they disagree. At
one LKMD meeting I attended, three or four out of the eleven men present
did most of the speaking while the others sat quietly. As the meeting progressed, one or two women occasionally voiced an opinion or agreement but
most of their conversation was carried out in whispers among themselves.
Nurani sat attentively with the women, participated in low-voiced discussion
with them, and was one of the few women who spoke up.

Of her participation in discussion, Nurani says she does not need to speak up
if she agrees with the men's statements, her presence only is important. Nurani
is not silenced in these meetings by men's "official" authority; her agreement is
needed for any plans to be approved, as is that of all the members. Rather she follows the Minangkabau pattern for public deliberations, a pattern that allots the
main speaking role to men but demands consensus among all members. If consensus cannot be reached, no decisions are made at the council meeting; people
return home to engage in further consultations until the issue is resolved.

Nurani gained political power in a state-controlled domain through her influence as an elder, landowner, and rice merchant, but there is little support for
women's presence in that domain. How does she feel about her position? Despite
her status as a community leader, Nurani is ambivalent about her role on the
council. She frequently complains that it is too much work for her to be on the
council. She told me she does not have time for council work because of her
responsibilities as a businesswoman and single mother. The meetings are always
late in the evening, she says, and she should be home taking care of her daughter (who was already out of high school at that time). Although she was
appointed to this position because of her status as a well-to-do "modern" businesswoman who is educated and of an elite lineage, her statements conveyed a
sense of ambivalence about stepping into an arena controlled by the state.

Nurani's attitude expresses the contradictions of political power at the "village
level" in West Sumatra. Her ambivalence about operating in a domain that has
been defined as public and masculine speaks to the tensions created by contradictory state, Islamic, and Minangkabau ideologies of gender. Not only are state
political and religious leaders predominantly men, women gain access to state
power primarily as wives of state officials. In these positions their political representation is usually limited to the sphere of "women's affairs," the issues of
home and health, and not broader political and international affairs of state.
Given the state model of men's authority, Nurani finds it difficult to justify taking on a leadership role within the village administration. Like other women
leaders in the community, she tends to downplay the extent of her power and
influence in village affairs.

Although women bridge community *adat* and state structures through their
participation in village government, their ability and desire to operate at that
level is compromised by the state model of men's authority. In fact, I was told

that women used to be embarrassed to participate in village government despite their leadership and capability in lineage affairs. Minangkabau men, in contrast, find less conflict in adhering to state gender ideology and have gained some advantage by it. The long history of colonial and state support for Minangkabau men's representation at the village level has reinforced the propriety of men's leadership in state-controlled village administration meetings. Practically, it has vested elite men with the power to operate outside lineage affairs in a capacity that few women experience. Although women have extensive power within the village, their ambivalence about holding positions in the state-mandated political structure attests to the ability of the state to create and instill new definitions and identities for its citizens. The hegemonic discourses of the state, reformist Islam, and global markets inscribe power as public and masculine, constraining rural Minangkabau women's ability to exert power in state-controlled domains.

NODES OF POWER

In this book I have pulled apart strands of social relations that are tightly entwined. Separating the various strands of agricultural, ceremonial, lineal, and family relations has enabled me to provide a more in-depth portrait of women's power in a rural Minangkabau village. By doing so I may have at times reduced the complexity of people's lives and simplified the density of power that operates in their lives. In this conclusion, I want to reweave some of these strands to show how individual practices and actions are produced by and result in the complex processes called social life.

In a West Sumatran rural village, power does not reside simply in titles and public offices. As we have seen, power even in a rural village is multiply constituted at a number of levels. Because power is multiply constituted, it is somewhat misleading to speak of different levels of power since all these arenas are connected and multiply constructed. Although Western narratives privilege the "public" aspects of power, power operates in many ways in the creation of human social relations (see Foucault 1979, 1980, Williams 1977, Ortner 1990). An emphasis on the "everyday" forms of power is useful as a way to direct attention to the multitude of ordinary, daily practices through which individuals contest and negotiate power. Yet even "everyday" power is limited as a conceptual tool because these small acts tend to be seen as small resistances thrown up against superior forces. I have argued that a more encompassing definition sees power invested in the ability to constitute and reconstitute (create and shape) social practice (see Fraser 1989, Margolis 1989, Moore 1992). Rather than seeing power oriented to a series of hierarchically aligned positions, the complexity of power in a rural Minangkabau village requires a re-vision of power as a multiplicity of nodes and interlinkages crisscrossing the village. I have visualized the particular nodes and linkages I describe for Taram in figure 8.1.

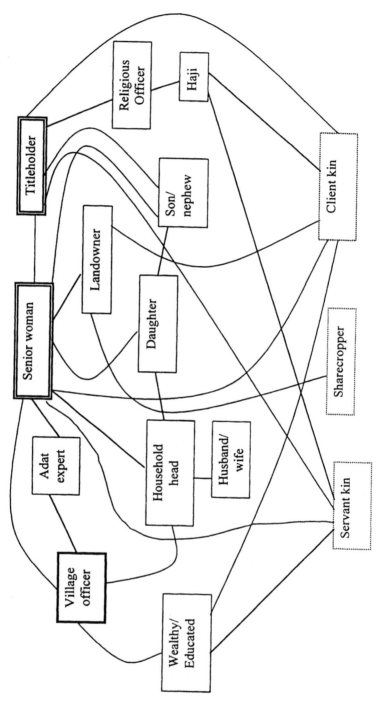

Figure 8.1 Nodes of Power

In this figure there are no categories labelled simply "men" or "women" because gender is always already socially defined and multiply constituted. The social identities that people occupy each have their own associations with power, but these shift over time through age and experience—for example, daughter to senior woman—and connection with other categories on the web. I have positioned senior women and titled men at the top of the web and connected them to other positions they can occupy as well as to those they have power over. Servant kin, sharecroppers, and client kin are positioned at the bottom, but they too have access to several other nodes of power (religious officer, household head, *haji*, wealthy/educated) that affects their relative standing in the community. Although I have not specifically included in this figure the various discourses that filter through and influence the community, these are apparent in the categories named. For example, *adat* expert represents local discourse; village officer, the state; *haji*, Islam; and so on.

In terms of a rural Minangkabau rice-farming village, power operates in multiple arenas in which gender, age, and rank figure prominently. Power is vested in senior women as well as senior men as the elders of their lineages, in elites as well as village officials, in wealth as well as in rank. Power operates in several nodes that are very much gendered. Women as "mothers" (*Bundo Kanduang*) of the lineage and men as "protectors" of the lineage each have certain rights and privileges, as do sons and daughters. Certain practices that privilege men coexist with practices and discourses that privilege women. Although gender ideology marks men and women with different rights and privileges, it does not encode men's hegemonic superiority. Terms such as "dominant" and "subordinate" fail to convey the complexity of power vested in elite men and women; they are incorporated in webs of power with many different orientations. Colonial, religious, and state practices further complicate the gendering of power by privileging certain forms of "official" and "public" power that have a decidedly masculinist cast. This privileging has created ambiguity in people's minds about the operation of power in state-sanctioned structures without, however, undermining women's power in the village.

For senior women and titled men, power resides in the ability to substantiate or set aside ideologies of relatedness, mutual assistance, and respect. It resides in the ability to maintain rank distinctions and to act as gatekeepers by defining and reinterpreting "custom" and controlling access to higher rank. Elites' power of approval means they can prevent client kin from using status symbols, such as large gold bracelets, large bridal headpieces, or water buffalo meat, that belong to the elite rank. Elite women control their own social identity and that of their sublineage through controlling daughters' marriages, through reaffirming and asserting their rights to ancestral property, by gaining access to more land, and by asserting their status at ritual events through the performance of mid- or high adat rituals.

Within the household power is not simply based on domestic relations; it is `embedded in kinship ties. Senior women are not simply mothers; they are elders in control of subordinate kin. Because of senior women's control of land, off-spring and kin must bargain with senior women for access to resources. Women's right to the produce from lineage land remains unchallenged. In fact, women take for granted their right to the harvest and do not ask anyone's permission concerning its use. Younger kinsmen seeking land to work must get the permission of the senior woman and may not always be successful if their mother's rice land is limited. A senior woman may be moved to help her offspring, but can never be forced to give up land that she controls. She makes the final decision, forcing her offspring to acquiesce to it.

Control of land also means that senior women have power over villagers who depend on them for access to land or wage labor. Through an extensive network of sharecroppers and laborers, wealthy elite women establish a powerful and influential presence in the village that can be realized in their ability to sway lineage deliberations or gain benefits for their family from village administration. For wealthy client women, their status as landowners with a sizable following of supportive families gives them greater influence in the negotiations with elites over ceremonial practice.

Matriliny and Power

Senior women's power is situated within and informed by matrilineal ideology. Matrilineal ideology forms the structuring principle that Minangkabau continually reconstitute through a variety of practices within the context of colonialism, the Indonesian state, and global markets. Materially the key practices that substantiate women's power include matrilineal inheritance and matrilocal residence, the practice of passing land and houses from mother to daughters, and the practice of daughters residing in or near their mothers' houses. Ideologically these practices include recognition of the right of elite woman as lineage elder to decide ceremonial practice, control subordinate kin, and manage and control ancestral land and houses. For men it includes recognition of the brother's right to protect house, land, and sister's children and forego rights in his wife's children. The operation of matrilineal practices in the village make understandable a mother's control of the matrihouse and the lands associated with it despite colonial and state efforts to put land into men's hands. It also makes understandable a daughter's ability to control a nuclear household and her land apart from her husband despite the state's insistence that her husband is the head of household.

Gender relations in a rural Minangkabau village provide an interesting contrast to those in a patrilineal society. Typically a married woman has little power as a daughter in her father's lineage and must continually struggle for recognition and rights as a person within her husband's lineage. Under matrilineal practice, although men marry out, they maintain a strong interest in the affairs of their matrilineage. The duality of men's relations to wives and sisters serves to diminish the tensions created by a husband's status as guest in his wife's house. Although a husband has little control over the affairs of his wife's matrilineage, his voice is equal to every other in his own matrilineage. Further, his responsibilities as mother's brother or titled man are important to the continuing prestige of the lineage. Minangkabau men as fathers and husbands have limited power but it is balanced by their primary identity and source of power as brothers in a matrilineage.

Some feminist theorists envision women as oppressed by the structures of household and family. Although this perspective has created compelling theories of marginalization, resistance, and borderlands, it is not an adequate representation of all Third World women. It tends to undercut the political implications of women's agency in their households and larger communities. For rural Minangkabau the picture is different. Minangkabau women constitute themselves, as heirs and heads of sublineages, producing their own meanings. They create and recreate households and matrilineal relations in which they are privileged with certain economic and social rights that men lack. Rural Minangkabau women are neither oppressed subjects of the state nor subordinate participants in a masculinist hegemony, but agents and actors in their own lives.

Neither is there one rural woman but a diversity of positions cross-cut by age, rank, and wealth. The differences in women's access to power underscore the multiplicity of women's subject positions in rural Minangkabau villages. Even mother-daughter relationships illustrate that neither "mother" nor "daughter" constitutes a single category of interest but depends on and reflects rank and wealth, education and careers. Both generations are aware of and articulate contemporary discourses, at the same time reconstituting their own sense of self and family in line with matrilineal practice.

MODERNITY AND THE VILLAGE

The Indonesian state is not a monolithic entity, yet the policies and practices that I have referenced in this book constitute a coherent ideology set in place to manage its citizens and their productive activities. State principles of equality and modernization, expressed through the media, in political speeches, and in the schools, have become part of Minangkabau consciousness. State ideologies create conflict between the housewife ideal and the position of *Bundo Kanduang*, between a middle-class lifestyle and the mud of farm work, between the possibilities of wealth and the constraints of rank. Nevertheless, as I have argued, Minangkabau *adat* as an alternative hegemony carries significant weight in the construction of people's identities. State and other discourses have not supplanted local meanings. Rather, as villagers negotiate their lives, they make use of these ideologies even as they weave them into the ideologies of Minangkabau rank and gender, kinship and matriliny.

In terms of elite-client relations, which I have examined from a number of perspectives, including lineal, ceremonial, and agricultural relations, they are all entwined within the ideology of relatedness (*kamanakan*). For example, women control land and thereby have power over their sharecroppers and laborers but that power is also bound by expectations of mutual assistance, generosity, and solidarity with kin. Sharecroppers are not just contract laborers; they are reconstituted under the trope of *famili* (kin) as part of the elite kin group. The changes in farm relations prompted by agricultural development have exerted subtle pressure on landowners and sharecroppers to redefine mutual obligations, intensifying a struggle over the rights and responsibilities of elites and client kin. But every *rupiah* paid for labor is not simply a token on the road to (late) capitalism. The elite-client relation and the ideology of relatedness remain important keys to the direction of change, demonstrating that even capitalist forces are reworked within the framework of matrilineal ideology.

In its efforts to gain control of its citizens, the Indonesian state has attempted to undermine village kinship. The ideology of equality encoded in the *Pancasila* provides grounds to challenge the kinship hierarchy. At the same time, the state recognizes and affirms social stratification based on the accumulation of wealth and prestige. Both elite and client families acknowledge the state principle of equality, but kinship rank continues to operate as a salient feature of social identity because, on the one hand, it is entwined with ideas of wealth and prestige, which the state validates, and on the other, it is bound by the ideology of relatedness, which *adat* affirms.

Because state ideology supports alternative readings of status, lower-ranked villagers use it to underwrite claims to higher rank. In post colonial Indonesia, the symbols and attributes of the elite are within the reach of larger numbers of client families. Elites have the advantage over clients historically because their wealth has allowed them to attain higher levels of education and to forge long-standing connections with state officials. Only elite men in the past were chosen to fill state positions and still today argue successfully that such positions rightly belong to them. Yet the availability of education, high-status jobs, and greater opportunities in business means that clients can find alternative routes to forge new social identities. In their efforts to negotiate status, clients like Anna or servant kin like Mariam take advantage of transnational connections, including their ties to the global market as entrepreneurs or "modern" successful farmers, their connections to Mecca through the *haj*, and their own budding connections to the state through civil servant positions.

Client kin draw on these connections as evidence of their respectability, success, and worthiness and argue that such attributes make them equals of elites. As I explored in chapter 7, these families negotiate for higher rank through a variety of means, the most visible occurring in the production and performance of ceremonial events. Elite women and men act as gatekeepers to prevent the erosion of their own claims to rank, but the more client families resemble elite families in their material success and positions of authority within the state, the more elites will be forced to accommodate the desires of their client kin. Client families use these global connections, however, not to overturn rank but to create distinction for their own families within matrilineal practice. The claims they make seek to broaden the definition of who is acceptable as elite kin and thereby who has access to elite power. Although client kin draw on ideologies of class and modernity to assert their claims, their actions are framed within the matrilineal ideology of rural Minangkabau communities.

For servant kin, the greater barriers to moving up in the kinship hierarchy have forced many of them ultimately to abandon the struggle to achieve a respectable identity in the village. For some, the simplest solution has been to move out of the village to urban areas where no one will question their background. In these locales they can be more successful using the state's ideology of equality and access to education or civil service to establish their place as Indonesian citizens. For others who stay in the village, the claims of modernity and the changing attitudes of elites like Irwati may lead to a more equalizing interpretation of adat.

Rural Minangkabau villages reconstitute the state's model for development and modernity in the context of their own rich body of practices and discourses. This process has resulted in complex conflicts and shifts in social identity and power within the village. Yet state hegemony is not complete. Minangkabau villagers tend to conduct their lives in ways congruent with state ideologies, the disharmonies downplayed, because people remember only too well the devastating results of the rebellion in the late 1950s and the numbers who died or were permanently imprisoned. But people in this rural village are not simply struggling against oppressive overlords, steamrolling development, or an all-powerful state. Neither can their actions simply be constituted as a form of resistance. The processes in this village reveal the multiplicities of power and the intricately woven responses to local and global structures.

The rural village I have presented here does not stand in for all Minangkabau villages; its members do not represent all Minangkabau in the choices that they make. The particular characteristics of Taram differentiate it from many other Minangkabau villages, from its thriving wet-rice agriculture, successful shift to cash cropping, vibrant social life, and interpretations of *adat*. Although Taram does contain many of the currents flowing through Minangkabau and Southeast Asian villages, its abundant rice land offers its inhabitants certain possibilities no longer viable in other areas of West Sumatra or Southeast Asia. Land is key to the maintenance and negotiation of status and rank, and the on-going reconstitution of a matrilineal ideology that empowers women. Women's control of land enables them to control and reconstitute kin relations and the ideology of relatedness to maintain their power and privilege as senior women.

Because this study focuses on social conflict and compromise—between generations, genders, and ranks—I have given only a partial version of rural Minangkabau life. Although I have argued for the complexities of power, rural life holds more complex meanings still than I have offered here. My experience in the village suggests that through the ideology of relatedness, ceremonial practice and lineage negotiations are more than just ways to gain loyal followers or to keep kin indebted. There are ways of maintaining community and expressing the importance of kin. Kinship frames people's lives, even as it frames the structure of the Minangkabau big house. The big house speaks to the power of the senior woman and the vitality of her offspring, the importance of her brother, and the strength of the bond with all her kin. It assures me that Minangkabau people will continue to find ways to articulate their vision of the world despite the powerful currents flowing through their lives.

Appendix

Notes on Minangkabau Kinship

Taram has a total of seven clans. Each clan is composed of three or four lineages (*payuang*, M.), and each lineage contains a number of sublineages (*kaum*). There are twenty-four lineages and approximately 160 elite sublineages (*kaum*) in the village. The seven clans in Taram are: Pitopang, Sumpadang, Piliang Gadang, Piliang Lawas, Sumabur, Bodi, and Melayu.[1] Of these clans, the four original clans were said to be Bodi, Piliang, Melayu, and Pitopang. Members of the other three elite clans arrived in Taram somewhat later than the first, according to Taram folk history.

All sublineages within the same lineage are thought to be related in the distant past, but few sublineages can identify their genealogical link with another sublineage. Individuals are not allowed to marry within their own lineage but may marry someone in the same clan, although this restriction is not consistently applied.

Although usage varies, depending on claims individuals are making about their closeness to other kin with titles, people in Taram usually use the term *kaum* and not *paruik* to refer to the group that shares an ancestral house, land, and title. For instance, people referred to ancestral land as *milik kaum*, owned by the *kaum*. A kaum was also said to be *saibu*, of one mother, referring to the relation to the eldest woman of the group. *Paruik* was rarely used in conversation, and only to identify a larger group of kin with more than one title. *Saparuik*, I was told, includes a larger group than the *kaum*. They are kin who are already separated into several *kaum* but are still considered to have a common ancestress.

The titled men and *Bundo Kanduang* of the clan system occupy ranked positions. The *Bundo Kanduang* and titled men of each clan are called the *pucuk* (head; *pucuk* refers to the tip of a leaf, shoot, or sprout). The titled man of a lineage holds the rank *penghulu tuo kampuang*. There are twenty-four *tuo kampuang*; each *penghulu tuo kampuang* has a number of *penghulu andiko* below

195

him who are the titled men of the sublineages. For each titled man there is a corresponding woman who holds the position of *Bundo Kanduang*.

The twenty-four *tuo kampuang* in Taram are referred to collectively as *penghulu ka ampek suku* ("titled males of the four clans," although there are now seven clans in Taram). According to Dt. Rajo, this clan system incorporates both the Koto-Piliang (hierarchical) and Bodi-Caniago (democratic) principles (see Josselin de Jong 1952, Kato 1982, and Ng 1987:23-24 for a discussion of these principles). The Taram clan system actually maintains both distinctions. The *penghulu* are arranged hierarchically: the twenty-four heads (*pucuk*) of the lineages make up the *adat* council for the village, each with an equal voice (democratic at council level), and each has higher status than the several *penghulu* below him. Yet in all ceremonial events and deliberations, all *penghulu* sit at the same level and are given identical trays of food, signifying that all are equal. There is no one *penghulu* in Taram who has the highest rank. There were 164 titles recognized in Taram in 1990 of which 120 were actively filled, according to a list of titles and ranks compiled for me by my consultant Dt. Rajo (a pseudonym). The remainder of the titles have been "put away" (*terlipat*) by the sublineage either because there was no one qualified or willing to claim the title or the family could not afford a ceremony to invest a candidate with the title.

Titles are distinguished names that begin with the term *Datuk* (Sir, abbreviated Dt.) followed in Taram by several royal appellations (and sometimes humorous adjectives) such as Sir Excellency the Tall King (*Datuk Paduko Simarajo nan Panjang*) or Sir Duke the Whining King (*Datuk Tan Simarajo nan Bangiang*). Titled men are not normally addressed by their birth name. In everyday conversation they are called simply Datuk, or a shortened form of their title, usually Datuk plus the last name in the title (in the first title above, it would be shortened to Datuk Panjang, or Sir Tall). When there are several titled men bearing the same last title, they are addressed by the short title followed by their birth name.

KINSHIP RANKS IN TANJUNG BATANG

Each clan within Taram has a number of client and servant families attached to it. Of fifty-eight sublineages in Tanjung Batang, twenty-five are elite rank (five of whom are newly titled), twenty-seven client, and six servant. The following chart lists the number of sublineages (families) of each rank belonging to each clan. These figures are only for those sublineages of each clan living in Tanjung Batang. Although I use three broad categories to identify kin groups in the village, there are further distinctions that are made in Taram. Newcomers are divided into those who have been adopted into an original clan (client kin, *orang bamamak*) and those who have been given permission to retain their own clan affiliation and title, if it is the same as one in Taram (*orang datang*). Despite having titles, the second group is distinct from the original clans and does not have

Table A.1 Number of Families from Each Clan Living in Tanjung Batang							
	Pito	*Spdg*	*Sum*	*P.L.*	*P.G.*	*Bodi*	*Mel*	*Total*
Elite	3	4	5	1	6	1	0	20
Newly Titled	0	0	1	2	2	0	0	5
Client	9	2	7	1	2	5	1	27
Servant	0	2	0	2	0	0	2	6

Note: Pito = Pitopang, Spdg = Sumpadang, Sum = Sumabur, P.L. = Piliang Lawas, P.G. = Piliang Gadang, Mel = Melayu.

the same influence in clan meetings because its members have only been in the village for one or two generations. Newly titled families are former client familes who have been given titles from the original clans within the last two or three generations. Their rank as elites has solidified, although it may take a few more years before their former rank is completely forgotten. For the purposes of this book, I collapse the newly titled into the elite category, while the *orang datang* are included in the client category.

NOTES

[1] I use the spelling given to me by my consultant for these clan names. In some other areas of West Sumatra, Sumabur is spelled Simabur.

Glossary

adat	social custom, beliefs and laws
baju kurung	long tunic or overblouse worn by Minangkabau women, usually made of sheer fabric with long sleeves and extending below the waist
bako	the matrilineage of one's father
bamamak	to be adopted into an elite lineage as client kin (M.)
baralek	ceremonial feast (M.)
beras	husked rice
bundo kanduang	mother, senior woman, ancestress, wise woman (lit., womb mother); also the name of the mythical queen of the Minangkabau
datuk	term of address for a titled man (*penghulu*), equivalent to "Sir"; abbreviated Dt.
dayang	to serve, or a member of the servant class
desa	village; also hamlet. Under new administrative rules, *desa* is the smallest unit of the Indonesian state and in many cases is equivalent to a hamlet. Prior to 1983, the village hamlets were called *jorong*. For Taram, *desa* refers to a hamlet.
gantang	measurement of rice, approximately three liters in bulk (abbreviated gt.)

haji	honorific title for one who has made the pilgrimage (*haj*) to Mecca. Villagers do not distinguish between men or women *haji*.
harta pusaka	ancestral property, including house, rice land, gardens, burial plot, ceremonial clothing and title (*harato pusako*, M.)
ibu	mother, also term of address for a woman; see also *mak*
ibu rumah tangga	housewife
kabupaten	district or regency (subdistrict of a province; West Sumatra is a province according to the administrative structure laid out by the Indonesian state)
kamanakan	one's nieces and nephews, or more generally one's relatives both fictive and "real" (Ind., *kemenakan*)
kampung	a neighborhood or housing cluster of related kin
Karang Taruna	neighborhood youth association
kaum	the smallest unit of kin comprised of an extended matrilineal group that shares ancestral property in common, is related to a common ancestress, and possesses a title in common
kecamatan	subdistrict of a kabupaten
kedai	small shop or food stall
kepala desa	village head or mayor
kepala keluarga	head of household
lambik ari	exchange labor group (M.)
mak	mother (M.)
mamak	mother's brother or kinsmen, or more generally, the members of an elite family
mendoa	to pray, also used to refer to a small ceremony in which only prayers are said
merantau	to migrate to areas outside one's home village
mufakat	consensus of all kin group members
musyawarah	group deliberation or consultation
nagari	village (M.) (Ind., *negeri*)

nenek	grandmother or grandfather
nikah	marriage; usually refers to the vows taken before an Islamic religious specialist
ninik-mamak	lineage elders
orang asli	original inhabitants, elites
orang bamamak	people who have been adopted into an elite lineage
orang datang	newcomers to the village
padi	unhusked rice
paduoan	land tenure arrangement whereby the produce is split in half between owner and worker; the Minangkabau term for sharecropping
Pancasila	the five guiding principles of the Indonesian state
pasumandan	woman married to a man of one's matrilineage, daughter-in-law
payuang	lineage, a group of sublineages sharing an unknown common ancestress (Ind., *payung*)
peci	rimless black velvet cap worn by men
pelaminan	highly decorated dais on which the bridal couple sits
penghulu	titled man, titular head of a matrilineal kinship group (M., *panghulu*)
pucuk	the tip of something, like a leaf, shoot, or sprout
rantau	traditionally, the outlying districts of the Minangkabau homeland; now refers to anyplace outside one's home village
rumah gadang	lineage house, lit., big house; a Minangkabau term that refers to the distinctive Minangkabau houses with peaked roofs resembling water buffalo horns
rupiah	Indonesian currency (abbreviated rp.); during 1989-90 the average exchange rate was $1 U.S. = 1,800 rp., during 1996, $1 U.S. = 2,800 rp.
salat	the obligatory prayer that must be performed five times a day in order to fulfill one of the pillars of the Islamic faith
sarong	a wrapped skirt made from a single piece of cloth

sawah	irrigated rice land
selendang	a long rectangular scarf worn by a woman around her neck or draped over one shoulder
sirih	an offering consisting of betel leaf and areca nut
songket	cloth embroidered with gold or silver thread
suku	clan
sunting	ornamental tinfoil headdress worn by a bride
surau	an Islamic prayer house
syariah	Islamic law
tanjung	village
tokéh	rice merchant, a local term apparently derived from the term for an employer or boss (*tauké*)
tolong-menolong	mutual aid
tunangan	engagement ceremony

References Cited

Abdullah, Taufik. 1966. Adat and Islam: An examination of conflict in Minangkabau. *Indonesia* 2: 1–24.

——. 1972. Modernization in the Minangkabau world: West Sumatra in the early decades of the twentieth century. Pp. 179–245 in *Culture and Politics in Indonesia*, ed. Claire Holt. Ithaca, N.Y.: Cornell University Press.

Abu-Lughod, Lila. 1990. Can there be a feminist ethnography? *Women and Performance: A Journal of Feminist Theory* 5(1): 7–27.

Ambler, John Sterling. 1989. Adat and aid: Management of small-scale irrigation in West Sumatra, Indonesia. Ph.D. diss., Cornell University.

Andaya, Barbara. 1994. The changing religious role of women in pre-modern South East Asia. *South East Asia Research* 2(2): 99–116.

Andaya, Barbara, and Yoneo Ishii. 1992. Religious developments in Southeast Asia c. 1500–1800. Pp. 508–71 in *Cambridge History of Southeast Asia*, ed. Nicholas Tarling. Cambridge: Cambridge University Press.

Anderson, Benjamin R. 1981. The idea of power in Javanese culture. Pp. 1–28 in *Culture and Politics in Indonesia*, ed. Claire Holt. Ithaca, N.Y.: Cornell University Press.

Aripurnami, Sita. 1996. A feminist comment on the Sinetron presentation of Indonesia women. Pp. 249–58 in *Fantasizing the Feminine in Indonesia*, ed. Laurie J. Sears. Durham, N.C.: Duke University Press.

Atkinson, Jane M., and Shelly Errington, eds. 1990. *Power and Difference: Gender in Island Southeast Asia*. Stanford: Stanford University Press.

Bachtiar, Harsja W. 1967. Negeri Taram: A Minangkabau village community. Pp. 348–485 in *Villages in Indonesia*, ed. Koetjaraningrat. Ithaca, N.Y.: Cornell University Press.

Behar, Ruth. 1995. Introduction: Out of exile. Pp. 1–29 in *Women Writing Culture*, ed. Ruth Behar and Deborah A. Gordon. Berkeley: University of California Press.

Benda-Beckmann, Franz von. 1979. *Property in Social Continuity: Continuity and Change in the Maintenance of Property Relations through Time in Minangkabau, West Sumatra*. The Hague: Martinus Nijhoff.

Benda-Beckmann, Franz, and Keebet von Benda-Beckmann. 1985. Transformation and change in Minangkabau. Pp. 207–34 in *Change and Continuity in Minangkabau: Local, Regional, and Historical Perspectives on West Sumatra*, ed. Lynn Thomas and Franz von Benda-Beckmann. Southeast Asia Series, no. 71. Athens: Ohio University.

———. 1988. Adat and religion in Minangkabau and Ambon. Pp. 195–212 in *Time Past, Time Present, Time Future: Perspectives on Indonesian Culture*, ed. H. J. M. Claessen and D. S. Moyer. Providence, R.I.: Foris Publications.

Benda-Beckmann, Keebet von. 1984. *The Broken Stairways to Consensus: Village Justice and State Courts in Minangkabau*. Cinnaminson, N.J.: Foris Publications.

———. 1990. Development, law, and gender-skewing. *Journal of Legal Pluralism and Unofficial Law* 30/31: 87–120.

Blackwood, Evelyn. 1995. Senior women, model mothers, and dutiful wives: Managing gender contradictions in a Minangkabau village. Pp. 124–58 in *Bewitching Women, Pious Men: Gender and Body Politics in Southeast Asia*, ed. Aihwa Ong and Michael Peletz. Berkeley: University of California Press.

———. 1997. Women, land and labor: Negotiating clientage and kinship in a Minangkabau peasant community. *Ethnology* 36(4): 277–93.

———. 1998. Tombois in West Sumatra: Constructing masculinity and erotic desire. *Cultural Anthropology* 13(4): 491–521.

———. n.d. Representing Women: The Politics of Minangkabau Adat Writings.

Bolyanatz, Alexander. 1996. Musings on matriliny: Understandings and social relations among the Sursurunga of New Ireland. Pp. 81–97 in *Gender, Kinship, Power: A Comparative and Interdisciplinary History*, ed. Mary Jo Maynes, Ann Waltner, Birgitte Soland, and Ulrike Strasser. New York: Routledge.

Bourdieu, Pierre. 1977. *Outline of a Theory of Practice*. Cambridge: Cambridge University Press.

Bray, Francesca. 1983. Patterns of evolution in rice-growing societies. *Journal of Peasant Studies* 11(1): 3–33.

Brenner, Suzanne A. 1995. Why women rule the roost: Rethinking Javanese ideologies of gender and self-control. Pp. 19–50 in *Bewitching Women, Pious Men: Gender and Body Politics in Southeast Asia*, ed. Aihwa Ong and Michael Peletz. Berkeley: University of California Press.

———. 1998. *The Domestication of Desire: Women, Wealth and Modernity in Java*. Princeton, N.J.: Princeton University Press.

Brown, Michael F. 1996. On resisting resistance. *American Anthropologist* 98(4): 729–35.

Butler, Judith. 1990. *Gender Trouble: Feminism and the Subversion of Identity*. New York: Routledge.

Carsten, Janet. 1997. *The Heat of the Hearth: The Processing of Kinship in a Malay Fishing Community*. Oxford: Clarendon Press.

Carsten, Janet, and Stephen Hugh-Jones. 1995. *About the House: Lévi-Strauss and Beyond*. Cambridge: Cambridge University Press.

Chu, Godwin, Alfian, and Wilbur Schramm. 1991. *Social Impact of Satellite Television in Rural Indonesia*. Singapore: Asian Mass Communication Research and Information Center.

Cole, Fay-Cooper. 1936. Family, clan and phratry in Central Sumatra. Pp. 19–27 in *Essays in Anthropology Presented to A. L. Kroeber*, ed. Robert H. Lowie. Berkeley: University of California Press.

Collier, Jane F., and Sylvia J. Yanagisako, eds. 1987. *Gender and Kinship: Essays toward a Unified Analysis*. Stanford, Calif.: Stanford University Press.

Collins, Jane L. 1986. The household and relations of production in southern Peru. *Comparative Studies in Society and History* 28(4): 651–71.

Coughenour, C. Milton. 1992. "Captured by" but not "prisoners" of capitalism: Strategies of limited-resource farm households in Sudan. *Journal of Asian and African Studies* 27(3/4): 202–15.

Dall, Greg. 1982. The traditional Acehnese house, Pp. 34–61 in *The Malay-Islamic World of Sumatra: Studies in Polities and Culture*, ed. John Maxwell. Melbourne: Monash University Centre of Southeast Asian Studies.

Deere, Carmen Diana. 1990. *Household and Class Relations: Peasants and Landlords in Northern Peru*. Berkeley: University of California Press.

Dick, H. W. 1985. The rise of a middle class and the changing concept of equity in Indonesia: An interpretation. *Indonesia* 39: 71–92.

di Leonardo, Micaela, ed. 1991. Gender, culture and political economy: Feminist anthropology in historical perspective. Pp. 1–48 in *Gender at the Crossroads of Knowledge: Feminist Anthropology in the Postmodern Era*, ed. Micaela di Leonardo. Berkeley: University of California Press.

Directorate General. 1977. *Cooperative Development in Indonesia up to 1976*. Jakarta: Directorate General of Cooperatives.

Djajadiningrat-Nieuwenhuis, Madelon. 1987. Ibuism and priyayization: Path to power? Pp. 43–51 in *Indonesian Women in Focus: Past and Present Notions*, ed. E. Locher-Scholten and A. Niehof. Dordrecht, the Netherlands: Foris Publications.

Dobbin, Christine. 1974. Islamic revivalism in Minangkabau at the turn of the nineteenth century. *Modern Asian Studies* 8(3): 316–45.

———. 1977. Economic change in Minangkabau as a factor in the rise of the Padri Movement, 1784–1830. *Indonesia* 23: 1–37.

———. 1983. *Islamic Revivalism in a Changing Peasant Economy: Central Sumatra, 1784–1847*. Scandinavian Institute of Asian Studies Monograph Series no. 47. London: Curzon Press.

Donham, Donald L. 1990. *History, Power, Ideology: Central Issues in Marxism and Anthropology*. Cambridge: Cambridge University Press.

Dove, Michael R. 1988. *The Real and Imagined Role of Culture in Development: Case Studies from Indonesia*. Honolulu: University of Hawaii Press.

Drakard, Jane. 1990. *A Malay Frontier: Unity and Duality in a Sumatran Kingdom*. Southeast Asia Program. Ithaca, N.Y.: Cornell University Press.

Durkheim, Emile. 1938. *The Rules of Sociological Method*. New York: Free Press.

Dwyer, Daisy, and Judith Bruce, eds. 1988. *A Home Divided: Women and Income in the Third World*. Stanford, Calif.: Stanford University Press.

Echols, John M., and Hassan Shadily. 1989. *Kamus Indonesia Inggris: An Indonesian-English Dictionary*, 3d ed. Jakarta: PT Gramedia.

Ellen, Roy. 1983. Social theory, ethnography and the understanding of practical Islam in South-East Asia. Pp. 50–91 in *Islam in Southeast Asia*, ed. M. B. Hooker. Leiden, the Netherlands: E. J. Brill.

Errington, Shelly. 1990. Recasting sex, gender, and power: A theoretical and regional overview. Pp. 1–58 in *Power and Difference: Gender in Island Southeast Asia*, ed. Jane M. Atkinson and Shelly Errington. Stanford, Calif.: Stanford University Press.

Esmara, Hendra. 1974. *The Economic Development of West Sumatra: Collected Papers.* Padang, Indonesia: Andalas University and Provincial Development Planning Agency, West Sumatra.

Fadlillah. 1996. Wanita, Malin Kundang, dan Feminisme. *Singgalang*, June 30: 3.

Faubion, James D. 1996. Kinship is dead, long live kinship: A review article. *Comparative Studies in Society and History* 38(1): 67–91.

Fett, I. 1983. Women's land in Negeri Sembilan. Pp. 73–95 in *Women's Work and Women's Roles: Economics and Everyday Life in Indonesia, Malaysia and Singapore*, ed. Lenore Manderson. Canberra: Australian National University.

Flax, Jane. 1990. Postmodernism and gender relations in feminist theory. Pp. 39–62 in *Feminism/Postmodernism*, ed. Linda Nicholson. New York: Routledge.

Folbre, Nancy. 1988. The black four of hearts: Toward a new paradigm of household economics. Pp. 248–64 in *A Home Divided: Women and Income in the Third World*, ed. Daisy Dwyer and Judith Bruce. Stanford, Calif.: Stanford University Press.

Foucault, Michel. 1979. *Discipline and Punish: The Birth of the Prison*. New York: Vintage Books.

———. 1980. *Power/Knowledge: Selected Interviews and Other Writings, 1972–1977.* New York: Pantheon Books.

Fox, James J., ed. 1980. *The Flow of Life: Essays on Eastern Indonesia*. Cambridge: Harvard University Press.

———. 1993. Comparative perspectives on Austronesian houses: An introductory essay. Pp. 1–28 in *Inside Austronesian Houses: Perspectives on Domestic Design for Living*, ed. James J. Fox. Canberra: Australian National University.

Fraser, Nancy. 1989. *Unruly Practices: Power, Discourse, and Gender in Contemporary Social Theory*. Minneapolis: University of Minnesota Press.

Gailey, Christine. 1987. *Kinship to Kingship: Gender Hierarchy and State Formation in the Tongan Islands*. Austin: University of Texas Press.

Gastellu, Jean-Marc. 1987. Matrilineages, economic groups, and differentiation in West Africa: A note. *Development and Change* 18: 271–80.

Geertz, Clifford. 1960. *The Religion of Java*. Chicago: University of Chicago Press.

Geertz, Hildred. 1963. Indonesian cultures and communities. Pp. 24–96 in *Indonesia*, ed. Ruth T. McVey. New Haven, Conn.: Human Relations Area File.

Ginsburg, Faye, and Anna Lowenhaupt Tsing, eds. 1990. *Uncertain Terms: Negotiating Gender in American Culture*. Boston: Beacon Press.

Gramsci, Antonio. 1971. *Selections from the Prison Notebooks of Antonio Gramsci*, trans. Quintin Hoare and Geoffrey Smith. New York: International Publishers.

Grewal, Inderpal, and Caren Kaplan. 1994. Introduction: Transnational feminist practices and questions of postmodernity. Pp. 1–33 in *Scattered Hegemonies: Postmodernity and Transnational Feminist Practices*, ed. Inderpal Grewal and Caren Kaplan. Minneapolis: University of Minnesota Press.

Gutmann, Matthew C. 1993. Ritual of resistance: A critique of the theory of everyday forms of resistance. *Latin American Perspectives* 20(2): 74–92.

Guyer, Jane I. 1986. Intra-household processes and farming systems research: Perspectives from anthropology. Pp. 92–104 in *Understanding Africa's Rural Households and Farming Systems*, ed. Joyce Moock. Boulder, Colo.: Westview Press.

Guyer, Jane I., and Pauline E. Peters. 1987. Introduction: Conceptualizing the household: Issues of theory and policy in Africa. *Development and Change* 18: 197–214.

Hadler, Jeffrey. 1998. Home, fatherhood, succession: Three generations of Amrullahs in twentieth-century Indonesia. *Indonesia* 65.

Hakimy, H. Idrus Dt. Rajo Penghulu 1994a. *Pegangan Penghulu, Bundo Kanduang, dan Pidato Alua Pasambahan Adat di Minangkabau*, 4th ed. Bandung, Indonesia: Remadja Rosdakarya.

———. 1994b. *Pokok-Pokok Pengetahuan Adat Alam Minangkabau*, 6th ed. Bandung, Indonesia: Remadja Rosdakarya.

Hall, Stuart. 1988. The toad in the garden: Thatcherism among the theorists. Pp. 35–57 in *Marxism and the Interpretation of Culture*, ed. Cary Nelson and Lawrence Grossberg. Urbana: University of Illinois Press.

Halperin, Rhoda H. 1994. *Cultural Economies Past and Present*. Austin: University of Texas Press.

Haraway, Donna. 1988. Situated knowledges: The science question in feminism and the privilege of partial perspective. *Feminist Studies* 14(3): 575–99.

Hart, Gillian. 1986. *Power, Labor and Livelihood: Processes of Change in Rural Java*. Berkeley: University of California Press.

———. 1989. Agrarian change in the context of state patronage. Pp. 31–49 in *Agrarian Transformations: Local Processes and the State in Southeast Asia*, ed. Gillian Hart, Andrew Turton, and Benjamin White. Berkeley: University of California Press.

———. 1991. Engendering everyday resistance: Gender, patronage and production politics in rural Malaysia. *Journal of Peasant Studies* 19(1): 93–121.

———. 1992. Imagined unities: Constructions of 'the household' in economic theory. Pp. 111–29 in *Understanding Economic Process*, ed. Sutti Ortiz and Susan Lees. New York: University Press of America.

Hart, Gillian, Andrew Turton, and Benjamin White, eds. 1989. *Agrarian Transformations: Local Processes and the State in Southeast Asia*. Berkeley: University of California Press.

Hefner, Robert W. 1990. *The Political Economy of Mountain Java: An Interpretive History*. Berkeley: University of California Press.

———. 1997. Islamization and democratization in Indonesia. Pp. 75–127 in *Islam in an Era of Nation-States: Politics and Religious Renewal in Muslim Southeast Asia*, ed. Robert W. Hefner and Patricia Horvatich. Honolulu: University of Hawai'i Press.

Heider, Karl G. 1991. *Indonesian Cinema: National Culture on Screen*. Honolulu: University of Hawaii Press.

Hobart, Mark. 1991. The art of measuring mirages, or Is there kinship in Bali? Pp. 33–53 in *Cognation and Social Organization in Southeast Asia*, ed. Frans Hüsken and Jeremy Kemp. Leiden, the Netherlands: KITLV Press.

Hooker, M. B. 1978. *Adat Law in Modern Indonesia*. Kuala Lumpur: Oxford University Press.

———. 1984. *Islamic Law in South-East Asia*. Singapore: Oxford University Press.

Hooker, Virginia Matheson. 1993. *Culture and Society in New Order Indonesia*. Kuala Lumpur: Oxford University Press.

Hüsken, Frans. 1989. Cycles of commercialization and accumulation in a Central Javanese village. Pp. 303–31 in *Agrarian Transformations: Local Processes and the State in Southeast Asia*, ed. Gillian Hart, Andrew Turton, and Benjamin White. Berkeley: University of California Press.

Hüsken, Frans, and Jeremy Kemp, eds. 1991. *Cognation and Social Organization in Southeast Asia*. Leiden, the Netherlands: KITLV Press.

Hüsken, Frans, and Benjamin White. 1989. Java: Social differentiation, food production, and agrarian control. Pp. 235–65 in *Agrarian Transformations: Local Processes and the State in Southeast Asia*, ed. Gillian Hart, Andrew Turton, and Benjamin White. Berkeley: University of California Press.

Jay, Robert R. 1969. *Javanese Villagers: Social Relations in Rural Modjokuto*. Cambridge, Mass.: MIT Press.

Johns, Anthony H., ed., transl. 1958. *Rantjak Dilabueh: A Minangkabau Kaba*. Southeast Asia Program, paper no. 32, Department of Far Eastern Studies. Ithaca, N.Y.: Cornell University.

Josselin de Jong, P. E. de. 1952. *Minangkabau and Negri Sembilan: Socio-Political Structure in Indonesia*. Leiden, the Netherlands: Eduard Ijdo N.V.

Junus, Umar. 1964. Some remarks on Minangkabau social structure. *Bijdragen tot de Taal-, Land-, en Volkenkunde* 120: 293–326.

Kahn, J. S. 1976. "Tradition," matriliny, and change among the Minangkabau of Indonesia. *Bijdragen tot de Taal-, Land-, en Volkenkunde* 132: 64–95.

———. 1980. *Minangkabau Social Formations: Indonesian Peasants and the World Economy*. Cambridge: Cambridge University Press.

———. 1984. Peasant political consciousness in West Sumatra. Pp. 293–325 in *History and Peasant Consciousness in South East Asia*, ed. Andrew Turton and S. Tanabe. Senri Ethnological Studies, no. 13. Osaka, Japan: National Museum of Ethnology.

———. 1993. *Constituting the Minangkabau: Peasants, Culture and Modernity in Colonial Indonesia*. Providence, R.I.: Berg Publishers.

Kandiyoti, Deniz. 1990. Women and household production: The impact of rural transformation in Turkey. Pp. 183–94 in *The Rural Middle East: Peasant Lives and Modes of Production*, ed. K. Glavanis and P. Glavanis. London: Zed Books.

Kantor Statistik dan BAPPEDA. 1989. *Sumatera Barat dalam Angka 1988* [West Sumatra in figures, 1988]. Padang, Indonesia: Kantor Statistik.

Karim, Wazir Jahan. 1992. *Women and Culture: Between Malay Adat and Islam*. Boulder, Colo.: Westview Press.

———. 1995. Introduction: Genderising anthropology in Southeast Asia. Pp. 11–34 in *"Male" and "Female" in Developing Southeast Asia*, ed. Wazir J. Karim. Oxford: Berg Publishers.

Kassim, Azizah. 1988. Women, land, and gender relations in Negeri Sembilan: Some preliminary findings. *Southeast Asian Studies* 26(2): 132–49.

Kato, Tsuyoshi. 1982. *Matriliny and Migration: Evolving Minangkabau Traditions in Indonesia*. Ithaca, N.Y.: Cornell University Press.

Kipp, Rita Smith. 1993. *Dissociated Identities: Ethnicity, Religion, and Class in an Indonesian Society*. Ann Arbor: University of Michigan Press.

Kipp, Rita Smith, and Susan Rodgers, eds. 1987. *Indonesian Religions in Transition*. Tucson: University of Arizona Press.

Kondo, Dorinne K. 1990. *Crafting Selves: Power, Gender, and Discourses of Identity in a Japanese Workplace*. Chicago: University of Chicago Press.

Krier, Jennifer. 1994. *Displacing Distinction: Political Processes in the Minangkabau Backcountry*. Ph.D. diss., Harvard University.

———. 1995. Narrating herself: Power and gender in a Minangkabau woman's tale of conflict. Pp. 51–75 in *Bewitching Women, Pious Men: Gender and Body Politics in Southeast Asia*, ed. Aihwa Ong and Michael Peletz. Berkeley: University of California Press.

———. forthcoming. The marital project: Beyond the exchange of men in Minangkabau marriage. *American Ethnologist*.

Lamphere, Louise. 1974. Strategies, cooperation, and conflict among women in domestic groups. Pp. 97–112 in *Woman, Culture and Society*, ed. Michelle Z. Rosaldo and Louise Lamphere. Stanford, Calif.: Stanford University Press.

Langenberg, Michael van. 1986. Analysing Indonesia's New Order state: A keywords approach. *Review of Indonesian and Malaysian Affairs* 20(2): 1–47.

Lea, Vanessa. 1995. The houses of the Mēbengokre (Kayápo) of Central Brazil: A new door to their social organization. Pp. 206–25 in *About the House: Lévi-Strauss and Beyond*, ed. Janet Carsten and Stephen Hugh-Jones. Cambridge: Cambridge University Press.

Lederman, Rena. 1990. Contested order: Gender and society in the southern New Guinea highlands. Pp. 43–73 in *Beyond the Second Sex: New Directions in the Anthropology of Gender*, ed. Peggy R. Sanday and Ruth G. Goodenough. Philadelphia: University of Pennsylvania Press.

Lehmann, David. 1986. Sharecropping and the capitalist transition in agriculture: Some evidence from the highlands of Ecuador. *Journal of Development Economics* 23: 333–54.

Lévi-Strauss, Claude. 1987. *Anthropology and Myth: Lectures, 1951–1982*, trans. Roy Willis. Oxford: Basil Blackwell.

Linnekin, Jocelyn. 1990. *Sacred Queens and Women of Consequence: Rank, Gender, and Colonialism in the Hawaiian Islands*. Ann Arbor: University of Michigan Press.

Littlewood, Paul. 1980. Patronage, ideology, and reproduction. *Critique of Anthropology* 15: 29–45.

LKAAM (Lembaga Kerapatan Adat Alam Minangkabau). 1987. *Pelajaran Adat Minangkabau (Sejarah dan Budaya)* [A study in Minangkabau *adat* (history and culture)]. Padang, Indonesia: LKAAM.

Loeb, Edwin M. 1972 [1935]. *Sumatra: Its History and People*. Kuala Lumpur: Oxford University Press.

Lutz, Nancy. 1992. Constructing the "modern" Indonesian woman. Paper presented at the Conference on the Narrative and Practice of Gender in Southeast Asian Cultures, Ninth Annual Berkeley Conference on Southeast Asian Studies, University of California, Berkeley.

MacAndrews, Colin, ed. 1986. *Central Government and Local Development in Indonesia*. Singapore: Oxford University Press.

Manderson, Lenore. 1980. Rights and responsibilities, power and privilege: Women's role in contemporary Indonesia. Pp. 69–92 in *Kartini Centenary: Indonesian Women Then and Now*. Monash University.

Maretin, J. 1961. Disappearance of matriclan survivals in Minangkabau family and marriage relations. *Bijdragen tot de Taal-, Land-, en Volkenkunde* 117: 168–96.

Margolis, Diane. 1989. Considering women's experience: A reformulation of power theory. *Theory and Society* 18: 387–416.

Martin, Richard C. 1982. *Islam: A Cultural Perspective.* Englewood Cliffs, N.J.: Prentice-Hall.

Mears, Leon A. 1981. *The New Rice Economy of Indonesia.* Yogyakarta, Indonesia: Gadjah Mada University Press.

Mohanty, Chandra. 1988. Under Western eyes: Feminist scholarship and colonial discourses. *Feminist Review* 30: 61–88.

Moore, Henrietta L. 1992. Households and gender relations: The modeling of the economy. Pp. 131–48 in *Understanding Economic Process*, ed. Sutti Ortiz and Susan Lees. Lanham, Md.: University Press of America.

Morfit, Michael. 1986. Pancasila Orthodoxy. Pp. 42–55 in *Central Government and Local Development in Indonesia*, ed. Colin MacAndrews. Singapore: Oxford University Press.

Naim, Mochtar. 1971. *Merantau*: Minangkabau voluntary migration. Ph.D. diss., Australian National University.

———. 1985. Implications of merantau for social organization in Minangkabau. Pp. 111–17 in *Change and Continuity in Minangkabau: Local, Regional, and Historical Perspectives on West Sumatra*, ed. Lynn Thomas and Franz von Benda-Beckmann. Athens: Ohio University Press.

Ng, Cecilia S. H. 1987. The weaving of prestige: Village women's representations of the social categories of Minangkabau society. Ph.D. diss., Australian National University.

———. 1993. Raising the house post and feeding the husband-givers: The spatial categories of social reproduction among the Minangkabau. Pp. 117–39 in *Inside Austronesian Houses: Perspectives on Domestic Design for Living*, ed. James J. Fox. Canberra: Australian National University.

Noer, Deliar. 1973. *The Modernist Muslim Movement in Indonesia, 1900–1942.* Singapore: Oxford University Press.

Oki, Akira. 1977. Social change in the West Sumatran village, 1908–1945. Ph.D. diss., Cornell University.

Ong, Aihwa. 1987. *Spirits of Resistance and Capitalist Discipline: Factory Women in Malaysia.* Albany: State University of New York.

———. 1990. Japanese factories, Malay workers: Class and sexual metaphors in West Malaysia. Pp. 385–422 in *Power and Difference: Gender in Island Southeast Asia,* ed. Jane M. Atkinson and Shelly Errington. Stanford, Calif.: Stanford University Press.

Ong, Aihwa, and Michael Peletz, eds. 1995. *Bewitching Women, Pious Men: Gender and Body Politics in Southeast Asia.* Berkeley: University of California Press.

Ortner, Sherry. 1974. Is female to male as nature is to culture? Pp. 67–87 in *Woman, Culture, and Society*, ed. Michelle Z. Rosaldo and Louise Lamphere. Stanford, Calif.: Stanford University Press.

———. 1981. Gender and sexuality in hierarchical societies: The case of Polynesia and some comparative implications. Pp. 359–409 in *Sexual Meanings: The Cultural Construction of Gender and Sexuality,* ed. Sherry B. Ortner and Harriet Whitehead. Cambridge: Cambridge University Press.

———. 1984. Theory in anthropology since the sixties. *Comparative Studies in Society and History* 26(1): 126–66.

———. 1990. Gender hegemonies. *Cultural Critique* 14: 35–80.

———. 1995. Resistance and the problem of ethnographic refusal. *Comparative Studies in Society and History* 37(1): 173–93.

Pak, Ok-Kyung. 1986. Lowering the high, raising the low: The gender alliance and property relations in a Minangkabau peasant community of West Sumatra, Indonesia. Ph.D. diss., Laval University.

Papanek, Hanna, and Laurel Schwede. 1988. Women are good with money: Earning and managing in an Indonesian city. Pp. 71–98 in *A Home Divided: Women and Income in the Third World*, ed. Daisy Dwyer and Judith Bruce. Stanford, Calif.: Stanford University Press.

Parpart, Jane L. 1993. Who is the 'other'? A postmodern feminist critique of women and development theory and practice. *Development and Change* 24: 439–64.

Peletz, Michael G. 1987. The exchange of men in nineteenth-century Negeri Sembilan (Malaya). *American Ethnologist* 14(3): 449–69.

———. 1988. *A Share of the Harvest: Kinship, Property, and Social History among the Malays of Rembau*. Berkeley: University of California Press.

———. 1995. Neither reasonable nor responsible: Contrasting representations of masculinity in a Malay society. Pp. 76–123 in *Bewitching Women, Pious Men: Gender and Body Politics in Southeast Asia*, ed. Aihwa Ong and Michael Peletz. Berkeley: University of California Press.

———. 1996. *Reason and Passion: Representations of Gender in a Malay Society*. Berkeley: University of California Press.

Pincus, Jonathan. 1990. Approaches to the political economy of agrarian change in Java. *Journal of Contemporary Asia* 20(1): 3–40.

Pramono, Dewi Motik. 1990. Woman and career in Islam. *Mizan* 3(1): 72–75.

Prindiville, Joanne. 1981. The image and role of Minangkabau women. Pp. 26–33 in *Southeast Asia: Women, Changing Social Structure, and Cultural Continuity*, ed. G. Hainsworth. Ottawa: University of Ottawa Press.

———. 1985. Mother, mother's brother, and modernization: The problems and prospects of Minangkabau matriliny in a changing world. Pp. 29–43 in *Change and Continuity in Minangkabau: Local, Regional, and Historical Perspectives on West Sumatra*, ed. Lynn Thomas and Franz von Benda-Beckmann. Athens: Ohio University.

Raffles, S. H., ed. 1835. *Memoir of the Life and Public Service of Sir Thomas Stamford Raffles*, vol. 1, new ed. London: James Duncan.

Raliby, Osman. 1985. The position of women in Islam. *Mizan* 2(2): 29–37.

Reenen, Joke van. 1996. *Central Pillars of the House: Sisters, Wives, and Mothers in a Rural Community in Minangkabau, West Sumatra*. Leiden, the Netherlands: Research School CNWS.

Reid, Anthony. 1983. Introduction: Slavery and bondage in Southeast Asian history. Pp. 1–43 in *Slavery, Bondage, and Dependence in Southeast Asia*, Anthony Reid with Jennifer Brewster. New York: St. Martin's Press.

———. 1993. *Southeast Asia in the Age of Commerce, 1450–1680*, vol. 2, *Expansion and Crisis*. New Haven, Conn.: Yale University Press.

Reiter, Rayna R. 1975. Men and women in the south of France: Public and private domains. Pp. 252–82 in *Toward an Anthropology of Women*, ed. Rayna R. Reiter. New York: Monthly Review Press.

Rieffel, Alexis. 1969. The BIMAS program for self-sufficiency in rice production. *Indonesia* 8: 103–34.

Robertson, A. F. 1980. On sharecropping. *Man* 15 (n.s.): 411–29.

Rosaldo, Michelle Zimbalist. 1974. Woman, culture, and society: A theoretical overview. Pp. 17–42 in *Woman, Culture, and Society*, ed. Michelle Z. Rosaldo and Louise Lamphere. Stanford, Calif.: Stanford University Press.

———. 1980. The use and abuse of anthropology: Reflections on feminism and cross-cultural understanding. *Signs: Journal of Women in Culture and Society* 5(3): 389–417.

Royal Netherlands Embassy. 1987. *Women and Development in Indonesia.* Jakarta: Development Cooperation Department.

Rudie, Ingrid. 1993. A hall of mirrors: Autonomy translated over time in Malaysia. Pp. 103–16 in *Gendered Fields: Men, Women, and Ethnography*, ed. Diane Bell, Pat Caplan, and Wazir Karim. New York: Routledge.

———. 1994. *Visible Women in East Coast Malay Society: On the Reproduction of Gender in Ceremonial, School, and Market.* Oslo: Scandinavian University Press.

Sacks, Karen. 1982. *Sister and Wives: The Past and Future of Sexual Equality.* Urbana: University of Illinois Press.

Sadanoer, Amilijoes. 1976. *Sociocultural Problems of Agricultural Development: A Survey on a Developing Provincial Area.* Singapore: Regional Institute of Higher Education and Development.

Salyo, Suwarni. 1985. Islamic influences on the lives of women in Indonesia. *Mizan* 2(2): 15–21.

Sanday, Peggy Reeves. 1990. Androcentric and matrifocal gender representations in Minangkabau ideology. Pp. 139–68 in *Beyond the Second Sex: New Directions in the Anthropology of Gender*, ed. Peggy R. Sanday and Ruth G. Goodenough. Philadelphia: University of Pennsylvania Press.

———. 1998. Matriarchy as a sociocultural form: An old debate in a new light. Paper presented at the Sixteenth Congress of the Indo-Pacific Prehistory Association, Melaka, Malaysia.

Sanday, Peggy Reeves, and Ruth G. Goodenough, eds. 1990. *Beyond the Second Sex: New Directions in the Anthropology of Gender.* Philadelphia: University of Pennsylvania Press.

Schiller, Jim, and Barbara Martin-Schiller, eds. 1997. *Imagining Indonesia: Cultural Politics and Political Culture.* Athens: Ohio University Center for International Studies.

Schneider, David M. 1961a. Introduction: The distinctive features of matrilineal descent groups. Pp. 1–29 in *Matrilineal Kinship*, ed. David Schneider and Kathleen Gough. Berkeley: University of California Press.

———. 1961b. Preface. Pp. vii–xvii in *Matrilineal Kinship*, ed. David Schneider and Kathleen Gough. Berkeley: University of California Press.

———. 1968. *American Kinship: A Cultural Account.* Englewood Cliffs, N.J.: Prentice-Hall.

———. 1984. *A Critique of the Study of Kinship.* Ann Arbor: University of Michigan.

Schneider, David M., and Kathleen Gough, eds. 1961. *Matrilineal Kinship.* Berkeley: University of California Press.

Schrieke, B. 1955. *Indonesian Sociological Studies: Selected Writings of B. Schrieke*, part 1. The Hague: W. van Hoeve.

Schwede, Laurel Kathleen. 1991. Family strategies of labor allocation and decision-making in a matrilineal, Islamic society: The Minangkabau of West Sumatra, Indonesia. Ph.D. diss., Cornell University.

Scott, James. 1985. *Weapons of the Weak: Everyday Forms of Peasant Resistance.* New Haven, Conn.: Yale University Press.

Sears, Laurie J., ed. 1996. Fragile identities: Deconstructing women and Indonesia. Pp. 1–44 in *Fantasizing the Feminine in Indonesia,* ed. Laurie J. Sears. Durham, N.C.: Duke University Press.

Sen, Krishna. 1993. Repression and resistance: Interpretations of the feminine in New Order cinema. Pp. 116–33 in *Culture and Society in New Order Indonesia,* ed. Virginia Matheson Hooker. Kuala Lumpur: Oxford University Press.

Sharma, Ursula. 1990. Public employment and private relations: Women and work in India. Pp. 229–46 in *Women, Employment, and the Family in the International Division of Labor,* ed. Sharon Stichter and Jane Parpart. Philadelphia: Temple University Press.

Sinaga, S. M. 1985. *Himpunan Peraturan Pemerintahan Desa & Kelurahan.* Jakarta: PT Bhuana Pancakarsa.

Sjahrir, Kartini. 1985. Wanita: Beberapa catatan antropologis [Women: Some anthropological notes]. *Prisma* 10: 3–15.

Stivens, Maila. 1985. Sexual politics in Rembau: Female autonomy, matriliny, and agrarian change in Negeri Sembilan, Malaysia. Occasional Paper no. 5. Centre of South-East Asian Studies. Canterbury, England: University of Kent.

——. 1991. The evolution of kinship relations in Rembau, Negeri Sembilan, Malaysia. Pp. 71–88 in *Cognation and Social Organization in Southeast Asia,* ed. Frans Hüsken and Jeremy Kemp. Leiden, the Netherlands: KITLV Press.

——. 1992. Perspectives on gender: Problems in writing about women in Malaysia. Pp. 202–24 in *Fragmented Vision: Culture and Politics in Contemporary Malaysia,* ed. Joel S. Kahn and F. Wah. Honolulu: University of Hawaii Press.

——. 1994. Gender at the margins: Paradigms and peasantries in rural Malaysia. *Women's Studies International Forum* 17(4): 373–90.

——. 1996. *Matriliny and Modernity: Sexual Politics and Social Change in Rural Malaysia.* St. Leonard's, N.S.W.: Allen and Unwin.

Stivens, Maila, Cecilia Ng, Jomo K.S., and Jahara Bee. 1994. *Malay Peasant Women and the Land.* London: Zed Books.

Stoler, Ann Laura. 1977. Class structure and female autonomy in rural Java. *Signs: Journal of Women in Culture and Society* 3(1): 74–89.

Strathern, Marilyn. 1987. *Dealing with Inequality: Analyzing Gender Relations in Melanesia and Beyond.* Cambridge: Cambridge University Press.

Sullivan, Norma. 1983. Indonesian women in development: State theory and urban kampung practice. Pp. 147–71 in *Women's Work and Women's Roles: Economics and Everyday Life in Indonesia, Malaysia, and Singapore,* ed. Lenore Manderson. Canberra: Australian National University.

Suryakusuma, Julia. 1996. The state and sexuality in New Order Indonesia. Pp. 92–119 in *Fantasizing the Feminine in Indonesia,* ed. Laurie J. Sears. Durham, N.C.: Duke University Press.

Swift, M. G. 1971. Minangkabau and modernization. Pp. 255–67 in *Anthropology in Oceania: Essays Presented to Ian Hogbin,* ed. L. R. Hiatt and C. Jayawardena. London: Angus and Robertson.

Syahrizal. 1989. Pola Hubungan Kerja Dalam Pertanian: Studi Kasus dalam Masyarakat Petani [The pattern of agricultural labor relations: Case study of a farm community]. Thesis, Andalas University, Padang, West Sumatra.

Tanner, Nancy. 1971. Minangkabau disputes. Ph.D. diss., University of California, Berkeley.

———. 1974. Matrifocality in Indonesia and Africa and among black Americans. Pp. 129–56 in *Woman, Culture, and Society*, ed. Michelle Z. Rosaldo and Louise Lamphere. Stanford, Calif.: Stanford University Press.

Tanner, Nancy, and Lynn L. Thomas. 1985. Rethinking matriliny: Decision-making and sex roles in Minangkabau. Pp. 45–71 in *Change and Continuity in Minangkabau: Local, Regional, and Historical Perspectives on West Sumatra*, ed. Lynn Thomas and Franz von Benda-Beckmann. Southeast Asia Series, no. 71. Athens: Ohio University.

Thomas, Lynn, and Franz von Benda-Beckmann, eds. 1985. *Change and Continuity in Minangkabau: Local, Regional, and Historical Perspectives on West Sumatra*. Southeast Asia Series, no. 71. Athens: Ohio University.

Tinker, Irene, and Millidge Walker. 1973. Planning for regional development in Indonesia. *Asian Survey* 13(12): 1102–20.

Tiwon, Sylvia. 1996. Models and maniacs: Articulating the female in Indonesia. Pp. 47–70 in *Fantasizing the Feminine in Indonesia*, ed. Laurie J. Sears. Durham, N.C.: Duke University Press.

Valle, Teresa del, ed. 1993. *Gendered Anthropology*. London: Routledge.

Van Esterik, Penny, ed. 1982. *Women of Southeast Asia*. DeKalb: Northern Illinois University.

Visweswaran, Kamala. 1994. *Fictions of Feminist Ethography*. Minneapolis: University of Minnesota Press.

Waterson, Roxanne. 1993. Houses and the built environment in island South-East Asia: Tracing some shared themes in the uses of space. Pp. 221–35 in *Inside Austronesian Houses: Perspectives on Domestic Design for Living*, ed. James J. Fox. Canberra: Australian National University.

Watson, C. W. 1987. *State and Society in Indonesia: Three Papers*. Centre of South-East Asian Studies, Occasional Paper No. 8. Canterbury, England: University of Kent.

———. 1991. Cognatic or matrilineal: Kerinci social organization in Escher perspective. Pp. 55–70 in *Cognation and Social Organization in Southeast Asia*, ed. Frans Hüsken and Jeremy Kemp. Leiden, the Netherlands: KITLV Press.

Weiner, Annette B. 1976. *Women of Value, Men of Renown: New Perspectives in Trobriand Exchange*. Austin: University of Texas Press.

Whalley, Lucy A. 1991. Who wears the veil? The politics of women's dress in West Sumatra, Indonesia. Presented at the Nintieth Annual Meeting of the American Anthropological Association, Chicago.

———. 1993. Virtuous women, productive citizens: Negotiating tradition, Islam, and modernity in Minangkabau, Indonesia. Ph.D diss., University of Illinois, Urbana-Champaign.

White, Benjamin. 1976. Production and reproduction in a Javanese village. Ph.D. diss., Columbia University.

———. 1989. Problems in the empirical analysis of agrarian differentiation. Pp. 15–30 in *Agrarian Transformations: Local Processes and the State in Southeast Asia*, ed. Gillian Hart, Andrew Turton, and Benjamin White. Berkeley: University of California Press.

Wieringa, Saskia. 1985. The perfumed nightmare: Some notes on the Indonesian women's movement. Working Papers. The Hague: Institute of Social Studies.

———. 1992. Ibu or the beast: Gender interests, ideology, and practice in two Indonesian women's organizations. *Feminist Review* 41: 98–114.

Wilk, Richard R., ed. 1989. *The Household Economy: Reconsidering the Domestic Mode of Production*. Boulder, Colo.: Westview Press.

Williams, Raymond. 1977. *Marxism and Literature*. Oxford: Oxford University Press.

Wolf, Diane Lauren. 1992. *Factory Daughters: Gender, Household Dynamics, and Rural Industrialization in Java*. Berkeley: University of California Press.

Wong, Diana. 1987. *Peasants in the Making: Malaysia's Green Revolution*. Singapore: Institute of Southeast Asian Studies.

Woodward, Mark R. 1989. *Islam in Java: Normative Piety and Mysticism in the Sultanate of Yogyakarta*. Tucson: University of Arizona Press.

Yanagisako, Sylvia. 1979. Family and household: The analysis of domestic groups. *Annual Review of Anthropology* 8: 161–205.

Yanagisako, Sylvia J., and Jane F. Collier. 1987. Toward a unified analysis of gender and kinship. Pp. 14–50 in *Gender and Kinship: Essays toward a Unified Analysis*, ed. Jane F. Collier and Sylvia J. Yanagisako. Stanford, Calif.: Stanford University Press.

Yanagisako, Sylvia J., and Carol Delaney. 1995. Naturalizing power. Pp. 1–22 in *Naturalizing Power: Essays in Feminist Cultural Analysis*, ed. Sylvia Yanagisako and Carol Delaney. New York: Routledge.

Index

About the Author

Evelyn Blackwood received her Ph.D. in cultural anthropology from Stanford University. She taught briefly at the University of Hawaii and is now assistant professor in anthropology and women's studies at Purdue University.

Breinigsville, PA USA
11 November 2010
249143BV00003B/1/P